S0-BWR-366

DISCARD

COMPUTER
SECURITY
MANAGEMENT

COMPUTER
SECURITY
MANAGEMENT

DONN B. PARKER

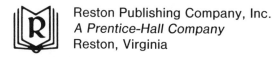
Reston Publishing Company, Inc.
A Prentice-Hall Company
Reston, Virginia

Library of Congress Cataloging in Publication Data

Parker, Donn B.
  Computer security management.

  Includes index.
  1. Computers—Access control. 2. Electronic data
processing departments—Security measures. I. Title.
QA76.9.A25P38   658.4'78   81-823
ISBN 0-8359-0905-0   AACR2

Editorial/production supervision and interior design
by Barbara J. Gardetto

© 1981 by
Reston Publishing Company, Inc.
A Prentice-Hall Company
Reston, Virginia 22090

All rights reserved. No part of this book may be
reproduced in any way, or by any means, without
permission in writing from the publisher.

10   9   8   7   6   5   4   3   2   1

Printed in the United States of America

To Lorna
    Diane
    David
    My mother, Miriam
    The memory of my father, Don
    and Aunt Louise

Contents

Preface

Ideas for this book started well before I received the assignment to write a security handbook for John O'Mara and his Computer Security Institute. The writing rapidly became a professional book manuscript as the concept of a how-to-do-it handbook faded from view amid the pages of more basic text on problems, concepts, theory, and, finally, practice. The history started 11 years ago with computer abuse research with which I am more generally associated. However, the primary purpose of the research has been to advance computer security by study of the problems that security is supposed to solve. This book is a logical outgrowth.

In addition to the research on computer abuse, a computer security program was developed at SRI International to apply what we were learning to assist organizations in using their computers more safely. As a result, this book expresses the ideas and methodologies coming from study of actual loss and experience in conducting many security reviews to develop computer security for clients.

If any single conclusion is to be drawn from the 11 years of research and consulting, it is that computer security is not primarily a technological subject. It is a subject of psychological and sociological behavior of people. As I have said repeatedly in my worldwide lecturing, computers do not commit errors, omissions, or crimes; only people can do these things that may subsequently be manifested in computers. Solutions to these problems also must come from people, their actions and their attitudes. These concepts are strongly emphasized in this book.

Only a few people assisted me. First, members of my family tolerated my long evenings and weekends of isolation. Secondly, SRI management agreed to do without some of the energy and attention I might have other-wise given to my SRI work. Finally, I thank specific people for special assis-tance: my wife, Lorna, for her many hours of typing; John O'Mara for guid-ance; Robert Courtney and Gerald Weinberg for tearing apart early drafts; Susan Nycum for her insights on the law; and copy editor Vickey Macintyre and production editor Barbara Gardetto.

Donn B. Parker

Introduction

In a more perfect world, computer security might readily be achieved by applying a finite list of do's and don'ts found collectively in books and manuals on the subject. Unfortunately, the task is not that straightforward. Computer security strives toward both protecting assets and limiting their loss from three basic threats: natural disasters (for example, extreme weather conditions), human errors and omissions (for example, incorrect tape labeling), and intentional acts such as fraud or sabotage. The first two threats are empirically predictable. We know from experience how to prevent them or control their severity, and thus how to limit the resulting losses. The cookbook approach of checklist do's and don'ts, cautiously adapted and applied to specific environments through much common sense and trial and error, works quite well except for securing the computer system itself, but more about that later.

The threat from intentional acts is not amenable to effective treatment by the cookbook approach in current use. The sad history of the war against crime is proof that traditional efforts of control have minimal effect. The "Maginot Line" syndrome of setting up massive protective efforts to correct obvious weaknesses but ignoring others invites perpetrators to "end run" such a line and to attack computer assets through remaining weak areas. The perpetrators know the cookbook safeguards, too, and merely subvert or circumvent them.

A different methodology must be employed to control intentionally caused losses. The checklist approach alone won't suffice. Robert Courtney, IBM corporate strategist for Data Security, has collected over 800 checklist safeguards, is still accumulating new ones, and is finding fault with already documented ones at such a high rate that their publication even in a loose-

1

leaf binder would be impractical. A ten-year study of computer abuse at SRI International reveals that new variations of intentional acts are continually being generated (Parker 1979). They are the same old crimes of fraud, embezzlement, theft, larceny, sabotage, espionage, and extortion. However, when computers are involved, these old crimes take on new characteristics that make them into totally new crimes. Automation of asset storage and processing has resulted in new occupations of perpetrators, new modi operandi, new crime environments, and new targets. In other words crime has become automated now that data processing has penetrated the environments in which crime has traditionally occurred.

This automation of crime has confounded the traditional security specialists and law enforcement and prosecution agencies (Parker and Nycum 1980). At the same time, the automation of the environments and processes subject to crime opens an exciting new opportunity to automate the safeguarding against crime. Can automation survive the onslaught of crime? Will the automation of security for the first time in history, bring financial and information crime under control? If such control is to be achieved, surely new security methodologies consistent with automation methodologies of systems and operations analysis must be employed.

The SRI study of the new phenomenon of computer abuse and automated crime has resulted in a new method of attacking the problem of all types of losses associated with computers. The traditional method of selecting safeguards from checklists found in many books on computer security can be effective against errors and omissions. However, a checklist method against the intelligent enemies' intentional attacks is ineffective, because the enemy uses a different checklist. In other words, computer crime perpetrators find vulnerabilities that were not anticipated in published checklists. Therefore, the computer security specialist must think like the enemy and be as innovative as he is. An effective method must anticipate that a game is being played, and the rules of the game are made by the enemy, not the security specialist. This calls for a method that includes development and use of threat scenarios based on experience and playing the role of the enemy.

Such an approach has many advantages. It avoids the unimaginative and ineffective cookbook method since it offers great flexibility in several dimensions. Its methodology can be applied to any size or type of computer system (defined here in the broadest sense to include staff, facilities, hardware, and software). Most discussions of computer security recommend safeguards that are suitable for the largest systems but that are difficult or impossible to scale down for the smaller system, for example, one separating responsibilities in positions of great trust. Other methods assume almost unlimited resources for security planning and for imposing recommended safeguards, whereas the method proposed here can be scaled to fit any budget. It can be used for planning and implementation even where little safeguarding previously existed; it can be used for compliance auditing; and it can be used for incremental increases in protection.

Some shortcomings and some difficulties need to be recognized, however.

First, the proposed method has not been widely tested. It has evolved over two years through three applications. Although it has never been fully implemented in the ideal form presented here, its results have been encouraging. Furthermore, it has been tested by the SRI computer security staff, who have had great experience in security planning and in conducting security reviews. Most important, this method is based on in-depth knowledge of and experience with victims, perpetrators, and others associated with actual losses. This information is a great aid in predicting the development of realistic and practical threat situations. There may be some concern that computer security specialists without this experience may have difficulty in developing scenarios. In fact, the success of this method does depend on some security experience and practice. Some critics may complain because the number of scenarios to sufficiently provide for all potential threats may be too large. It will be seen, however, that scenarios can be generalized to reduce the number needed, and that this method will still be able to treat threats more comprehensively than the cookbook method. The threat scenario method is not very different from methods used by experienced electronic data processing (EDP) auditors who implicitly play out scenarios when they evaluate controls and safeguards. The method presented here merely formalizes this process, and thus makes the scenario approach an explicit one.

Some readers may think that more emphasis than is appropriate is being placed on intentional acts, versus accidental acts. After all, losses from accidental acts are said to be significantly higher than losses from intentional acts. It might also be argued that since the author's principal area of study is computer-related crime, this discussion might direct readers toward a presumably less serious problem. Of course, a universal problem with books on computer security is that the subject is so broad that no two authors are likely to be expert enough in all aspects of security to do them justice. One book may treat data base management security very well, while another may do a thorough job on physical security. Certain topics are bound to be left in the background, regardless of the comprehensive treatment claimed by any given author.

With this concern in mind, I warn the reader that this book mentions only superficially such important subjects as natural disasters, insurance, operating system security, and some others. On the other hand, it emphasizes and covers extensively some new concepts of computer security, it treats accidental and intentional acts as separate problems (a controversial idea), and it closely examines methods of analyzing threat and risk and methods of organizing the computer security function. It also examines methods of conducting a security review, selective rather than comprehensive application of quantitative risk assessment, and principles of safeguard selection.

This book focuses on security against intentional acts rather than against errors and omissions. The reasons are thoroughly explained in the text. No one knows whether either of these problems predominates, but surely it is more challenging to deal with the schemes responsible for intentionally caused losses. In addition, I believe that protection from intentional perpetrators, while only marginally increasing the cost over protection from accidents, provides protection from both types of loss, whereas protection against accidents does not include effective protection from intentionally causes losses. This relationship works in one direction but not the other.

To get through this book the reader must live with my prejudices and limitations. He may not agree with my concepts, conclusion, and emphasis, but I guarantee challenging and stimulating reading.

SECTION I
COMPUTER SECURITY AND THE ORGANIZATION

Chapter 1
Why We Have Security Problems

Security Needs in Transition

Before the need for computer security was recognized, business, government, and institutional organizations were concerned with general security, which had to do with the physical protection of assets through such means as locks, barriers, and uniformed guards. These assets consisted of both personnel and physical assets, which included buildings, yards, vehicles, and their physical contents such as products, parts, supplies, paper records, and money. Protection of negotiable assets was of particular importance. Negotiable assets were, and are today, stored in vaults, and various safeguards have been used to protect them from robbery, larceny, and burglary.

Protection from accidental loss and white-collar crime—particularly from fraud against businesses—has been primarily the responsibility of line managers, assisted by auditors and security personnel. Businesses such as financial institutions that experience a large amount of white-collar crime assign some of the security responsibility to protection departments, which maintain a staff of detectives and undercover informants. The director of security for a large transportation company once boasted that he had more undercover agents than visible agents in his security department even though industrial security, in others' view, depended primarily on armed guard activity and only secondarily on undercover agents.

Some types of assets still require this form of protection, so that traditional protection departments continue to provide valuable services. However, large amounts of assets and representations of assets—including money—that are now stored in computers and that are moved about electronically require other methods of protection. Primary records for tangible assets such as contents of warehouses are also stored in computers and transmitted electronically. In this computerized transition to electronically stored assets and representations of assets, the focus of crime and the locale of accidental losses have also shifted. When asked why he robbed banks, Willie Sutton, the famous bank robber, is supposed to have replied, "Because that's where the money is." We can anticipate that increasing numbers of amateur white-collar criminals and professional criminals will focus on computer and telecommunications systems for their ill-gotten gains. The computer transition is leading to major changes in security, auditing, and management functions.

The early computer technologists assumed that their employers' computers functioned in benign environments. Their major concerns were accidental losses from errors, omissions, and natural disasters. As the EDP-business environment becomes more vulnerable to hostilities in the forms of both accidentally and intentionally caused losses, EDP management must assume increasing responsibility for protection. Advanced organizations have already developed EDP security specialists within their data processing divisions and some are similarly developing EDP auditing specialists (primarily within the audit division, although some of these specialists report to the highest level of data processing management). Even the traditional protection departments in these most advanced organizations are developing EDP security capabilities.

Unfortunately, the traditional protection and audit methods are no match for computer-related abuses, errors, omissions, and natural disasters. Traditional security has been a matter of devising safeguards in reaction to specific losses. That is to say, when a loss occurs, a new safeguard is introduced to protect from that loss in the future. EDP simply cannot afford this luxury, because integrating applicable safeguards after the design, development, and implementation of computer hardware, software, and computing facilities are completed would entail impractical, expensive, and in some cases, impossible major revisions. Therefore, anticipatory planning and the use of models, systems analysis, and automated tools have become necessary. Even so, the new safeguards cannot keep pace with the accelerating transition to automation and to electronic forms and representations of assets.

Problems for Computer Security

As technology advances, development of important supportive functions that protect the technology from intentional losses is lagging behind. One reason is that the human capability to manage the development of complex systems of today is being taxed to its limit. If we knew how to manage technologists better, we could achieve greater integrity of their products.

Auditing, another supportive function, is also lagging behind the advancement of technology, as documented in the system auditability and control reports produced by SRI International for the Institute of Internal Auditors and funded by International Business Machines (SAC 1977). Although many auditors are learning to audit batch-operated computer systems, at the same time, technology is racing ahead with real-time, on-line, integrated-file, distributed computer, and telecommunications systems. Each time technology changes by a small amount, the auditor's world turns upside down and the auditor's independence is further eroded. Technologists now stand between the auditor and the electronically stored documents. Because the auditor does not know the technology in sufficient depth to work independently, he must rely on the trustworthiness of computer programmers, operators, tape librarians, and maintenance engineers. This dependence violates a basic audit principle. Like EDP, auditing requires a high degree of specialization and team activity, and auditors are only starting to understand this. In addition, data processing management is only beginning to recognize the existence, purpose, needs, and value of auditors. Now that they have been introduced to one another, auditors and EDP management must learn to understand each other's language, jargon, and technology.

Computer security is another supportive function that is not keeping up with the advancement of technology. There is no practical way to technically protect multi-access computer systems from programmed compromise. Meanwhile, we are rapidly moving to on-line, distributed computer systems in which there appears to be even less hope of providing the security needed to assure technical protection of data, programs, processes, and computer users without great increases in cost.

Despite this lag in supportive functions, the potential for protecting organizations against accidental losses does not appear to be inhibited. Throughout its history the EDP community has attempted to control errors and omissions, so that controls have been a fundamental part of the design, development, and implementation of hardware, software, data communications, and computer facilities. The control of accidental losses has had great cost benefit value in dealing with recurrent losses and in developing well-known controls and safeguards with few, if any, unsolved problems. Losses from errors and omissions are accepted by management as a cost of doing business, are anticipated in budgets, and are expected to be overcome. In contrast, protection from intentionally caused losses is a new phenomenon in EDP, neither financially nor psychologically anticipated, still to be fully understood, and fraught with the lack of practical solutions.

A fundamental problem with cases of intentionally caused losses is the transition in forms of negotiable assets needing protection. This is not a new phenomenon in itself, for such transitions have taken place now and then throughout recorded history, and possibly before that, when mankind first began bartering goods and services. The concept of money in the form of precious objects and metals appeared much later. Relatively soon thereafter, the volume of precious metals became too heavy and awkward to easily transport. These metals were therefore placed in vaults and small pieces of paper were produced to represent the precious metals in business negotiations. The paper alone has worked so well that recently it was decided that the precious metal need not represent negotiable assets except in international trade. As a result, the United States has gone predominately to a paper based system of money, checks, warrants, notes, and negotiable securities. To this growing list have been added plastic money in the form of credit cards and plastic and magnetic money in the form of magnetic stripe credit and debit cards.

Automated Crimes

We are now in the midst of perhaps the most important transition in history as we move rapidly toward adopting a system of electronic money wherein negotiable assets take the form of electronic pulses and magnetic patterns stored and processed in computer systems and squeezed through telephone lines. With the advent of electronic funds transfer systems, including automated teller machines and point-of-sale terminals, much of our money is no longer in paper form and is no longer stored in traditional safes and vaults or under mattresses. The new vaults are computer systems, and the electronic money is moved about through data transmission lines. If business crimes and abuses follow Willie Sutton's example and focus on where the money is, then we can be sure that they will focus on computer and telecommunication systems. Even though we may identify these new crimes under the traditional labels of fraud, theft, larceny, embezzlement, sabotage, espionage, and extortion, everything except the names will be changed: the occupations of the perpetrators, the environments in which crime occurs, the methods of perpetrating crime, and the form of assets involved are all new.

The rapid advancement of computer technology and data communica-

tions has been identified as a major factor affecting the safety o
tivities. The early technologists were engineers and scientists w
experience with crime. The technology was open and its trade
assets were relatively unprotected. Computer programs became ı
of assets that were freely exchanged and traded among the techn. ... community. The first computer organizations such as SHARE and GUIDE would not have developed as they did without this relatively free exchange of software. Later, in the early 1960s, business management began to understand computer technology enough to realize that programs represent valuable corporate assets needing protection and cost evaluation. Programmers, however, still assumed that software was basically owned by the person who created it, whether or not an employer happened to be paying him for doing it. Even today, this concept persists among some programmers. A similar view was held about computer services, but to a lesser degree. Programmers assumed that computer services were to be used as they saw fit, especially since they were the only ones who knew how to use the computer. Thus, if a computer was idling, it could be used for any personal purpose by those who knew how to use it. This concept also widely persists today.

These benefits were built on the idea that everyone connected with computer technology had noble and socially acceptable purposes. We were all working for the same goals, primarily for the advancement of computer technology. As soon as the technology proliferated and entered environments in which traditional business crime had flourished, however, business and government administrators became aware that their organizations depended on the safe use of computer technology, that computers could function in hostile environments, and thus that they needed to introduce new security and auditing methods. But the hardware, software, and system concepts have advanced and changed so rapidly that there has been hardly enough time to provide for the new needs of safe use of the technology relative to the value it represents through the amount of assets stored and processed in computer systems.

A rapidly developing use of the technology made available more and more used computers, along with peripheral devices and computer time-sharing services. Before long, the hardware and its use became subjects and objects of criminal activity. New ways were found to convert the hardware and its use into direct economic gain through illegal activities. With the recognition that software is an important asset, there has developed a software industry that puts prices on computer programs, which have become a new type of asset to be the focus of criminal activities and other abuses.

Computers were first used to execute single programs and then serial batches of programs. From a security and audit point of view, computers could be treated as a simple transition from previous manual and unit record equipment. The computer was merely a black box sitting in a room that could easily be physically protected and controlled. Auditing was done by comparing data before they entered the system with computations after reports were removed from the system. That this approach was not sufficient became evident with the development of parallel processing, interaction of computer programs, and the sharing of data files by different application programs. Such activities could be performed only through complex computer system programs that grew so large and multifaceted that their operation, maintenance, and expansion could not be predicted (and sometimes not controlled).

During these advancements in the early 1960s enough people were working with computer systems and were processing sufficient assets to create opportunities for unauthorized acts, some of which could be classified as crimes. The first federally prosecuted computer crime occurred in 1962 in Minneapolis, Minnesota, when a programmer changed the demand deposit accounting system on an IBM 1401 computer to eliminate the overdraft reports from the records of his personal checking account. Awareness of the possibilities of computer abuse nonetheless grew slowly during the 1960s, even with the publicity and sensationalism of reported computer crimes in the public media, since these were considered rare novelties.

The advancement from parallel processing to parallel input, the multiplexing of input and output, and finally the real-time, on-line interaction through communication circuits to users at personal and remote job entry terminals left systems almost totally unprotected, for few practical safeguards were available. This situation was first experienced in classified military use of computers, for which few sufficient means of safeguarding classified processing in multi-access, multilevel security systems could be found. As a result, to this day, processing is limited mainly to costly, single-level classification systems. Nonmilitary, business, and government activities have not been constrained by law or regulation to this degree, even though they may have highly sensitive computer applications.

The advancing technology was used with little regard for safety until a major turning point occurred with the discovery of the Equity Funding Insurance fraud in 1973, in Los Angeles. The third phase of this largest known business fraud had depended on the use of computers, and part of the deception was based on the inability of external auditors and examiners to audit within a computer system. After this case became known and sensationalized extensively in the public media as a computer crime, many new professional audit committees were formed in order to develop an approach to auditing that recognized the need for looking inside computer systems and computer storage media. That activity is still trying to catch up with the advancing technology in what appears today to be a close race. With even the most advanced commercially available computer systems, there is no known practical way of technically protecting the user organizations from intentionally caused losses if the perpetrators have sufficient technological skills, knowledge, access, and resources. A rapidly growing number of people have just such capabilities. In addition, now that more computer systems are being interfaced to dial-up telephone networks, a whole new range of technology and vulnerability has been added to systems in which we are already unable to prove or maintain integrity. This is the current environment in which this book is being written. I hope that it will help advance the state of the art of EDP security and auditing sufficiently to allow those concerned to catch up and keep up with the rapidly advancing technology and its increasingly sophisticated use.

Chapter 2

EDP as the Focus of Power in the Organization

"Information Is Power"

"Information is power" is an old maxim that takes on important new meaning when we think of the vast possibilities for concentrating information and using it with computer systems. The security specialist should therefore be sensitive to and aware of the role of EDP in his organization. The computer security specialist must know how and where to seek support for his work and the resources and services he needs to perform his job. If EDP management is strong and in a favored position in the organization, the security specialist might seek support for his needs through that organization. If the security department itself is particularly strong, he might obtain adequate support there. The computer security specialist must also understand the strengths, weaknesses, and politics of an organization if he is to determine potential loss and is to deal with discovered losses.

In the past, higher management considered EDP to be a necessary irritant in performing certain tasks of accounting, inventory control, and so forth. The high frequency of errors and system failures caused significant problems for management and embarrassed the organization. Because few members of management wanted the responsibility for such activity, it was often given to the engineering department, which then had to process both engineering and business data. The history of many organizations will no doubt show considerable movement of EDP responsibility among various department heads. From the outset, data processing also required significant investment in equipment and manpower, even though it was considered merely a service function like copying or printing.

Today the situation is different. Organizations have learned to go beyond routine data processing. Computers are used extensively in planning activities, for example, in determining the impact on sales and profits of various departmental budget alternatives. Much operational and accounting data is stored only on magnetic tape or in computer systems and would be difficult to recreate from any other source. Reliability, accuracy, and freedom from errors and failures have increased considerably, and methods and procedures in EDP have become more standardized. The result has been fewer embarrassments and greater respect for EDP management. In addition, the costs of processing data and of increasing staffs have made the EDP budget far more significant than in the past. The EDP organization has become a focus of power, as Peter Drucker has noted: "The systematic and purposeful acquisition of information and the systematic application, rather than science or technology, are emerging as the new foundations for work productivity and effort throughout the world" (Drucker 1969).

The use of computers in planning activities imparts authority to the department in charge of the planning. Even though managers may not act directly on the results of data processing, they use the technology and the resultant information that supports their positions. The managers with the facts will get the attention of the president of the organization, and conversely, top management will seek advice from those who have the information or are capable of obtaining it. The new role of EDP as the focus of power and source of readily available facts has caused higher management to become increasingly interested in controlling the EDP function rather than in relying directly on lower level management to gain the information from a variety of sources. Power is therefore shifting to parts of the organization that are already organized and sophisticated enough to recognize the importance of EDP and to know how to use it effectively.

Gottlieb and Borodin have observed that,

> Presumably, technocrats derive their power when politicians and decision makers do not have the expertise to question their conclusions, which are based on highly technical arguments. Just as important is the ability to define the set of alternatives that are being considered in a given situation. This issue of the power of technicians came to the fore with the development of nuclear weapons, but it applies also to computer and systems analysts. Boguslaw writes, "It is in this sense that computer programmers, the

designers of computer equipment, and the developers of computer languages possess power to the extent that decisions made by each of these participants in the design process serve to reduce, limit, or totally eliminate active alternatives. They are applying force and wielding power in the precise sociological meaning of these terms." (R. Boguslaw 1965). But most of those who consider the question, although recognizing the dangers, conclude that there has been no surrender of power to experts and planners, and that the major decisions on the economy, social welfare, and military matters are continuing to be made by those who have the responsibility for them. (Gottlieb and Borodin 1973)

Types of Information Systems

For the past several years, great debates have raged over the centralization, decentralization, and distribution of computer systems. The controversy over centralization and decentralization has to do with both managerial control and types of computers and computer configurations to be used. Distributed computing, independent of who controls it, means that data acquisition, conversion, and storage are as close to the data source and computer output usage as possible, and are facilitated by centralized telecommunications to interconnect an organization's functions.

The present trend is for organizations with centralized data processing to think about decentralizing, and organizations with decentralized data processing to think about centralizing. Too often, these changes are thought to be technological issues stemming from technological capabilities. In fact, the technology supports both centralized and decentralized configurations as well as distributed or integrated data processing. Often the most problematic issue is management control, especially when managers of other functions think that the centralized data processing division has too much power or limits their use of EDP; therefore, attempts are made to decentralize and fragment data processing to put the power, choice, and degree of using EDP in the hands of the various departments. On the other hand, a strong, high-level manager may gradually capture parts of a decentralized configuration and, using many good technical arguments, may show how considerable money can be saved by centralizing the data processing function through the economy of scale.

Many organizations move from centralized mode to decentralized mode only when there are sufficient standards, controls, and discipline, as a result of long-term centralized operation. One reason for centralizing a previously decentralized operation is that discipline, uniformity, and adherence to standards have broken down. Centralization is often justified to restore these necessary attributes for cost effective data processing.

Both decentralized and distributed computer configurations are attractive to the user and to people in the organization served by computers. Shortening the distance between data processing and the users has many advantages. Users also prefer to have their own data processing experts. This preference often causes conflict between a centralized data processing organization and the users because it represents a challenge to the central control over the use of computers. When users have their own capabilities—especially programming—they feel much more independent and believe that they can control the reliability, quality, and safety of the services they are using. When data processing representatives of two of the largest banks in the world debated the merits of decentralization underway in one of the banks and centralization underway at the other, the technical superiority of one over the other could not be established.

To the computer security specialist, however, there is a difference. Centralized systems are not as difficult to secure as the other two, since they have a limited number of workers confined around a single computer in a single room or building. In contrast, decentralized and distributed operations require varying levels of security at numerous small sites where computing may be done on an informal basis by a small staff. Work assignments are more difficult to separate here. In addition, this kind of computing often entials the use of telecommunications, which creates an additional significant burden for security. Maintaining varying security standards across a number of relatively independent parts of an organization causes a severe problem for the computer security specialist, who must have sufficient jurisdiction over all computing areas to be effective, for he has to be aware of and sensitive to organizational changes, their purpose, and their impact on security at several sites.

As the "information is power" maxim becomes increasingly applicable to EDP, the technology will undoubtedly be abused, especially by those who consider the computer a symbol of power, or worse, a means of deception and intimidation. The manager who comes into a meeting with a thicker stack of computer listings than anyone else may be attempting to intimidate his colleagues. The concept that computer data are authoritative and correct can be used for purposes of deception. Although many such problems are ethical issues and of little concern to the computer security specialist, some of them can be considered unauthorized acts that require correction and sanctions against the perpetrators. Thus the computer security specialist should have information sources strategically placed throughout an organization if he is to obtain the intelligence he needs to ensure the safety of the organization.

Chapter 3

Computer Security Organizational Relationships

In maintaining security it is important to understand the relationships between EDP services and the rest of an organization. Individuals being served as well as other parts of an organization can both hinder and assist security operations. Thus, the computer security specialist should maintain good relations with all such areas, examples of which can be seen in the idealized organization chart in Figure 3-1. The function of each area and its relationship to computer security are described below, along with possible benefits and problems. Relationships within the data processing organization are also treated.

EDP Activities

Users

The user departments are the suppliers of data, receivers of computer output, and the entities for whom the data processing is performed. Some departments only supply data and others only receive data. All are considered users here. A payroll department that handles timekeeping as well is

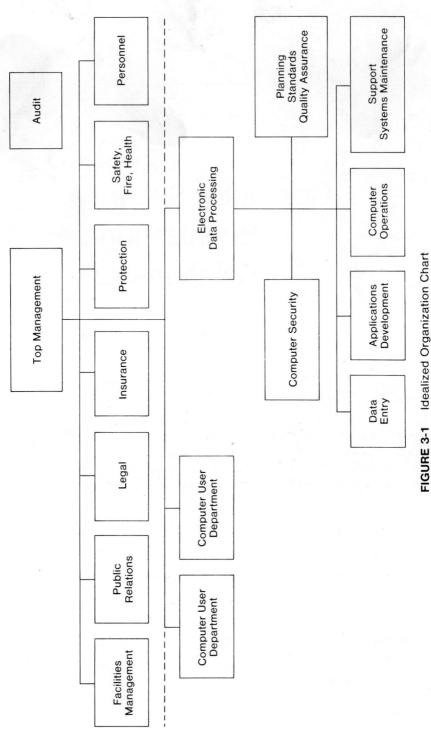

FIGURE 3-1 Idealized Organization Chart

both a producer of data and a receiver of output, and needs specialized production programs. The computer security function should also be a heavy user of the computer services, but primarily as a receiver rather than as a generator of data. On-line system access control security requires only a few inputs but many outputs of journals, operations statistics, and exception reports. The security department of a large transportation company, for example, has a computer program that produces daily reports of the movement and location of "hot" (high-priced, low-volume) cargoes that need extra protection.

Many problems and misunderstandings may arise between an EDP service and its users. Users frequently demand more service than can reasonably or otherwise be provided, while EDP personnel sometimes think that users cause them difficulties and bothersome extra work. Some users are short on praise and long on criticism, while on the other side, some EDP personnel focus on their technology rather than the aims of the organization and for this reason are resented by the users. In this type of relationship the best that the EDP service organization can expect is to go relatively unnoticed.

One possible source of serious conflict between EDP and the users is the question of accountability for security and controls. EDP must supply a sufficiently secure environment, computer system, and associated EDP services. The user must assume responsibility for adequate security in the supplying of data and the use of output. The user must also state the needs and pay the price for instituting controls in the applications programs. The EDP service systems analysts and programmers are responsible for controls in programs that are system oriented and must implement controls needed by the users.

When data are handled manually in both the user department and computer center, batch totals generated in the user department must be entered in the computer and checked against data totals in the computer. Both organizations need verification of correct input and must share this responsibility. On the other hand, only the user department is responsible for controlling out-of-range data emanating from source errors, and the data processing service is responsible for controlling out-of-range data caused by computer input and operations errors.

Obviously accountability and responsibility for security must be shared to a certain extent by the users and EDP service. The computer security specialist should make sure that all aspects of security have been explicitly and comprehensively assigned between the user and the EDP service. Technical language can cause confusion over assignments as well since some of the EDP technologists' jargon may be unintelligible to the users and vice versa. The security specialist must have a basic understanding of the technical jargon on both sides.

EDP Employees

The relationships between people in different EDP occupations have considerable bearing on computer security, for out of 700 reported cases of computer abuse, half of them involved collusion (Parker 1979). Collusion is high because no one person possesses the skills, knowledge, and access needed to carry out a technological crime. Therefore, choosing controls that will effectively impede collusion requires an understanding of the differences in jobs performed by employees and their interpersonal relationships.

Thus far, patterns of collusion indicate that typical abuses exhibit three major characteristics: overall knowledge of the system environment involved, capability to perform the technical acts, and opportunity to convert technical acts to removable gain. At least one individual has to know how unauthorized gain can be accomplished and how all the controls or methods of detection can be overcome. Usually managers or systems analysts have this overview. The technical acts are performed mainly by the people responsible for data entry, computer, and peripherals operation and programming. Conversion to removable gain can be accomplished by those having access to computer output and to negotiable assets such as checks or property controlled by computer, particularly inventory. These people are the disbursement clerks, inventory control clerks, buyers, tellers, and customers who are considered to be direct or indirect computer users.

Controls that keep the three types of perpetrators apart or that limit the possibilities for combining skills, knowledge, and opportunity also increase the need for collusion. This makes abuse more complex and thus more dangerous for them to perform. Detailed descriptions of EDP occupations and the vulnerabilities they represent are provided in Appendix F. Exposure analysis described in Chapter 11 is a means of identifying potential threats based on skills, knowledge, and access. Collusion, however, is not analyzed in great detail because of the various combinations of occupations that can be involved. That is a subject for further analysis.

Interpersonal relationships are also important for security. Security can be increased if managers become aware of and sensitive to interpersonal relationships, including sexual, family, hobby, business, sports, social and competitive interests among their employees. Computer security specialists should also be prepared to aid managers and encourage them in this regard. In addition, the expert advice and writings of industrial psychologists should be followed.

Although the computer security specialist may leave the concern for individual relationships to the appropriate managers, knowing the general relationships between departments or occupations can help him choose and develop safeguards such as badging, access devices, and methods of separating work areas. He should recognize that certain antagonistic relationships among EDP employees are related to differences in their occupations and functions. For example, antagonism commonly exists between programmers and computer operators. Each depends on the other for successful job performance; at the same time, they function in greatly different environments, have different pay scales, are at different professional levels, and have different educational backgrounds.

Figure 3-2 shows some of the common complaints among occupations, which can lead to losses if one employee sabotages another either playfully or maliciously. On the other hand, some antagonisms have a positive security effect in that they reduce the likelihood of collusion; however, encouraging antagonism is not a recommended means of control. The point is that more formal interaction that fosters distant but effective relations with good methods of resolving problems can benefit security.

Independent Consultants

In 1978 a computer security consultant violated his position of trust in a bank in Los Angeles to gain vital information that enabled him to steal $10.2 million. This computer-related crime is an example of another problem computer security may have to contend with. Consultants brought in from outside an organization may be a potential threat. Normally a consultant is retained to solve a problem vital to the organization. Because of the nature of such problems, the consultant is often entrusted with important information. An organization should be aware of the possible dangers of such a position and should not be satisfied to merely say, "Well, you have to trust somebody!" Security consultants and external auditors are in particularly sensitive positions of trust.

The computer security administrator should be involved in engaging consultants. The integrity, past record, and confidentiality practices of consultants—especially discreetness in discussing past engagements—should be important considerations. An agreement about confidentiality is essential, for an organization should be assured of the security of its working papers and documents in consultants' offices and during travel. Limiting the movement of a consultant within organization facilities and applying the need-to-know principle will help to minimize security risks. In addition, an employee assigned to work closely with a consultant can provide further control over documents and activities.

Higher Management

Higher management generally refers to all management in a direct line over EDP services and over the computer security specialist. The line management will be the same in both cases except that a security specialist might report to the security or protection division in the organization.

Complaints From → To ↓	Operators	Programmers	Media Librarians	Data Entry Clerks	Source Data Preparers	Users	Vendors' Maintenance Engineers
Operators		Job failures; failure to report errors	Unrecorded removals and submissions			Job failures; failure to report errors	Misuse of equipment; failure to report errors
Programmers	Poor program design; misleading or absent instructions		Misleading or absent instructions	Poor input formats; poor instructions	Poor input formats; poor instructions	Lack of problem understanding; poor documentation	Programs; improper use of equipment
Media Librarians	Slow or incorrect media selection	Loss of media; incorrect labelling				Loss of media	Poor handling of media
Data Entry Clerk	Data errors causing reruns	Data errors unanticipated in program design; program entry errors	Loss of media assigned to them			Data entry errors causing erroneous output	Misuse of equipment

Source					
Data Preparers	Data errors causing reruns	Data errors and out-of-range data not anticipated in program design		Poor legibility on data forms	Data errors causing reruns and incorrect output
Users	Inconvenient run schedule demands; poor job instructions	Unclear or absent problem specifications; inconvenient program change demands	Misleading or absent instructions	Inconvenient work schedule demands	Poor instructions; inconvenient work schedule demands
Vendors	Inconvenient equip. maint. sched.; equipment failures	Equipment failures		Inconvenient equip. maint. sched.; equipment failures	

FIGURE 3-2   Potential Antagonistic Relationships Among Employees

25

TABLE 3-1

Major Concerns of Top Management*
(221 respondents each picked two items, total 200 percent)

	Percent of Respondents
Insufficient controls	40
Complexity	30
Lack of user involvement	25
Lack of standards	24
Fraud exposure	21
Lack of independent review	20
Low return on investments	17
Other	13
No concerns	5

* *"Systems Auditability and Control,"* Institute of Internal Auditors, Altamonte Springs, Fla., 1977.

The mandate for security and the example of security support set for the rest of the organization is the responsibility of higher management; therefore, the effectiveness of the security specialist is highly dependent on higher management's position and practices. Clear commitments in the form of support for standards and policies should be produced by management or produced by others and approved by management. In a study of systems auditability and control done for the Institute of Internal Auditors by SRI International (SAC 1977), an international survey of top management in 1500 large businesses and government agencies brought to light a number of management's concerns for EDP (see Table 3-1). A number of top management's concerns fall into the computer security specialist's domain. Fraud exposure, which ranks fifth on the list, stands out in particular since management is normally concerned primarily with cost and performance.

The survey also found that only 17 percent of all reporting organizations submitted reports of accidental losses to higher management. It is not surprising, then, that top management believes that losses associated with EDP are minimal. Most of those surveyed have no routine procedures for reporting losses and no methods for measuring or estimating losses. Since a major responsibility of the security function is to keep management informed of material losses, a formal method for recording losses and reporting them in meaningful ways to top management will ensure a beneficial, close relationship between the security specialist and management.

In another survey, organizations with and without auditors were asked

TABLE 3-2

Assuring that EDP Applications contain Adequate Controls*
(249 respondents, two items picked, total 200 percent)

	Organizations With Auditors	Organizations Without Auditors	All
External Auditors	79	62	75
Users	64	63	64
Internal auditors	78	0	59
EDP	38	27	36
Management	21	20	21
Others	9	8	9
None	5	8	5

* *"Systems Auditability and Control,"* Institute of Internal Auditors, Altamonte Springs, Fla., 1977.

to identify departments that should be held accountable for the control of EDP applications (Table 3-2). Since computer security specialists were not uniquely identified in this survey, they do not appear on the list. It is somewhat discouraging to see internal auditors in third place. The ranking of EDP in fourth place and users in second place is consistent with the general agreement that users are primarily accountable for the adequacy of controls. A staffed security function is becoming increasingly important for EDP services, and this need should be recognized by higher management.

Other Departments of Concern

Protection, Health, and Fire Safety

Electronic data processing has been a totally foreign technology to personnel concerned with plant protection, health, and fire safety. The data processing organization should train these people to understand the basic aspects of computer technology in order to assure adequate protection and service. Some of the physical protection, health, and fire safety responsibilities related to computers should be assumed by the EDP function, especially if a computer security specialist is on the EDP staff. In fact, protection and fire safety organizations should work closely with the computer security specialist in providing a secure and safe environment for the computer operation. Physical security for the EDP facilities begins with a secure and safe environment, which should be the responsibility of the plant protection, health, and fire safety organization(s). This environment includes all rooms, walls, and areas surrounding the building that houses the data processing facilities, as well as the immediate neighborhood. This topic will be treated in detail later.

Audit

Audit departments are rapidly increasing their EDP capabilities, and the EDP department should encourage this development since the audit function can help EDP management assure compliance with security policies. The audit function must have the responsibility for reviewing computer security to assure management that protection is adequate and complies with policy. The EDP function could provide, at least on a temporary basis, various specialists in computer technology to transfer needed technical knowledge and skills to the audit function.

A few EDP managers might consider audit a threat, especially those who assume that audit will force a whole new level of complex constraints and controls onto the computer operation that EDP management is barely able to control adequately in its present state. This does not have to be the case if audit and EDP management work closely together, and in fact, a more effective EDP service and increased reliability and security are bound to result from such a relationship. How the two can cooperate is described in other chapters.

Insurance

Although specialized insurance is now available for EDP services, it is complex and requires knowledge of insurance and computer technology if coverage is to be appropriate. Unfortunately, the insurance executives of an organization are rarely familiar enough with data processing to ensure such coverage without the close support of EDP management. In many cases, EDP management, particularly the computer security specialist, has to seek the attention and assistance of the insurance executives to assure adequate insurance coverage. Obviously, the computer security specialist needs to be familiar with the various forms of EDP insurance.

Legal

The legal staff of an organization can help the computer security specialist make sure that safeguards, controls, and security techniques are consistent with the legal requirements of the organization. EDP management should encourage its legal department to study the special needs of EDP services—in particular, liability, property rights, and bonding of employees—to assure the most favorable resolution of any legal problems that may arise. Increasing numbers of attorneys in private practice have become expert in EDP legal matters and their assistance can assure compatibility of EDP services and the law. An excellent book on this subject is *Your Computer and the Law,* by Robert Bigelow and Susan Nycum (1976).

Public Relations

Now that computers have great visibility in the media, many kinds of significant events can arouse the interest of newspapers, radio, and television. Contingency plans should be established with the public relations department of an organization to assure that losses are reported properly and that such reports do not reflect adversely on the organization. Careful reporting is particularly important in cases of major losses (including criminal acts) associated with the EDP operation. All EDP employees should be briefed periodically concerning proper procedures for dealing with inquiries from the media. A company's public relations department, which should obviously have a basic understanding of EDP, can be most helpful in this respect.

Personnel

Three functions of personnel departments are pertinent to computer security: hiring, employee relations, and employee services. Hiring procedures might help to identify individuals known to be risks. A continuing study of computer abuse at SRI International indicates, however, that few of the known computer criminals would have been screened out before employment by means of reasonable screening methods, so that the screening process can be expected to identify only the obvious career criminal and unstable person. Competent personnel departments normally have the skills and knowledge to carry out such screening, but they must be particularly cognizant of the trustworthiness demanded for positions in data processing. The computer security specialist can help by ranking job positions and by indicating trust requirements in job descriptions related to data processing. It would be desirable for him to interview all final applicants for positions of high trust. The computer security specialist should work with the personnel department regarding employee relations through initial and periodic briefings for employees, employment termination practices, and services for employees that might help deter acts resulting in losses.

Facilities Management

Facilities management is concerned with providing work space, air conditioning, utility services, and furnishings. This function should not be confused with facilities management of computer services. The security specialist should work with this department to make sure that the environment and services are conducive to security. For example, the layout and assignment of work space should minimize movement of people through the work spaces of others, and reliable air conditioning and utility services should be provided along with secure containers for sensitive assets. This department also looks after the proper destruction of data media trash, removal of clutter, and cleanliness.

Executive Security Policy

On July 27, 1978, the U.S. Office of Management and Budget issued to all heads of agencies Transmittal Memorandum No. 1 under Circular No. A-71 on Security of Federal Automated Information Systems. This memorandum established a comprehensive policy regarding establishment of computer security programs in all nondefense computer centers, a procedure for adopting security standards, a requirement for security in all hardware and software procurements, plus guidance on conducting risk analyses, performing security audits, developing contingency plans, and establishing personnel security policies. Various roles are specified for the National Bureau of Standards, General Services Administration, and Civil Service Commission.

This memorandum is a significant milestone for computer security in the federal government, for it is a well-conceived document worthy of general use. It is presented below in modified form because it could be used by top management to establish computer security policy in any organization that uses computers. The agencies' roles have been replaced by the appropriate departments in a typical business organization.

To: Heads of Departments That Supply, Use, or Provide Assistance to Electronic Data Processing Services

Subject: Security of Electronic Data Processing Systems and Services

1. _Purpose_. This memorandum promulgates policy and responsibilities for the development and implementation of computer security programs. More specifically, it:
   a. Defines the division of responsibility for computer security between the electronic data processing department, computer security function, personnel department, and top management.
   b. Establishes requirements for the development of management controls to safeguard personal, proprietary, and other sensitive data in electronic systems.

    c. Establishes a requirement for the organization to implement a computer security program and defines a minimum set of controls to be incorporated into each department's computer security program.

    d. Requires the computer security function to develop and issue computer security standards and guidelines.

    e. Requires the protection department to issue policies and regulations for the physical security of computer facilities consistent with standards and guidelines issued by the computer security function. Requires that specifications for the procurement of electronic data processing equipment, software, and related services include security requirements and that all procurements meet the security requirements.

    f. Requires the personnel department to establish personnel security policies for personnel associated with design, operation, or maintenance of computer systems, or having access to data in computer systems.

2. *Background.* Increasing use of computer and communications technology to improve the effectiveness of organization programs has introduced a variety of new management problems. The public and numerous boards of directors have expressed concern about the risks associated with electronic processing of personal, proprietary, or other sensitive data. In some instances, computer and communications technology has been misused to perpetrate crime. In other cases, inadequate administrative practices along with poorly designed computer systems have resulted in improper payments, unnecessary purchases, or other improper actions. The policies and responsibilities for computer security established by this memorandum supplement other related organization policies.

3. <u>Definitions.</u> The following definitions apply for the purposes of this memorandum:

    a. "Automated decision-making systems" are computer applications that issue checks, requisition supplies, or perform similar functions on the basis of programmed criteria, with little human intervention.

    b. "Contingency plans" are plans for emergency response, backup operations and post-disaster recovery.

    c. "Security specifications" are a detailed description of the safeguards required to protect a sensitive computer application.

    d. "Sensitive application" is a computer application that requires a degree of protection because it processes sensitive data or because of the risk and magnitude of loss or harm that could result from improper operation or deliberate manipulation of the application (for example, automated decision-making systems).

    e. "Sensitive data" are data that require a degree of protection owing to the risk and magnitude of loss or harm that could result from inadvertent or deliberate disclosure, alteration, or destruction of the data (for example, personal data, proprietary data).

4. *Responsibility of top management.* Top management is responsible for assuring an adequate level of security for all organization data, whether processed internally or externally. This responsibility includes the establishment of physical, administrative, and technical safeguards to adequately protect personal, proprietary, or other sensitive data. It also includes assuring that automated processes operate effectively and accurately. In fulfilling this responsibility top management shall establish policies and procedures and assign responsibility for the development, implementation, and operation of the computer security program. The organization's computer security program shall be consistent with all organization policies, procedures, and standards. In consideration of problems that have been identified in relation to existing practices, the computer security program shall at a minimum:

a. Assign responsibility for the security of each computer installation operated by the organization, including installations operated directly by or on behalf of the organization to a management official knowledgeable in data processing and security matters.

b. Establish personnel security policies for screening all individuals participating in the design, operation, or maintenance of computer systems or having access to data in computer systems. The level of screening required by these policies should vary from minimal checks to full background investigations commensurate with the sensitivity of the data to be handled and the risk and magnitude of loss or harm that could be caused by the individual. These policies should be established for contractor personnel as well. Personnel security policies for employees shall be consistent with other policies.

c. Establish a management control process to assure that appropriate administrative, physical, and technical safeguards are incorporated into all new computer applications and significant modifications to existing computer applications. This control process should evaluate the sensitivity of each application. For sensitive applications, particularly those which will process sensitive data or which will have a high potential for loss, such as automated decision-making systems, specific controls should at a minimum, include policies and responsibilities for:

(1) Defining and approving security specifications prior to programming the applications or changes. The views and recommendations of the computer user organization, the computer installation, and the individual responsible for the security of the computer installation shall be sought and considered prior to the approval of the security specifications for the application.

(2) Conducting and approving design reviews and application

systems tests prior to using the systems operationally. The objective of the design reviews should be to ascertain that the proposed design meets the approved security specifications. The objective of the system tests should be to verify that the planned administrative, physical, and technical security requirements are operationally adequate prior to the use of the system. The results of the design review and system test shall be fully documented and maintained as a part of the official records of the organization. Upon completion of the system test, an official of the organization shall certify that the system meets the documented and approved system security specifications, meets all applicable policies, regulations and standards, and that the results of the test demonstrate that the security provisions are adequate for the application.

d. Establish a program for conducting periodic audits or evaluations and recertifying the adequacy of the security safeguards of each operational sensitive application including those which process personal, proprietary, or other sensitive data, or which have a high potential for financial loss, such as automated decision-making applications. Audits or evaluations are to be conducted by an organization independent of the user organization and computer facility manager. Recertifications should be fully documented and maintained as a part of the official documents of the organization. Audits or evaluations and recertifications shall be performed at time intervals determined by the organization, commensurate with the sensitivity of information processed and the risk and magnitude of loss or harm that could result from the application operating improperly, but shall be conducted at least every three years.

e. Establish policies and responsibilities to assure that appropriate security requirements are included in specifications for the acquisition or operation of computer facilities, equipment, software packages, or related services. These requirements shall be reviewed and approved by the management official assigned responsibility for security of the computer installation to be used. This individual must certify that the security requirements specified are reasonably sufficient for the intended application and that they comply with current computer security policies, procedures, standards, and guidelines.

f. Assign responsibility for the conduct of periodic risk analyses for each computer installation, including installations operated directly by or on behalf of the organization. The objective of this risk analysis should be to provide a measure of the relative vulnerabilities at the installation so that security resources can effectively be distributed to minimize the potential loss. A risk analysis shall be performed:

(1) Prior to the approval of design specifications for new computer installations.

    (2) Whenever there is a significant change in the physical facility, hardware, or software at a computer installation. Criteria for defining significant changes shall be commensurate with the sensitivity of the information processed by the installation.

    (3) At periodic intervals to be established by the organization, commensurate with the sensitivity of the information processed by the installation, but not to exceed five years, if no risk analysis has been performed during that time.

g. Establish policies and responsibilities to assure that appropriate contingency plans are developed and maintained. The objective of these plans should be to provide reasonable continuity of data processing support should events prevent normal operations. These plans should be reviewed and tested at periodic intervals of time commensurate with the risk and magnitude of loss or harm that could result from disruption of data processing support.

5. *Responsibility of the Computer Security Function.* The Computer Security Function shall develop and issue standards and guidelines for assuring security of automated information. Each standard shall, at a minimum, identify:

a. Whether the standard is mandatory or voluntary.

b. Specific implementation actions that departments are required to take.

c. The time at which implementation is required.

d. A process for monitoring implementation of each standard and evaluating its use.

e. The procedure for departments to obtain a waiver to the standard and the conditions or criteria under which it may be granted.

6. *Responsibility of the Electronic Data Processing Department.* The manager of the Electronic Data Processing Department shall:

a. Issue policies and regulations for the physical security of computer facilities consistent with standards and guidelines issued by the computer security function.

b. Assure that procurement requests for computers, software packages, and related services include security requirements.

c. Assure that specifications for computer hardware, software, related services, or the construction of computer facilities are consistent with standards and guidelines established by the computer security function.

d. Assure that computer equipment, software, computer room construction, guard or custodial services, telecommunications services, and any other related services meet the security requirements established and are consistent with other applicable policies and standards.

7. *Responsibility of the Personnel Department.* The Personnel Department with assistance from the Computer Security Function shall establish personnel security policies for personnel associated with the design, operation, or maintenance of computer systems, or having

access to data in computer systems. These policies should emphasize personnel requirements to adequately protect personal, proprietary, or other sensitive data, as well as other sensitive applications.
Requirements for personnel checks imposed by these policies
should vary commensurate with the sensitivity of the data to be handled and the risk and magnitude of loss or harm that could be caused
by the individual. The checks may range from merely normal reem-
ployment screening procedures to full background investigations.

SECTION II
THE NATURE OF COMPUTER COMPUTER SECURITY

Chapter 4
Concepts and Definitions

Security is a fuzzy concept that has resisted standardization efforts, partly because there are so many types of assets, threats, and conditions of risk. Assets and potential threats can be categorized, and corresponding security domains, principles, functions, methods, and safeguards can be developed, but effectiveness and completeness of safeguarding, identification of all material threats, and risk assessment fall short of the urgent needs. Attempts are now being made, however, to apply analytical methods to a difficult and diverse subject.

Security Definitions

Security is an ill-defined term in the technical literature. It has been used to denote protection and well-being of political entities, as in the term "national security." It may also refer to industrial protection provided by the security or protection departments of organizations. Police forces having limited responsibilities are also sometimes called security forces. The standard lexical definition equates security with freedom from danger, fear, anxiety, uncertainty, economic vicissitudes, and so forth.

Security, confidentiality, and privacy are often confused. For example, the term "computer privacy" is often incorrectly used to mean computer security. Privacy, however, refers to a social issue involving a human right and is not to be confused with security. Confidentiality is the state of being private or secret. Confidentiality is established in relation to a particular classification of data and a corresponding set of rules authorizing and limiting collection, dissemination, and storage of data. In other words, privacy is assured by imposing rules of confidentiality for the use of personal data that are safeguarded by security actions and functions.

Security is made up of six functions: avoidance, deterrence, prevention, detection, recovery, and correction. They are described in Chapter 5, except avoidance, which is treated below. Many domains of security as implied by the terms computer security, computer system security, data security, physical security, operational security, procedural security, terminal security, and telecommunications security are associated with the safe use of computers and freedom from loss. Computer security and data security are commonly used generic terms, but in addition computer security may mean security inside a computer and data security may refer to any body of data, computerized or not. Table 4–1 defines the terms and domains of security referred to throughout this book.

One final distinction to be made is that a safeguard can be automatic (automatic security) or manual (manual security). A manual safeguard requires real-time dependence on the correct, authorized activities of one or more people. An automatic safeguard functions without human intervention except for starting, stopping, monitoring, testing, and possibly replenishing.

Risk Avoidance

The principal function of security can be thought of as the reduction of risks to acceptable levels. An equally valid, additional function of security is avoidance of risk. Avoidance is an obvious part of the broader goal of making organizations safe in their use of computers. Analysis of the risk equation within this more basic goal illustrates the value of risk avoidance as a basic security concept.

The risk equation is $R = L \times P$, where R is risk in terms of expected loss, L is potential loss, and P is probability or expected frequency of loss. Applying the principal function of security reduces R by reducing L and P. Security including risk avoidance within the broader goal includes the possibility of making a risk equal zero by making $L = O$ or/and $P = O$.

TABLE 4-1
Definitions of Security

TERM	DOMAIN	SAFEGUARD EXAMPLES
Computer security	Generic.	
Computer system security	Functions of the CPU and attached peripheral and storage devices. Resident operating system software.	Storage access control. Privileged function levels. User and program access control. Exception reporting. Program-calling protocol control.
Data security	Not used in this book.	
Physical security	Rooms, adjacent hallways, buildings and immediate vicinities housing computer systems, telecommunications, environmental maintenance and control equipment, power facilities equipment, data preparation and entry equipment, supply storage and EDP personnel work areas.	Entrance and exit control of people and materials. Fire, water, heat, cold, chemicals, earthquake, lightning, radiation, explosion, and physical force controls.
Operational security	EDP, telecommunication environmental control and power equipment operation activities.	Operation log-keeping. Emergency or anomaly instructions documentation and training. Recovery program.
Procedural security	EDP, user, vendor and management personnel.	Personnel identification methods and procedures. Security briefings for people in positions of trust. Background screening. Intelligence gathering.
Terminal security	Terminal equipment, personnel and adjacent areas.	All safeguards described above are applicable.
Telecommunications security	Telecommunication equipment, personnel, transmission paths and adjacent areas.	All safeguards described above are applicable. Transmission path redundancy. Cryptography.

This would make $R = O$ and avoid the need for safeguards altogether.

This line of reasoning leads to the conclusion that the first step in a security review should be risk avoidance by making both L and P equal zero. This can also be accomplished in the two succeeding steps of risk assessment; assets identification (Chapter 9) by making $L = O$ and threats identification (Chapter 10) by making $P = O$.

Risk avoidance as a first step consists of analyzing the safety of the organization in its business and undertakings. Are there activities of the organization that should be stopped because the risks are inherently too high? For example, in selling its excess computer time, an organization might dangerously expose its data and programs, and might inadvertently provide physical and logical (terminal) access to others. The need for security may cause this activity to be terminated and help to avoid many risks.

Are there any activities of an organization that should not be computerized? Some current applications or ones planned for computerization might have to be done manually if sufficient security in computer use is not possible. Here, too, avoidance may be exercised to eliminate a risk. However, note that in this case a computer security problem may be avoided at the expense of some other security problems. That is, avoidance of computer security problems may merely create new problems for other types of security. The result may or may not be overall avoidance of risk for the organization. Reduction of risk is more likely if the activity is more safely done manually than by computer. At the same time, risk avoidance in one context may merely shift risk to a larger context.

The computer security specialist has an opportunity to avoid risk by participating in the decision to authorize new computer applications before system design starts. At this initial stage he can challenge or at least question the prudence of starting a system development when risk is unacceptably high. The specialist, however, would require considerable insight into future potential threats in order to make such a challenge.

Assets

Identification of what must be protected should be the next step in making an organization secure from loss. Since computer security is a branch of security of the organization, only a subset of all assets is to be considered. These assets are presented in Table 4–2 in generic form but in no particular order of importance or risk. The complex subject of risk is treated in Chapter 9. This is a deceptively simple list, which can be expanded greatly when specific items are tabulated under each generic category and when each form and location are identified. For example, a large data processing de-

TABLE 4-2

Assets Subject to Computer Security

Data processing staff
Computer system services
Computer-related facilities
Power, water, and communication utilities
Computer and peripheral equipment
Supplies and data storage media
System and utility computer programs and documentation
Application computer programs and documentation
Data
Safeguards

partment may have thousands of computer programs, each in source language and object or machine language, copies of which may be found in programmers' desks, the program listing library, punch card files, tape library, on-line program test library, on-line production library, and backup storage facilities.

Two highly important items on the list are often overlooked. First, the protection of people is paramount. In this case, the people are the data processing staff members. Secondly, no other assets can be protected unless the safeguards protecting them are also protected, in the sense that they will work reliably and that subversion of them is resisted.

Some assets may need no protection because they are not subject to potential or active threats of loss. Therefore, identification of assets has meaning only when coupled with potential and active threats.

Threats

A threat is an indication of an impending undesirable event; for example, a threat can be an expression of intent to inflict injury or damage. Three types of threats are recognizable: (1) potential threats, for example, a data entry clerk might be able to press the wrong key; (2) active threats, for example, data entry clerk threatens to press the wrong key if his demands are not met; and (3) accomplished or actualized threats, for example, a data entry clerk has pressed the wrong key.

In addition, threats can be classified according to type of act. The three types are natural disasters, errors or omissions, and intentional acts. The last two categories also include disasters caused by people such as fires, floods, and explosions. For protection purposes, the types of acts can be classified simply as accidental and intentional. Many intentional acts are classified as crimes such as fraud, theft, embezzlement, extortion, larceny, and mischief when the perpetrators are convicted.

One's approach to improving security will differ greatly for the two main types of security: protection from accidents and protection from intentional acts. The distinction made between accidents and intentional acts and treating them as separate problems will become obvious later in this chapter. Although separate treatment has a great effect on safeguarding and prevention, it has little effect on recovery after a loss, because at that point the cause becomes irrelevant. The two problems must be treated in parallel and their combined effects must be considered in assessing the total risk, potential losses, and economic justification of avoiding both types of threats by adopting appropriate security measures.

Characteristics of Accidental and Intentional Acts

Frequency. Incidence of errors and omissions in computer service organizations is usually sufficiently high to warrant statistical analysis of loss cases. A limited number of cases, however, is often tolerated because the expense of reducing loss any further is not cost effective. Analysis can be used to identify the major locations and sources of errors and omissions. From statistical data on the incidence of accidents we can calculate probability and expected loss from these problems.

Conversely, the low incidence of intentionally caused losses makes statistical analysis difficult. Only in limited cases, such as credit card and some other payment frauds, has the incidence been high enough to warrant statistical analysis. Most intentional acts, especially those involving significant losses, are detected so infrequently that attempts to calculate probability, expected loss, nature, patterns of location, and source are difficult. Therefore, quantitative risk analysis at the present time can be used successfully in few situations. Although past experiences might be projected into potential situations for the purpose of calculating statistical probabilities, their overall usefulness would probably be minimal.

Unsolved Problems. Few cases of accidentally caused losses remain unsolved. Efforts to control unintentional losses have been made throughout the development of electronic data processing, so that adequate solutions are known for most common errors and omissions. Most of the causes of errors and omissions are obvious and the solutions equally obvious. It remains to apply these solutions in a cost-effective manner.

In contrast, significant security problems concerning intentionally caused losses remain unsolved. The technical security of currently available computer systems is inadequate against attacks from potential perpetrators (such as systems programmers) who have sufficient skills, knowledge, and opportunity. Moreover, general purpose computer operating systems are basically unpredictable. Therefore, proving the integrity of a system and guaranteeing freedom from unauthorized changes or enhancements are not possible at this time. Neither practical prevention nor adequate detection capabilities are currently known for such sophisticated attacks as Trojan Horse methods, salami techniques, data leakage, logic bombs, asynchronous attacks, or post system failure attacks (Denning and Denning 1977). Another problem to be solved is how to verify the identity of legitimate remote system users. Where technical safeguards are inadequate, therefore, more difficult and less satisfactory methods of safeguarding must be developed for protection from intentional acts.

Act Complexity. Accidentally caused losses derive from single, isolated acts. Each incident is, in general, unrelated to other loss incidents. On the other hand, an intentionally caused loss commonly results from sequences of dependent and independent authorized and unauthorized acts. The loss may stem from intentional efforts capitalizing on observed errors and omissions. Many perpetrators deliberately increase the complexity of intentional acts in order to avoid detection or apprehension.

Singularity of Source. One person usually is responsible for an error or omission even though other people may cause extenuations, whereas more than one individual frequently perpetrates an intentional act. Half the known cases of computer abuse have involved collusion. Compared to manual, or noncomputer-related fraud, embezzlement, and other such acts, collusion is more prevalent in the computer crimes, primarily because computer crimes require more skills, knowledge, access, time or resources, than any one person usually possesses in the technically oriented environments of the computer systems. Security strategies and safeguards must be far more elaborate when one attempts to deal with the possibility of collusion.

Complexity of Perpetrator Behavior. Behavior that causes errors and omissions is relatively simple, for it is related to conditions prevailing at the instant of the act. After the act, the perpetrator need, at most, defend only the weakness that resulted in error. In contrast, the behavior of most people performing intentional acts is highly complex. Interviews with twenty-three people who intentionally perpetrated computer crimes have revealed that personal problems or goals preceded their search for the vulnerable points of a particular computer system or work environment (Parker 1976a). Searching or studying a system for vulnerabilities is, however, only one facet of the complex behavior pattern of intentional perpetrators. Once motivated to penetrate and use a system to his own ends, a perpetrator plans, plots, gathers information, organizes, conspires, and finally rationalizes all of his intentional acts. Effective security must address all of these issues.

Using Errors for Intentional Acts.   An error threat could be applied to each loss, which could also have an intention threat associated with it. The error threat could easily become intentional as demonstrated by the following example. A person who has committed an error might conclude that if it recurred, it could result in advantage to him. He could subsequently "let the error happen again," and thus would convert the erroneous act into an intentional one, even though it could be considered a passively intentional act. His next move might be to compromise or avoid a safeguard designed to detect and record the "error." This move would convert his act to an active one, the prevention of which must include protection of the safeguard from compromise as well as protection of the asset subject to loss. This scenario demonstrates the need to consider all error threats to be intentional threats. An appropriate safeguard can then be chosen by means of a risk analysis based on all possible threats.

Sources of Security Assistance.   Accidentally caused losses have been extensively studied and discussed in the technical literature for many years. However, most technical literature that claims to treat accidental and intentional acts primarily addresses accidentally caused losses. Professional societies and governmental organizations dedicated to the prevention of intentionally caused losses have only recently focused on the problems associated with computer technology. The American Society for Industrial Security, the U.S. Justice Department, the International Association of Chiefs of Police, National Crime Prevention Association, and Surety Association of America have only begun to seriously or significantly address the criminal aspects of computer use.

Security Checklists.   Much of the literature relies heavily on checklist or cookbook approaches to computer security (Krauss 1972; Martin 1973; Patrick 1974). Strategy is based on the concept of implementing the well-known safeguards and controls identified in the checklists. Although this approach is particularly helpful in handling errors and omissions, it is neither sufficient nor effective in dealing with intentionally caused losses. Perpetrators can easily learn of the safeguards and controls identified in checklists; thus their methods for compromising the system can be designed to avoid them. Merely installing a safeguard named in a checklist is not sufficient protection from intentional acts. Such a checklist rarely includes information concerning the need and means of protecting the safeguard itself from attack or compromise.

Strategy and Safeguard Independence. Each possibility for error or omission can be effectively treated in isolated ways, because one loss will be only sequentially any other loss. On the other hand, each possibility for intentionally caused losses must be covered comprehensively to have any effect. As a result, all possible acts leading to the loss must be taken into account. A safeguard against an intentional act will often have impact on other types of acts or losses, but it may only partially supply adequate protection. Techniques for the prevention of a particular loss could lead to the formulation of a security strategy involving many safeguards, possibly multiple rings of safeguards. Further, imposing a safeguard must be considered in terms of its potential for creating other possible vulnerabilities. If a safeguard fails to deter a perpetrator, he will often simply neutralize it, seek ways around it, or seek other vulnerabilities.

Safeguard Compromise. It can generally be assumed that the integrity of the safeguard aimed at preventing accidental losses will be ensured and sustained. Safeguards may fail as a result of errors, but in general these errors will be independent of the errors that the safeguard is preventing. Safeguards are, however, vulnerable to intentional attack as part of the perpetrator's strategy in carrying out an intentional act. Thus safeguards should not be compromised or they will become part of the total loss that they are meant to prevent or detect. In this sense, a safeguard must be considered an asset to be protected if it is to perform adequately when needed.

Level of Protection. The level of protection that a safeguard offers against an accidental act can be readily determined from the one-for-one, act-safeguard relationship. A higher incidence of accidents would no doubt facilitate the calculation of loss probability. In intentionally caused acts, the level of protection is determined on the basis of a combination of possible acts and safeguards associated with a given asset. Lack of statistics makes effectiveness difficult to determine.

Achievable Protection Level. Accidental losses can be largely prevented or, at least, can be minimized for a wide range of possibilities. One reason is that the success of protection can be accurately measured from incidence statistics, and the appropriate security then can be instituted on the basis of the need that is determined. Because there are few unsolved protection problems with accidental losses, it is possible to control incidents to any degree desired, within the limits of economic considerations.

A high level of protection from intentionally caused losses is difficult to achieve because our knowledge of vulnerabilities is incomplete. An individual estimate of loss could be affected by many factors, including the difficult-to-determine completeness of protection. The escalating one-upsmanship and increasing sophistication of perpetrators' methods make reliable measurement impossible.

Potential Perpetrators. The potential perpetrators of accidental loss can be easily identified. These are persons having the access and authorization to perform an act that might result in an accidental loss. Conversely, potential perpetrators of intentionally caused losses are difficult to identify. They include not only those identified in connection with accidentally caused losses, but also the larger numbers of people who might have an opportunity to gain the necessary skills, knowledge, and opportunity to perform an unauthorized act. For example, wherever remote terminals are used, impersonation alone would account for a large number of people who might be able to attack a computer system.

Potential Perpetrator Capabilities. Accidentally caused losses tend to correlate with minimum skills, knowledge, and resources of potential perpetrators, and of course opportunity is a significant factor. Intentionally caused losses, however, can be correlated with maximum possible skills, knowledge, opportunity, resources, and time to commit the act. The perpetrator's search for attack possibilities and the security specialist's matching search for protective devices constitute a game in which each side pits its maximum capabilities against those of the other side.

Loss Limits. Accidentally caused losses are limited in size. Where the size of the loss can vary, the probability of detection and termination of the loss grows in proportion to the size of the loss. The victim is ordinarily able to observe, measure, and limit accidental losses in a timely manner. However, detection of intentionally caused losses in a timely manner is not necessarily related to the size of the loss. Exceptionally large losses can go undetected when the perpetrator puts forth significant effort to conceal the losses. In addition, as criminal methods become increasingly automated, it will be possible for large losses to occur in a matter of milliseconds; people may not be able to react quickly enough to that kind of situation.

Detection. Perpetrators of accidentally caused losses have no conscious intention of erring before and during their acts. Therefore, if an attempt is made to avoid detection, it occurs after the loss. Less fear of detection, less reluctance to report the loss, and greater cooperation with the victim in recovery are evident in accidental loss situations than in intentional acts. Interviews have revealed that perpetrators greatly fear unanticipated detection before, during, and after their acts, so that much of their efforts and resources go into prevention of detection. Thus detection of intentionally caused losses becomes a greater challenge than it is for accidentally caused losses and should occupy a greater amount of the security specialist's attention.

Two Theoretical Approaches to Probability of Loss

The difference in risk between accidental and intentional acts can be shown in mathematical terms, even though this procedure is highly theoretical and not intended for practical use. Given are an asset subject to accidentally or intentionally caused loss, its environment, and a population of potential perpetrators with known skills, knowledge, access, resources, time, and motivation. The probability P of a particular type and size of loss L from any possible independent accidental acts a_i ($i = 1, 2, \ldots n$) with probabilities of their occurrence $p(a_i)$ is

$$P(L) = \sum_n p(a_i) - \prod_n p(a_i)$$

This suggests that a safeguard that reduces the probability of an act a_i for any value of i will reduce P(L).

The probability P of a particular type and size of loss L from any possible independent intentional acts a_i ($i = 1, 2, \ldots n$) with probabilities of their occurrence $p(a_i)$ is

$$P(L) = \underset{n}{\mathrm{Max}} \left\{ p(a_i) \right\}$$

This conclusion is based on the theoretical premise that any potential perpetrator will perform rationally in choosing the one act showing the greatest probability of success. This suggests that an entirely different result would occur from installing a safeguard that reduces the probability of an intentional act a_i for any i. If it were the act with greatest probability, it would have the most significant effect on P(L) by directly reducing it by the amount that would cause the act of next largest probability to determine the value of P(L). If the probability of any other act was to be reduced, there would be no change in P(L). Therefore, safeguards have no effect except for those that reduce the probability of the act with greatest probability of occurrence.

Two Security Strategies

Two different security strategies are suggested by these theoretical conclusions. An optimum strategy for reducing accidentally caused events in an organization is to reduce the probabilities of that combination of acts that reduce P(L) by the greatest amount to an acceptable level, given limited security resources. An optimum strategy for safeguarding against intentional acts that reduces P(L) to an acceptable level is to reduce the probability of the act with maximum probability followed in sequence by reducing the probability of subsequently maximum probability acts until security resources have been expended, or P(L) is reduced to an acceptable level, whichever occurs first.

Applying any safeguard that reduces the probability of any accidental act will incrementally increase security. However, a safeguard that reduces the probability of an intentional act may not increase security unless it reduces the probability of the one act that represents the maximum probability of occurrence. Thus, security from intentional acts is no greater than the weakest link. This is the major difference between the two kinds of problems, assuming equal loss among all acts.

The most obvious weakness in this argument is the assumption that potential perpetrators regularly select the act having the greatest possibility of success. In addition, identification of the weakest link requires that all possible perpetrators and all acts relative to loss of a particular asset are known.

Any strategy that is applied only for accident prevention or only for intentional act prevention cannot be fully effective, because many safeguards, some with minor modification, serve both purposes. A combined strategy offers a significant advantage over currently used strategies that are organized only around computer center functional approaches (physical, operational, procedural, and system) to security strategy. The steps to be followed in applying a combined strategy are:

1. Select the intentional act with largest probability of occurrence.

2. Apply safeguards to reduce the probability.

3. Identify the accidental acts also affected.

4. Repeat Steps (1), (2), and (3) for the newly identified intentional act with largest probability until probability of intentionally caused loss is reduced to an acceptable level.

5. If the probability of accidentally caused loss is still not lowered to an acceptable level, apply safeguards to reduce the probabilities of the combination of acts that reduce the probability of accidental loss to an acceptable level.

The alternatives of applying safeguards against accidental loss first or applying safeguards without regard to accidental or intentional act differences are less effective. Safeguards aimed only at accidental acts will be ineffective against intentional acts, primarily because these safeguards are generally installed only to protect an organization from the compromise of assets and not to protect the safeguards themselves from compromise. In addition, a particular procedure in implementing safeguards may not be responsive to the strategies of the potential perpetrators who are looking for the simplest and safest route to achieve success.

Failure to use the recommended strategy results in the Maginot Line Syndrome: A monolith of obvious and traditional safeguards will be installed, and the perpetrator will merely bypass it by finding the weakest link not yet addressed by the victim organization.

Illustration of Accidental and Intentional Act Prevention

One method of implementing access control is to require passwords for entry into an on-line system from a terminal. To prevent purely accidental access in a benign environment, identities can be verified simply by entering a minimal length password or name. Prevention of intentional, unauthorized access to the system requires the following additional measures:

- Make passwords of sufficient length to reduce exhaustive search attempts.
- Assign randomly generated passwords to reduce guessing by analysis of dependence between password content and password holder characteristics or knowledge.
- Make input of passwords nonvisible to avoid observation or scavenging.
- Hold frequent briefings of password holders concerning safekeeping of passwords.
- Make password administration safe through separation of duties; invocation of need-to-know principle; appropriate transport and storage of passwords; and specific authorization of duties to accountable and trusted employees to avoid spoofing, coercion, degradation of care, and unauthorized physical access attempts.
- Provide for covert signaling by a user under duress.
- Encrypt on-line system password files and compare password in encrypted form in privileged mode computer operation to prevent technical compromise.

- Limit guessing attempts of unauthorized passwords by imposing time delays between input attempts and disconnect after three failed attempts.

- Record and verify password use periodically with password users to avoid password theft and unauthorized use.

- Analyze patterns of password use and failed access attempts for deviations from normal experience to detect unanticipated attacks.

- Test all protection mechanisms frequently and prepare and follow contingency plans to avoid attacks when system or operational failures occur.

- Perform frequent, random, independent, and visible audits to inhibit potential perpetrators and ensure safeguard integrity.

- Impose sanctions against violators.

These additional safeguards are not new, but are seldom found together in a single source. Similarly, subsets have been implemented, but are not generally found in a single computer service organization. For prevention of accidental access, only a few are needed. For prevention of intentional acts, all are needed; however, total implementation of all safeguards may still fail to protect many high-risk environments. Many more detailed specifications are needed for such items as levels of encryption effectiveness, pattern analysis of password use, password length, and audit techniques.

Level of Protection

It is difficult to set the level of protection needed in intentional loss incidents. It can be expressed, however, in terms of the work factor—that is, the effort required by an anticipated perpetrator with specified skills, knowledge, and resources who might have access to facilities where the incident could be perpetrated. There is no equivalent meaningful term such as work factor for perpetration of errors. If there were, it would probably have negative value since in most cases performing a task erroneously takes less effort than performing it correctly. The work factor is the sum of the efforts required to perform the least number of easiest acts and to compromise or avoid the necessary safeguards.

Some have argued that a sufficient level of security in the protection of an asset is achieved when the work factor is greater in cost than the value of the asset to the perpetrator. But this rule is neither practical nor adequate. Determining the work factor in terms comparable to the value of the asset is difficult enough, but determining the value of the asset to any potential perpetrator is not generally possible. Finally, this rule assumes that any given perpetrator is rational, totally knowledgeable, uses good judgment, and applies this rule with consistency. This seldom occurs in practice. The security methods in this book combine accidental and intentional acts by assuming that what appear to be accidents could also be caused by equivalent intentional acts. To avoid partial solutions and suboptimization, assume the worst, and the solutions will take care of the lesser problems.

Chapter 5
Security Functions

As noted in Chapter 4, the six basic functions of security are avoidance, deterrence, prevention, detection, recovery, and correction. The EDP security department of a large organization should be chartered to engage explicitly in each function or should be divided into subdepartments specializing in each function. In smaller organizations the functions must be shared. The talents and skills required for deterrence are clearly different from those needed for recovery or the other functions. In contrast, prevention and correction require similar skills and talent. Avoidance is a function to be carried out before consideration of safeguarding, and therefore, was treated in Chapter 4.

Security Dimensions

Security has other dimensions as well. It is perhaps most often defined in terms of physical, operational, procedural, managerial, personnel, and technical safeguards. Operational, procedural, and managerial safeguards are commonly combined under the operational category. This is convenient for

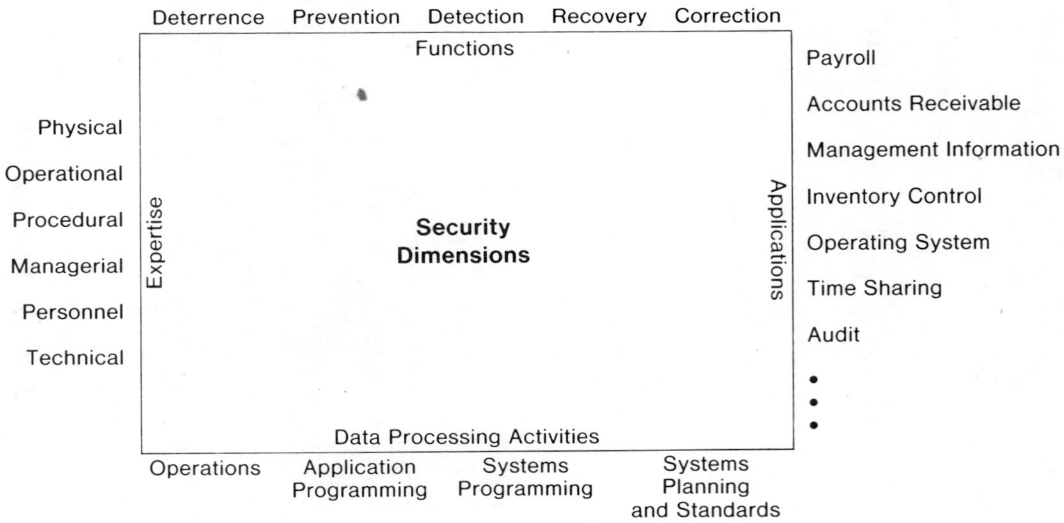

FIGURE 5-1 Dimensions of Computer Security

identifying and associating security specialties of people engaged in security work. Physical security has long been the domain of plant protection or guard departments and the profession is represented by the American Society for Industrial Security. Systems and procedures analysts are specialists who can adapt to operational, procedural, and managerial security. Personnel specialists can deal with personnel security, and systems and application programmers and analysts and electronic engineers can deal with technical security. This type of breakdown would be an aid in staffing and training a computer security organization. It is important to recognize, however, that all security specialists must deal with the security functions identified above, whereas a particular function need not involve all specialists.

Security can be analyzed by means of data processing activities of operations, application programming, systems programming, and systems planning and standards. This breakdown can be helpful in applying security to data processing departments, and it provides a way of budgeting resources to organizations receiving the benefits and suffering the cost, and possibly suffering reduced performance related to security measures. Here, too, we must note that all security functions play a role in each activity, but that all activities do not play a role in each function.

Finally, security can be analyzed in relation to computer applications requiring security. Security can be broken down into payroll security, accounts receivable security, time-sharing security, and so forth. This breakdown can help an organization assure consistency of data protection through complete processes, for degree of security consistent with sensitivity and value of assets and for completeness in covering all assets.

This is not to deny that these other breakdowns are valuable from time to time in developing a security program and system of protecting computer-related assets. However, a more thorough and logical treatment of security concepts can be achieved here by using security functions as a framework. The four dimensions of security are summarized in Figure 5–1.

Security functions are not independent. Detection methods, devices and practices are strong deterrents when visible and known to potential, intentional perpetrators. Recovery and correction include reestablishment of prevention and detection methods, devices, and practices.

Priority of Security Functions

Priorities and reasons for security functions can be established in a security program. Table 5–1 lists the functions of security in order of highest to lowest priority for the beginning security program and for a specific vulnera-

TABLE 5-1

Priority for Security Functions

New Program	Specific Vulnerability
Basic recovery	Deterrence
Major vulnerability prevention	Prevention
Detection of less obvious events	Detection
Capability for later correction	Recovery
Deterrence for the long term	Correction

bility. Generally recovery has first priority. If none of the other functions are present, an organization must at the very least be able to recover and not go out of business from a loss. Therefore, a data processing alternative plan and production data and program files backup are essential. An organization's next priority would be prevention to at least keep obvious bad things from happening. Detection is next, for it assures that losses that would not be obviously evident are discovered on a timely basis for optimum recovery. Correction refers to the placement and restoration of prevention and detection capabilities after recovery. Finally, a new program should consider methods of deterrence. Some say deterrence against accidental or intentional acts deserves higher priority, for prevention is never assured nor even likely to work.

The correctness of the above priorities can be seen in comparison with other orderings. Deterrence, for example, does not immediately assure the prevention of loss. Correction is obviously a secondary function for a starting program and takes place only after a loss demonstrates the precence of a particular vulnerability that had not been adequately detected, prevented, and recovered. Detection is needed at first only for events that are not immediately obvious. For example, explosions are readily observable. On the other hand, excessive heat requires detection unless it can do no damage until manifested in fire in continuously observable areas. Detection should not be limited to discovery of loss events but is essential in determining whether prevention methods and devices are working. This latter function of detection is known as instrumentation and will be discussed later along with the principles of security. A beginning security organization should focus on preventing major losses ahead of detection, and normally it will devote the largest share of security resources to this function. Recovery is first a stop-gap measure and later becomes an impotant backup capability.

A problem that might arise when other functions are given high priority is seen in the case of one insurance company EDP organization, that decided that except for a few basic prevention measures such as a guard at the main entrance, all security efforts and resources would be directed toward recovery. Losses were of little concern as long as adequate recovery could be achieved. This simplistic approach soon changed after someone attacked the computer memory module with a screwdriver. Recovery was a first priority until experience and maturity showed that new priorities had to be, developed.

The prioritization of functions is applicable to an initial or stop-gap security approach. In a full security program, however, all functions must achieve equal priority. In dealing with a specific vulnerability, priorities should be ranked differently. First try to reduce a vulnerability by deterrence. This is certainly the most socially redeeming action because it will keep people from committing harmful acts or even thinking about them in the first place. If deterrence is not enough, then attempt to prevent a vulnerability from resulting in loss. When prevention fails, then at least be aware that loss events have occurred through detection. Even if prevention is assured, it is important to know whether attacks have been made against protected assets or against prevention mechanisms. This is important for planning and security justification purposes. Therefore, even if it were achievable, absolute prevention does not preclude the eventual need for detection of attacks. This position will be discussed more fully in a later section.

If deterrence, prevention, and detection are not sufficient (and they never are), then appropriate resources must be allocated to recovery and finally to correction in order to minimize the possibilities of future occurrence.

Resource Allocation to Security Functions

Allocating resources for protection from a particular vulnerability is difficult because vulnerabilities are difficult to isolate and treat separately; the same is true of security functions. The example of a salami attack (described in Appendix E) on a large payroll system amply demonstrates this problem. The hidden code (a Trojan horse) in a payroll computer program or utility subprograms used by the program has been used to cause small amounts of money, hours worked or sick, or vacation credits to be debited randomly from large numbers of employee accounts and added to favored accounts without violating or subverting controls. This type of attack illustrates part of the broad range of vulnerabilities created by unauthorized access to computer programs in a computer facility, for purposes of modification in this case, or for theft of programs or their destruction in acts of vandalism or sabotage. The unauthorized access could be in the form of physical access to programming offices or program storage areas. It could also be in the form of direct, physical computer access or access from an on-line terminal at a distant location. This latter type of access might result from password administration weaknesses. The difficulty of treating any one of these vulnerabilities in isolation is obvious.

The same problem arises in performing security functions, where deterrence might include offering confidential financial counseling to possible perpetrators. Prevention could include employee badging, physical intrusion alarms, physical access control, terminal access password protection, and computer program isolation. Detection could include confirmation of accounts, test decking, integrated test facilities, and programmer access logging coupled with programmer work-profile analysis. Recovery might include accounting of losses and making restitution to victim employees, while correction might involve changing policies and procedures and introducing new safeguards and controls.

The difficulties of allocating resources to particular vulnerabilities and among the security functions on a cost-and-risk benefit basis are great. What basis would exist to apply any set division of resources to deterrence, prevention, detection, recovery, and correction? On the other hand, overlooking any one of the security functions could seriously reduce the total security effort effectiveness. Overemphasis of any subset of the functions or vulnerabilities can result in serious suboptimization.

Poor budgeting and responsibility assignment in an organization can also lead to serious security deficiencies and suboptimizations, particularly when security responsibilities are shared by departments with separate budgets. Before considering this combinatorial problem, we should examine each security function in detail.

Deterrence

The noun "deterrence" derives from the verb "deter," which means to discourage from acting by fear or consideration of dangerous, difficult, or unpleasant attendant circumstances or consequences. Particularly important to the context there is the connotation of fear, which can be defined as an unpleasant emotional state characterized by anticipation of pain or great distress and accompanied by heightened autonomic activity. Its synonyms include dread, fright, alarm, dismay, consternation, panic, terror, and horror. Another meaning of fear is also relevant here, that of profound reverence and awe, as in "Fear of the Lord is the beginning of wisdom" (Psalms 111:10). Respect for authority is important.

Let us now identify what and who we fear in the computer context:

- Schedule overruns
- Budget overruns
- Personal injury
- Detection
- Computers
- Sickness
- Management
- Policemen
- Auditors
- Enemies
- Peers
- God

As indicated elsewhere (Parker 1976a), the profile of the computer criminal includes fear of unanticipated detection. Thus, possible sources of fear are important considerations in developing computer security.

Value of Deterrence

Some would argue that deterrence is of little value, because an individual intent upon perpetrating an act will do so, illegal or not. That may be generally true for career criminals, but it is not the case for the amateur white-collar criminal, who, according to known experience, is the predominant type of computer criminal. Once enough intent has developed sufficiently, deterrence obviously loses its value, but the whole idea of deterrence is to combat intent before it reaches that critical point.

After concluding that an unshareable problem must be solved and failing to find socially acceptable solutions, the amateur white-collar criminal, and to a lesser degree the career criminal, goes through a period of anomie. Anomie is the state in which normative standards of conduct and belief are weak or lacking; it is commonly characterized by disorientation (confusion in values), anxiety, and isolation. During this period deterrence has its greatest value because it can force an individual to deal with his problem in acceptable ways or to share it with others who could help him, for the solution by violation of trust will present too many unacceptable or disagreeable outcomes.

Deterrence prevents intent from reaching the degree necessary to carry out a violation of trust. Deterrence also confronts a person with the fact that he would violate a trust more valued than his problem solution. If the deterrent says loudly and clearly enough, "Do Not Enter Under Penalty of Law," he will recognize the implications of his desire to solve his problem in criminal ways, and he will not follow that course of action. Therefore, deterrent forces work against the necessity of problem solution in wrongful ways. This occurs during the period of anomie.

Deterrent Values of Safeguards

Detailed below are examples of safeguards, their deterrent effectiveness, and methods of improving deterrent value.

Background Investigation (Vetting). The fact that an employer has information about an employee that is not associated with his work implies that any change in his life style or personal problems is discoverable and that he is a "known quantity." An individual will hesitate to act against a victim who has considerable information about him. Improving the effectiveness of the deterrent value can be accomplished in two ways. Employees should be made aware, through an employees' manual, of the type of personal information stored by an organization. This also meets one of the criteria for privacy protection. Secondly, the times at which different information is collected should be varied so that any miscreants will be kept off balance by not knowing when possible incriminating evidence might be discovered.

Employee Counseling. The deterrent value of counseling employees, whether in drug, alcohol, or gambling abuse programs or confidential family or financial advisory services, is personal problem elimination or reduction. If people can be made to share their problems with expert personal problem solvers, legitimate solutions can be found and potential criminal acts can be avoided. Even where such services are available, their existence, successes, and assurance of confidentiality may be unknown or overlooked by the individual needing help.

The deterrent value of employee counseling can be increased by advertising on bulletin boards, in newsletters, and at employee briefings. Counseling services should be recognized as important safeguards and should be considered part of a computer security plan and program. It would be useful for all EDP employees in high positions of trust to have an annual interview with a competent psychologist. A psychologist should at least be made available for interviews at specified times and employees should be encouraged to participate in interviews by having managers set an example and sign up first. There should be a rigid regulation that nothing in the interviews will be revealed to any other person. However, the psychologist may find interviews with employees helpful when interviewing their managers.

Security Briefings. Because loss situations occur infrequently and security doesn't normally add to productiveness or performance, employees easily forget their responsibilities and the need for being alert to loss. Periodic security briefings will address this problem by sensitizing employees to the possibilities of losses. The deterrent value of briefings can be improved by emphasizing consequences of losses for the organization and for employees. Laws, codes of conduct, and possible sanctions should be described and reviewed. A healthy, reasonable dose of fear can be helpful. Participation in such briefings can also increase the impact on employees. Scenario playing, written quizzes and guest speakers can be effective.

   Codes of Conduct.   The deterrent value of rules of acceptable and unacceptable behavior is especially appealing because of the low cost. However, if the rules are to have deterrent value, management must visibly practice them and violations must be dealt with decisively and fairly. The code must be promulgated or at least strongly endorsed by top management. Suggested codes are provided in Appendixes A and B.

   Laws and Regulations.   Now that the deterrent value of laws and regulations has become a subject of wide interest (Parker and Nycum 1980), increasing emphasis is being placed directly on individual violators within organizations, as seen in legislation such as the Privacy Act of 1974, Foreign Corrupt Practices Act of 1977, and Senator Abraham Ribicoff's 1979 computer crime legislation in the U.S. Senate, and in the privacy and computer crime legislation actions in the states. However, the deterrent value of these laws will not be effective unless people are aware of them and understand their scope and meaning. This requires frequent briefings and written reminders, and might best be done by an organization's legal counsel or by a representative of the criminal justice agencies such as a prosecutor, an FBI agent, or a police detective. Awareness is the key to the deterrent value of laws and regulations (Parker 1980). Known computer criminals frequently are not aware of, or try to ignore the law-breaking aspects of their acts that could brand them as criminals. They believe they are "solving problems, not intentionally breaking laws."

   Audit.   One of the greatest values of auditing is deterrence. Every known computer criminal involved in financial fraud or theft has indicated that "beating the auditors" was part of the crime. If they had not been able to anticipate auditors' activities, they would have been deterred from their acts. The key to the deterrent value of auditing is unpredictability of the auditors' activities. Since one-third of computer criminals are managers, even they must be subjected to surprise audits to the greatest degree possible. Top management must put heavy weight on this unpredictability factor in assuring that their auditors are effective. Anyone in a position of trust must not be able to accurately predict where auditors will look next and the degree of detail and methods they will use.

   In addition, the deterrent effect can be enhanced if auditors are highly visible and participate in the observation of organizational activities. In high risk activities such as funds transfer, many large organizations, especially financial institutions, use the Chinese Army technique of assigning large numbers of auditors on a full-time basis.

Separation of Duties.   Distributing high risk assignments among two or more employees is one of the most common safeguards. It is sometimes referred to as the "maker, checker, signer concept." One worker makes or completes an item, another checks it and a third accepts responsibility for it. Where automation reduces the need for large numbers of employees and separation of duties is difficult, the alternative method of dual control or redundancy can be substituted.

The deterrent value of these techniques at the same time creates the need for collusion in perpetrating a crime. Collusion can be discouraged by generating a healthy level of mutual suspicion among people working together in high positions of trust. Employees should know they will be held partly responsible for failure to notice the unauthorized acts of others, and can be informed of their responsibility in their job descriptions or in their performance reviews. One responsibility of a computer security administrator should be to review and recommend security-related items in all job descriptions.

Physical Access Control.   Access to high risk areas is normally restricted by means of prevention controls backed up by detection capabilities. Physical access to restricted areas may also be controlled in deterrent fashion by merely telling people they will be punished if found in areas in which they don't belong.

Deterrence can be enhanced in any access control situation by making the controls more formidable. For example, uniformed and alert-looking guards would be more effective then receptionists without uniforms. Large, bold signs carrying messages such as "Unauthorized Persons Keep Out" and "Restricted Access Area" are useful. The reason for restricted access should not be displayed except for safety precaution, as in the case of radiation hazards. Exposing the breaking of access rules to the view of people also might deter an individual.

Logical Access Control.   Logical access control refers to the restriction on access to the use or contents of a computer. Such control should be applied to the use of terminals, submission of computer programs for execution, data entry, and report generation. Here the power of the computer can be used as a deterrent.

Computers are ideal for monitoring and detecting deviations from normal activity that might indicate attempts at unauthorized access. Unlike human beings, the computer never tires or fails to note even the smallest detail. Yet it is an ideal data reduction device that can be used to reduce volumes of exception data into summary form for priority action of the security specialist.

The computer user will be deterred from unauthorized access if he knows that his actions are being monitored and that he will probably be caught before he can achieve his ultimate goal. Therefore, deterrence can be increased by informing users they are being monitored in several unspecified ways. In addition an effective deterrent will inform users that detection reports are read and that action is taken. Users may test detection capabilities out of curiosity or for malicious purposes, but if no action is taken against them, the detection capability will be less than expective.

Logic and Storage Partition. A privileged instruction mode and storage partition using address limit registers, logical locks, and keys or virtual system concepts are powerful safeguards within a computer system. The greatest deterrent value here is a high work factor in compromise attempts. Complexity also discourages compromise.

Deterrence can be enhanced by reducing interest in and heroism associated with beating the system. Unauthorized game-playing should be held in contempt. The concept should be fostered that the computer is a vault for safekeeping information, and not the object of a game! Those who have mastered the complexity of a system should understand that their knowledge places them in high positions of trust and responsibility.

These are only a few of the many safeguards that have deterrent values. Further values of safeguards are examined in Chapter 12.

Application of Deterrence

The purpose of deterrence is to reduce the threat to assets that then reduces the vulnerability of the assets to loss. Vulnerability can include a low work factor situation that makes it easy and attractive for a perpetrator to cause a loss of assets. Deterrents appropriate for errors and omissions differ from those for intentional, unauthorized acts. In the former, the objective of the deterrent is to increase the skills, attentiveness, care, and positive motivation of people whose activities may cause errors and omissions. These objectives can be achieved through training, positive experience, sufficient rewards for and acknowledgement of good performance, imparting of accountability and responsibility for results, and providing reasons for loyalty and identity with the organization. These are all the responsibilities of line management, from the highest executive to the lowest employee.

Intentional, unauthorized acts that could result in losses are prevented primarily by reducing motivation and importance of reasons for performing such acts. This can be done by keeping people unaware of gain to be made and by reducing the need and desire for unauthorized gain. A high degree of protection from an unauthorized act is considered a passive deterrent. The type of active deterrence considered here takes place before an act is contemplated. A high profile of asset protection is a valuable passive deterrent except for the individual who is motivated by the challenge of committing an unauthorized attack. A safeguard will be a valuable passive deterrent if it is unavoidably visible, so as to discourage further thought of performing unauthorized acts.

Deterrence is less effective against career criminals whose livelihoods depend largely on crime. Active deterrence would have had to have been applied before he began his career of crime. The current 60 percent rate of recidivism in the United States indicates that sanctions may inhibit or re-direct the career criminal but will not stop him. In general the career crimi-nal takes pride in his wrongdoing and remains acceptable by his peers. In contrast, amateur criminals suffer shame, loss of respect and anguish in confrontations with their friends, associates, victims, and family.

Deterrence methods are based on three assumptions about causes of computer abuse. First, people in positions of trust and with computer skills, knowledge, access, and resources may be influenced by others to engage in unauthorized acts. This is particularly applicable to EDP employees and any employees who use computer services: a bank teller, welfare worker, or loan officer doing favors for customers, often in collusion with EDP employ-ees. Changing loan payment dates for a customer in financial difficulties by making unauthorized changes in master file data might be easily done by a programmer, who could rationalize his act because it was so easy to do. No one may have told him that the technical act was wrong; he might also argue that it could have happened accidentally anyway.

Another common way of rationalizing unauthorized acts is to rest on the higher ethic principle, which allows a trust to be violated for a more noble cause than maintaining the trust. Thus serious fraud can result from seemingly innocuous acts performed for ennobling purposes. Many EDP technologists in particular are naive about such matters because they focus on technical rather than on social and business matters, and they assume their technology exists in a benign rather than hostile environment. This at-titude may be changing.

To deter people in high positions of trust from committing an unauth-orized act, an organization should impart a desired set of values to these people—including all EDP technologists. For example, convince program-mers in a bank that they are bankers first and technologists second. Inform EDP employees of the business function, its mores, values, and ethics. En-courage employee-employer and customer-vendor loyalty and respect—it works both ways. Educational awareness and increased sensitivity can be achieved through newsletters, advertising, explicitly stated policies and pro-cedures, and oral briefings. As stated earlier, every EDP employee should undergo at least annual briefings and be required to review documented pol-icies and procedures and should sign statements testifying to his under-standing and acceptance of his position of trust and to his having complied with requirements. (Sample statements are presented in the appendixes A and B.)

The second cause of computer abuse is personal or business problems. The deterrents for the preceding cause are applicable here as well. In addition, advice and material aid can be given to individuals to help them solve their problems as stated in another section. Examples of problems that might motivate an employee toward computer abuse include financial, legal, marital, filial, psychological, medical, alcoholism, drug addiction, gambling, employment related, education, housing, and recreational problems. Aid should be offered on a confidential basis.

Professor Donald Cressey, a noted criminologist who interviewed hundreds of convicted embezzlers, concluded several years ago that the two most important motivational factors were needing to solve an unshareable problem and being able to verbalize their acts to conclude they were not criminals (Cressey 1971). His conclusion supports the recommendation here for confidential advisory and real aid.

Verbalization is especially important, and thus needs closer examination. In relation to verbalization, security can be thought of on three levels: no security with admonitions to avoid losses (the honor system); no security with confrontation of wrongdoing (the confrontation system); and the generally accepted system presented in this book of using prevention and detection methods. The honor system works only in limited, high peer pressure, cultural environments. However, confrontation can be a powerful passive deterrent relative to verbalization. For example, with little expense an employer can label assets as proprietary and thus clearly signal to the trusted employee that his unauthorized act with the asset is a wrongdoing. This makes it difficult for the employee to verbalize his act as acceptable behavior.

A common practice in the computer programmer office of large companies illustrates this point: Metal labels bearing serial numbers are affixed to desks, chairs, filing cabinets, and tables, and identify them as company property. It would be difficult for an employee to verbalize the taking of this furniture as acceptable behavior. At the same time, sitting on a $47 labeled table may be a box of punch cards identified only with a programmer's name written across the top with a felt pen. The punch cards contain a copy of a program that cost $300,000 to develop. This obvious inconsistency in labeling makes a strong point for confrontation.

An inexpensive but valuable passive deterrent would be to label all copies of computer programs, data, documentation computer equipment, and storage media (disks, tapes, RAMs, and PROMS). Labels might read "Property of [Company]" or "Property of [Company]. Unauthorized modification, destruction, disclosure, taking, or use is punishable by law." The labels can be placed on lead comment cards at the beginning of card decks, preprinted or computer-printed on all pages of listings, printed in manuals, or printed and affixed to the protected asset. One possible criticism of labeling is that the perpetrator will remove the labels; on the contrary, it confronts him with the realization that he is engaging in a possible criminal act.

An additional value of labeling assets is that if the labeled asset or copy is taken and becomes an issue in litigation, whether the label is present or not the victim's legal position is strengthened. This aspect of labeling is especially important because more computer programs are becoming the subjects of litigation.

The third cause for computer abuse derives from individuals attempting to reach goals in socially unacceptable ways or to reach goals that in themselves are unacceptable. The deterrents discussed above are applicable here as well. In addition, opportunities for upgrading skills and knowledge and for advancement should be opened to employees, who should be made fully aware that such opportunities and their benefits are fairly offered.

Management should be aware that many tasks in automated environments can be routine and monotonous, and that many EDP technologists are people who need mental challenges. A dangerous employee can be one who is overqualified and occupies a position of trust. He may be the one to seek unauthorized outlets for his untapped imagination and skills. In addition, management has a responsibility not to assign an employee to a position of trust that exceeds his known level of resistance to temptation.

The visibility of preventive measures has been identified as a passive deterrent, and its deterrent value has been hotly debated by industrial and national defense security professionals. Does greater benefit derive from a visible protective measure or from a secret one? This issue is discussed in Chapter 12, which treats the principles of security. It suffices to say that showing employees in position of trust that performing unauthorized acts would require great effort and especially could be detected with a high degree of probability are great deterrent forces. The visibility of detection capability is effective in that the greatest fear of the white-collar or amateur criminal is unanticipated detection. Some white-collar criminals trapped in a pattern of continuing crime reach a point at which they desire to be caught and thereby end the stress and problems they are trying to solve. A computer criminal once told me that he knew he would be caught after taking the first million dollars, but that he was attempting to steal enough to make back enough through gambling to return the money to the bank before discovery (Parker 1976b). Arrest was a great relief to him and the best solution to his problems. Another computer criminal told me that he planned to get caught in such a way that he might receive a suspended sentence and be able to go away and enjoy the $1,000,880 he had embezzled. His plans did not work out, however, for he had to serve five and a half years in San Quentin Prison (Parker 1976b).

Among twenty-five computer criminals I have interviewed, all except for these two indicated that they feared detection and being exposed as criminals (after verbalizing that they really weren't criminals) to their families, friends, and business associates.

An interesting but impractical experiment would be to invest all security resources in detection capability in a computer facility and system. All people representing a potential threat because of their skills, knowledge, and access would be informed that no preventive security measures would be taken; however, if an unauthorized act were attempted, the perpetrator would surely be detected and caught. Such a test might show the value of detection over prevention.

Deterrence should be extended to nonemployees as well. However, here the position of trust becomes one of broad social trust and therefore is not directly controllable by a single organization. Making customers and vendor's representatives aware of their responsibilities as citizens and showing a formidable security capability are most important actions. Using the fear of detection as a passive deterrent is also of great value among nonemployees.

Prevention

Prevention is the traditional security function most valued, but of course, its value is conditioned on cost effectiveness. The cost of the prevention must be less than the expected loss that could be sustained without the prevention. Absolute prevention is only a theoretical concept. Increasing intensity of attack by the perpetrator will eventually reach a point of success, when efforts result in destruction of the assets (if the goal of the perpetrator is to obtain the assets in usable form). Absolute prevention means that any perpetrator would fail in any attempt to accomplish his goals.

Within artificially defined frameworks, absolute prevention by definition can be obtained. For example, an on-line computer transaction system could be designed whereby the users of the transaction terminals would have limited capabilities to perform their functions but do no more. Suppose the framework of the prevention domain is to assure that no spurious programmed results are possible and that only authorized data assets are available for transactions. Then if the transaction system prevents the entering of programs or prevents unauthorized commands from the transaction terminals, the defined unauthorized acts would be absolutely prevented, assuming the continuous, correct functioning of the system. A terminal operator might conceivably await a specific type of system failure that precludes the correct functioning of the system safeguards, and then enter and execute unauthorized commands.

Another problem for absolute prevention is how it can take into account all possible attempts a perpetrator might make, for if he is sufficiently intent on achieving his goal and is prevented in one way, he will find another. Therefore, when all attempts to gain a defined set of assets are considered, absolute prevention must also mean universal prevention. In the example above, if the perpetrator failed to achieve his goals through the transaction terminal, he could resort to gaining access to a terminal with computer programming capability.

A more practical goal for prevention is to force the potential perpetrator to seek other means of accomplishing his goals. This approach is called relative prevention. Another possibility is partial prevention, the purpose of which is to impede the perpetrator in his activities toward his goal. This provides a deterrent effect by wearing down the perpetrator or causing him to deplete the resources he is willing to expend.

In another dimension, prevention can be termed either a technical or a procedural function. Technical prevention, which is essentially automated, requires a minimum of human, real-time activity to maintain the preventive capability. A password system for computer entry would be a useful technical or automated prevention safeguard in this case. Procedural safeguards require the real-time functioning of people to prevent unauthorized acts. For example, a guard providing access control would be a procedural safeguard. An automatic mantrap and identification verifier could replace the guard and thereby provide technical prevention. In general, technical prevention is more desirable than procedural prevention. The latter will be vulnerable because it relies on the real-time functioning of people who are inherently unstable and unreliable.

The commonly used closed circuit television (CCTV) monitoring method illustrates the weakness of procedural preventions. Remote, automatic cameras wired to TV monitors in a guard office (shack) allow guards to view critical areas such as limited access and emergency doors. A guard watches the monitors and if a breach of security occurs, he takes preventive action. Unfortunately the method does not work. Observation shows that no individual can be attentive to four or ten or a dozen monitors for a long enough period of time to be effective. Furthermore, most monitors are mounted above eye level on a wall behind the desk. Television manufacturers learned early that at that level of viewing sore necks are inevitable.

CCTV is only effective when used in conjunction with alarms. Then CCTV helps a guard evaluate whether further action is needed. But the alarm must direct the guard's attention to a monitor in the first place.

Three levels of prevention can be useful: (1) intensive prevention, the goal of which is to prevent unauthorized acts from even the most sophisticated and persistent attackers; (2) confrontation prevention, which employs enough safeguards to make any perpetrator aware that he is performing or attempting to perform an unauthorized and possibly illegal act; and (3) little prevention, which involves removing assets from direct temptation. It is obvious that the costs of prevention can escalate significantly from level 3 to level 1. A rational decision to agree on which level of prevention to impose in protecting any particular asset will simplify security planning and implementation.

Detection

Most preventive measures will not be effective unless detection is incorporated in the security system. Detection alone is usually insufficient. Timely detection is the process of determining that an unauthorized act is impending, is in progress, or has occurred recently enough to prevent or to significantly limit losses. There is little value in detection of easily heard bomb blasts; the damage has already been done. However, detection of fire is a basic security function because effective measures can then be employed to limit the loss. Detection also provides a means of recording evidence to determine the cause and source of a detected actual or potential loss.

The interesting theoretical exercise previously described of basing the entire security program on detection rather than prevention is pertinent here also. All persons coming in contact with the computer organization and those within it would be informed that although they would not be stopped from performing unauthorized acts, if they did perform the acts, they would be caught and sanctions would be imposed. The temptations in this approach would probably be too much for some computer people to resist.

Detection normally accompanies prevention safeguards. For example, a password system for terminal access to a computer should always journal failed access attempts in order to detect possible unauthorized activities. Technical or automatic detection is generally superior to manual detection because computers are ideal detection devices and humans are poor detectors owing to the routine, repetitive, and high-speed nature of electronic data processing. Deduction and evaluation are, however, still jobs primarily for humans using the computer as a tool. No rigid rules can be established in choosing technical or manual detection. For example, most heat and smoke detectors are coupled directly to fire suppression safeguards. However, where the fire suppression method might be expensive or cause damage if used unnecessarily, a delay and direct instigation by human action are favored.

Detection methods should neither embarrass innocent persons nor fail to allow for timely notice and evaluation. Volume or frequency of detection reports to humans should not saturate their ability to discriminate, deduce, and react. Some exception reports from a computer have this problem. Some computer systems are designed to print out indications of all deviations from normal activity for clerical scrutiny. This output can result in daily listings thick enough to measure in edge-inches. No one could possibly handle all this material effectively. Instead, the detail should be saved on tape and the computer used to reduce and summarize the data into several pages for human attention and to provide a data retrieval method for selected detail. Such a process might also make it practical for a higher level individual to read the report and take effective action.

It is important that the recorded results of detection be saved for future use. A means of filing detection results, especially voluminous results, should be developed in such a way that their retrieval is possible. The computer is an obvious, useful device for this purpose.

Now and then the importance of detection is overlooked. The leader of a research staff designing safeguards for a secure computer operating system was once asked why there were no detection and exception reporting features being developed as well. He replied that their safeguards were so effective that they could not be breached and thus eliminated the need for detection. Another probable reason he might have had was that prevention is the more challenging and intellectually interesting pursuit, and implementation of detection and reporting capability is tedious, routine work. The value of detection of attacks against even totally effective safeguards to apply sanctions against perpetrators was overlooked.

Recovery and Correction

If deterrence, prevention and timely detection are not practical or are not totally effective in dealing with a security problem, then recovery and correction of the weaknesses are essential.

Recovery is needed for a wide range of events and activities. Computer production jobs must be designed to recover from hardware failure, software bugs, operator error and data errors. These problems and recovery from them occur several times every day. Long-running production jobs have check-point restart capabilities every few minutes of running time or after processing batches of data. This capability limits the cost of recovery. A production job that runs several hours without check points is usually considered poorly designed. It has been claimed that providing some engineering applications involving large data arrays with check points would be more costly than taking the chance of long-running periods. Such issues are frequently debated by operations and programming staffs. It is wise for the computer security specialist to avoid such issues as long as all parties are aware of the consequences and are prepared to deal with them.

Recovery from other, less frequent and sometimes more catastrophic events occupy more time of the computer security specialist. This recovery can be expensive, difficult, and tedious. Recovery commonly takes place in an environment where people are confused, upset, and not functioning effectively. Confusion can delay and even prevent effective recovery. Security planning should therefore include the testing of threat scenarios to anticipate the failure of safeguards and possible alternative results. Documented recovery plans that are readily available are necessary to restore systems and their operation.

The cost of recovery can be significant and should be taken into account in determining the cost of a potential loss. This can be difficult. For example, the loss of a competitive advantage because of an industrial espionage theft of data should include the cost of a lost product, legal cost if a suit is contemplated, development costs, unusable production facilities, and advance sales commitment problems.

Corrections to security should be implemented immediately after recovery, when management will have the greatest motivation to support the cost of corrections. Overreaction may occur because of the recent, vivid memory of the incident and painful recovery process, so that the security specialist must approach recovery objectively at such times to maintain a sense of balance and perspective.

Contingency Backup Alternatives

Many organizations are becoming so dependent on continuous availability of their computer services that loss of a few days can sometimes be fatal. The amount of time that an organization can go without computer services is referred to as Maximum Time to Belly Up (MTBU). One large savings and loan association became concerned about MTBU after installing a highly automated on-line teller terminal system and experiencing chaotic periods after only one or two hours of down time. A study revealed that the company could endure up to seven or eight days of down time and successfully recover, whereas nine or ten days would probably lead to bankruptcy.

This increasing dependency has been revealed to top management in many organizations so that major contingency planning is now common in security programs. Because of the enormous cost of a backup computing capability, many organizations have sought alternative solutions. Many companies in metropolitan areas share the same problem and search for joint solutions. For example, three groups of companies have been formed in

France. Sixteen companies in Manhattan formed a company to develop a backup capability but failed, while others in Milwaukee, Los Angeles, and Philadelphia have started organizing similar ventures. These efforts have been spurred forward by reports of attack such as occurred in Italy during 1977–1979 when extreme leftist terrorists attacked twenty-six computer centers with submachine guns, Molotov cocktails, and plastic explosives. The FBI warned at the time that international terrorism could appear in the United States.

In New York City the Contingency Planning Corporation was formed in 1978 to plan and build a backup facility. It has since gone out of business, but in its study of alternatives, Robert V. Jacobson, president, reported ten alternatives:

1. Do nothing. Beyond insurance, accept the risk.

2. Store replacement hardware. This assumes that adequate facilities will be found to make the equipment operational. Although many manufacturers do not guarantee replacement of equipment within specified times, they can come close to delivery at about the same time that stored hardware could be moved to an operational facility from a warehouse. Storing the hardware too close to existing computer facilities raises the question of what may be destroyed in a disaster causing the need for replacement.

3. Bilateral aid agreement. A computer backup capability can be obtained through an agreement with another organization for mutual backup. This arrangement has not been effective in most cases because the two computer systems must stay mutually compatible over time, and each must be able to accommodate the workload of the other. Even if the critical work load of each could be reduced by an average of fifty percent, that would represent a problem. Moreover, on-line, real-time applications are difficult to move.

4. Multilateral aid agreement. Problems here are similar to those of the bilateral agreement.

5. Dual EDP sites. Creating a second, nearly duplicate facility and system could be the most expensive solution unless expansion is needed anyway. Then the cost would be somewhat less. Other important decisions would have to be made on how to split the workload and whether to separate the centers by one mile, twenty miles, fifty miles, or more.

6. Multiple EDP sites. This solution usually takes the form of replacing a single large computer system with a distributed system of smaller computers. The decision to do this is normally based on

other more significant factors, and increased backup capability is a side benefit.

7. Empty shell. Destroyed computer equipment is often easily and quickly replaced in a matter of a few days. The critical requirement is a facility with sufficient power, air conditioning and communications capabilities, assuming the victim's facility has been destroyed. The solution is to build a complete facility in a safe location leaving it empty until needed.

8. Vendor-supplied EDP services. Several data processing service organizations offer guaranteed computer services as a backup on a contract basis. Compatibility and geographic distances are prime considerations.

9. Shared contingency empty shell. Cost of an empty shell is shared under this option.

10. Shared contingency facility and computer system. This is the solution of greatest interest to groups of businesses in large cities. These businesses cannot afford the few days required to obtain new equipment.

The need for backup is growing, but obtaining it is difficult, costly, and complex. Security review methods presented in this book are essential steps toward the best solutions.

A backup capability is only one of many issues to consider in recovery. A more complete list is provided below. A number of planning items must be considered for each issue:

- Precontingency preparation
- Actions during the contingency
- Actions after the contingency
- Recovery priorities
- Responsibility assignments
- Resources needed
- Cost

A contingency will rarely result in total destruction or failure. Recovery is needed primarily from lesser, isolated problems that affect only part of the EDP function. Therefore, a set of recovery plans is needed for the more likely single problem or combinations of contingency problems as well as for total destruction or failure. This approach requires a risk analysis and extensive planning and preparation, which are treated in Chapter 11.

Recovery Issues

Staffing. Concern for the safety of people comes first. The basic rule in physically dangerous situations is evacuation of workers from the danger areas as quickly and as orderly as possible. This requires evacuation routes, assignments of actions to be performed on the way out, proof of complete evacuation, regrouping at a safe site, medical aid, communication with workers' families, identification and assignment of available staff for recovery, authorization to return to work areas or assignment to alternate work areas, finding and hiring and training supplemental workers, and payroll and insurance payment adjustments.

Evacuation from a dangerous area is a cardinal rule. Workers should never be told to stay and battle the problem. After people are safe and the problem has been assessed, the solution to the problem can begin. This rule should be followed even for a small wastebasket fire. A manual fire extinguisher should be used for only one primary purpose—to clear a path to safety. After everyone is safe it may be used for fire suppression. In addition, workers can be assigned to perform emergency duties as long as they do not threaten worker safety. For example, emergency power shutoff switches should always be placed at the evacuation doors from a computer room, and operators should be instructed to shut off power as they leave in an emergency. Food, bedding, and first aid equipment should be stored in a protected place to support operations staff if surrounding disasters leave a computer center intact.

Removal of Cause of Contingency. If the cause of a contingency is not momentary, it should be removed in an organized and preplanned fashion. However, all emergencies and all situations cannot be anticipated in plans. Individual initiative by qualified people should be encouraged.

Facilities and Neighboring Site. Safe facilities must be restored or found in the recovery process. Establishment of a computer room with open space and backup independent power and air conditioning might be enough to allow recovery from localized problems. For example, when a gasoline bomb completely destroyed an IBM 360/40 computer system located at one end of a long, large room, the empty end of the room was restored and a replacement computer system was installed and running within six days.

Many disasters don't occur in computer rooms, but in a neighboring site. Computer rooms usually contain few low-temperature, flammable materials. Fire is more likely in adjacent areas where it can still do great damage. As Bob Courtney has pointed out, "the computer is baked instead of burned in these situations."

Possible contingencies may not be obvious and may produce unexpected results. For example, tornadoes or strong winds can produce air pressure differentials that create problems in air ducts or might cause aluminum floor panels to fly into the air. In one case it was discovered that two buildings thought to provide mutual backup were in the same orientation as tornadoes that pass through the area so that a tornado that strikes one building is likely to strike the other. An airplane from above or a truck from the side or loading area below can also be hazards. Furthermore, increasing danger from international terrorists is anticipated. The attacks on computer centers in Italy described previously indicate that terrorists understand the vulnerabilities resulting from loss of computer services. Should computer centers prepare to defend themselves from this type of attack? If they do, to what lengths will they have to go? Lightning and polluted air or water are other often-overlooked problems mentioned in Chapter 10.

Utilities. Contingencies may also result from remote happenings. On-line systems are vulnerable to damage of local telephone switching centers, vehicles damaging power or telephone poles, and excavation and ground shifts that damage underground lines. A close working relationship with utility companies, sheriff, FBI, police, and fire department is essential.

Utility lines and terminal, switching, or distribution boxes are highly vulnerable and must be protected to the same degree as the computer and air conditioning equipment. Motor generator sets, emergency lights, air intakes, and uninterruptable power supplies (UPS) come under this category as well.

Computer Equipment. Recovery requires minimizing damage, repair, and replacement of computer equipment. Computer systems made up of equipment from different vendors complicate planning and recovery. Cables can be as difficult to replace as equipment. Simple plastic equipment covers to protect from dripping or spraying water, extra portable water pumps and air conditioners are valuable equipment. Maintenance facilities and spare parts must be available.

Supplies. Replacement of specially printed forms is often overlooked in recovery planning. They are essential, and considerable time may be needed to replace them. Many supplies are stored in rooms that are not under surveillance or automatically protected. Some flammable supplies are mixed in with fire-resistant supplies. Packed paper forms are surprisingly resistant to fire. Magnetic tapes are more susceptible to damage from humidity than heat or water alone. Other important information can be gained from articles, brochures, and books and from conversations with computer and supply vendors.

Documentation.   In order to operate a computer facility must have documentation. This includes operation instructions, program and equipment specifications, operations journals and records, and so forth. Most important in an emergency are the recovery plan and instructions. These must be readily available but safe from destruction. They must also be familiar to and understood by those who will have to use them.

Operating System, Utilities and Production Programs.   Computer programs must be safely backed up with remotely stored copies. The most difficult problem is to assure that backup copies are the latest updated versions. A further advantage is flexible software adaptable to the widest range of system configurations possible. This provides the possibility of continued operation if a part of the system is lost or if backup is needed on a wider range of other computer centers' systems or a restored system. An alternative is to have reduced performance versions of critical software that will run on minimal or most commonly available system configurations. These must be periodically tested, of course, since computer programs "age" rapidly.

Data.   Data must also be safely backed up. Much data currently used for processing can be found in various forms in other parts of an organization in original documents and paper and microfilm copies and can sometimes be recreated at the source. However, the cost of reentering the data into computer readable form can be high. Having backup data in different format or order because of program changes after the data were stored creates another problem which can be solved by writing conversion programs or using a generalized conversion package. However, the time, effort, and cost must first be anticipated. In any case, a safe site and regular delivery of updated backup files must be basic requirements.

Financing.   Recovery from purchasing new equipment, supplies, repairs, and retaining extra workers and services can be costly. Therefore a contingency account representing highly liquid assets or a line of credit should be available and quick access planned. This contingency is separate from insurance coverage considered below.

Customer Services.   The objective of recovery is to restore customer services with as little loss as possible. This requires active participation of all departments and organizations depending on computer services and organizations responsible for supplying data. Each must have its own recovery plans, which should be based on various lengths of periods of unavailable EDP services. Effective communication with users must be established in order to obtain reports of contingencies and progress during recovery.

Security. EDP services can be considerably more susceptible to various additional losses during recovery periods. Many safeguards and controls are inoperable, confusion and nonstandard operations prevail, and strangers are called in to assist. Several reported computer crimes included sabotage as the first stage of fraud or a cover-up of damaging evidence. Additional and more costly security is required during recovery by deputizing employees, obtaining assistance from auditors, and hiring outside services.

Reporting and Journaling. Two important but often overlooked requirements are to keep records of significant events during recovery and to report these events to appropriate agencies and higher management. Contingencies occasionally result in disputes, insurance claims, and litigation requiring evidence admissible in court. Keeping records and reporting events should be explicitly assigned responsibilities.

Audit and Legal. A full operational and financial audit should be performed as soon after recovery as possible to assure compliance with law and regulations and integrity of computer applications. After recovery, application systems should be treated with suspicion until confidence is fully restored.

Cleanup. Debris left from the contingency and recovery process should be moved aside and left for low priority clean-up tasks unless it represents a hazard. Adding workers to perform this work also increases the exposure of assets to further loss.

Public Relations. A publicly known contingency can represent a great embarrassment to the victim, harm an organization's image, cause a loss of customers, and attract wrongdoers. Procedures should be established for maintaining confidentiality, identifying official spokesmen, and issuing press releases. An organization with a public relations department should ask the department to participate. In some cases, it may be important to retain a public relations agency or consultant. An example of a well-handled catastrophe was the major fire experienced by IBM's Hawthorne Computer Facility several years ago. IBM produced a brochure describing the fire, problems encountered, and recovery procedures that succeeded and failed. Although the cause was never determined, it put IBM in the responsible role of helping others avoid similar problems by reporting the experience rather than being the embarrassed victim.

Insurance. A contingency plan requires action on insurance claims during recovery. Policies should be kept in a safe place, and an appropriate insurance program should be established as part of computer security planning.

This list should not be considered complete, for continuing experience with contingencies will produce new items that will have to be taken into account.

Security Factors for Computer Site Selection

Many organizations are building second sites either to expand their computer services as a backup capability or to modernize their operations with new computer facilities. These activities represent great opportunities to increase security. The first action after such a decision is to engage in a fact-finding task by visiting proposed sites and other computer-using organizations that have made similar moves; visit local law enforcement, health, civil defense, fire, civic planning, utilities, and weather agencies; obtain information from security products vendors; and consult with specialized consultants and government agencies on special problems.

The following factors should be considered.

Ground Hazards. Determine proximity to earth faults, unstable soils, river beds, water table, flood or lava routes, tornado routes, high fire hazards and sources of radar, and atomic radiation. This may require retaining a variety of special consultants such as geologists and visiting government agencies such as the U.S. Geological Survey.

Protection Services. The capabilities of the local law enforcement, fire, and criminal prosecution agencies should be assessed. Where are they located? What type of experience have they had? How soon could they respond to a problem? Local attorneys and fire underwriters can also provide opinions on these local agencies. Be sure to contact police, sheriff, national guard, FBI, and postal authorities as well as the local prosecutor and U.S. Attorney. Increasing numbers of computer-associated crimes are coming under federal jurisdiction.

Utility Services. Meetings with local electric power, water, gas, and sewage agencies or companies are needed to assure adequate services. Water pressure, continuity of electrical power and gas services, alternate sources, and costs of all services are most important. Contact other organizations with computers in the area to learn about their experiences. Seek two sources or alternative routes of each service within economic constraints. Be certain that routes of these services to the computer site are well protected.

Communications Services. Both data and voice communication services can be highly variable relative to geographic location. How far away is the telephone company data communications expert? What alternative services are available? Can a selected computer site be served economically by two switching centers? Examine the circuit routes to the site. What experience have other data communications users had? Determine the optimum distance and safety of routes from sources of data and users of computer output.

Local Site Environment. Most communities have an area master plan indicating intended use of land areas. Political forces and plans can be identified during the process of obtaining building permits and meeting environmental impact requirements.

Avoid high-crime areas. Stay away from colleges and universities where riots and protests commonly occur. Liberal antibusiness groups are attracted to such areas. Avoid proximity to heavy ground traffic and airport traffic where vehicles pose a threat. Avoid areas where large gatherings of people occur, such as stadiums and large meeting facilities. At the same time make certain ground and air transportation are available for fast and safe evacuation and for aid from outside the community. Avoid areas near industrial or government facilities where dangerous chemicals, smoke, or dust are produced. Also test the area for microwave levels. Costly screening of computer centers has been required for sites placed too close to airport radar facilities.

Select a location where computer equipment vendors have adequate service for maintenance and repair. This means that locating near other users of the same equipment is desirable. Be sure that backup storage of data, programs, and supplies can be safely arranged, including routes to and from backup facilities.

Select a site and plan buildings to assure a lower profile to public attention than neighbors. Be sure that a stranger approaching from any direction and intent on causing harm would find more attractive targets. The building and site should have a low profile and should be the least conspicuous structure in the neighborhood.

External Facilities Security. The building should be as functional and unpretentious as possible. It should have only a few markings or indications of its use. It should have as few windows as possible, a wide, well-lighted perimeter area free of places of concealment with minimal numbers of egress points. The building should be built to resist fire and ground lightning strikes and should be protected against explosions and projectiles. The facility should be limited in various uses so that few employees and outside contacts are needed. Vendor contacts and labor-intensive activities such as programming and data entry should be located at other sites. To the greatest degree possible, consider the computer center as a minimally manned, utility-type service for users at remote locations.

These recommendations will be difficult to follow in their entirety. Some are mutually conflicting, others may conflict with other requirements or objectives of a business or agency. The computer security specialist, however, must strive to meet his goals just as others in the organization strive to meet theirs. All compromises of security needs must be identified and rational acceptance of the risks must be explicitly agreed upon by top management.

Chapter 6
Computer Security Organization

An organization, whether it is a business, institution, or branch of government, can be divided into line-management functions and staff functions. Line management is directly concerned with carrying out the business function of the organization. In manufacturing, for example, design, manufacturing, distribution, marketing, accounting, data processing, and sales are line functions. Personnel, building maintenance, planning, research, and protective services are considered staff functions. Computer security is generally a staff function, particularly in a computer-service bureau or time-sharing company devoted primarily to providing data processing services.

Organizations have traditionally had protective services, risk management for insurance planning, fire and safety departments, and auditing departments. Computer security is a new specialty that can overlap with all of these functional areas. Therefore, confusion as to its role is only natural.

It is difficult to agree on standard or accepted forms of organizations. Organizations are made up of human beings having various strengths and weaknesses. Furthermore, organizations are engaged in many different, sometimes unique activities requiring variations in organizational structure. Thus the vice-president for finance in one organization may be a strong individual who oversees a wide range of functions, such as treasury, control, accounting, receiving, printing, and data processing, whereas in another organization, strength may be distributed horizontally among several top-level managers. Therefore, computer security may be placed in the organization primarily on the basis of personal management strengths and interests.

Many textbooks have discussed various management schemes such as vertical structures, horizontal structures, and matrix structures where functional and administrative aspects of all activities crisscross. Therefore, when new functions are needed in an organization, they tend to be placed according to some combination of both functional justification and personal strength of individual managers. Organization charts representing idealized businesses and government agencies are used here to indicate the various ways in which computer security might function within the organization. Although the two charts shown in Figure 6-1 and Figure 6-2 may not resemble any particular organization, they will serve our purposes. They also show alternative locations for computer security (identified in dotted line boxes).

The general functions that have a close relationship with computer security are as follows.

Organization Functions

Protection services.   These functions, which have alternative names such as plant security, security, and guard services, are concerned with the physical protection of the organization and sometimes with the investigation of theft, larceny, robbery, espionage, and sabotage. The protection service manages the uniformed guard force and includes various investigators and occasionally undercover operatives. In railroad companies this function is carried out by a sworn police force with power of arrest established by law. In other organizations the function is commonly supplied by an outside vendor such as Burns, Wakenhut, or Pinkerton's.

Insurance.   This function is sometimes called the risk department. It can be a large, formal organization or merely one function handled by the treasurer, depending on the size and complexity of the insurance needs. Its purpose is to plan and obtain insurance, manage claims, and attempt to obtain lower premiums for insurance.

Fire, Health, and Safety.   Fire, health, and safety may be three or two separate operations or a single operation, depending on the size of an organization. These divisions are responsible for meeting all government

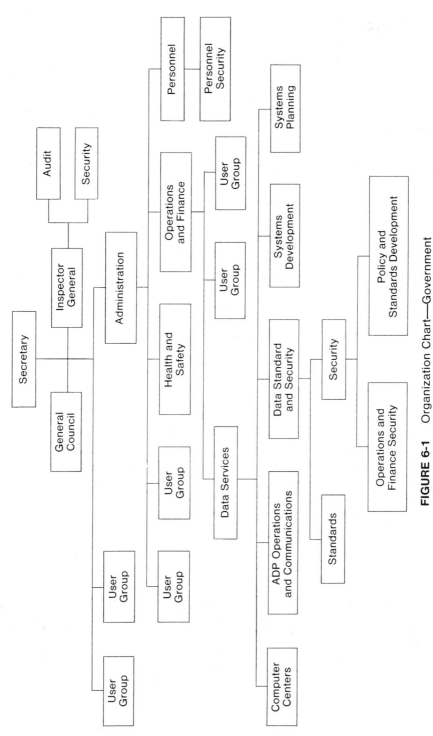

FIGURE 6-1 Organization Chart—Government

85

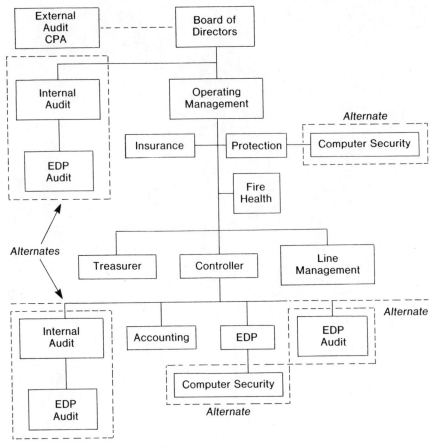

FIGURE 6-2   Organization Chart—Business

regulations concerning fire, health, and safety hazards. They plan, install, and inspect safeguards.

Audit.   In the private sector and some local governments, external auditors in the form of certified public accountants are retained by the highest level of management to conduct periodic audits of organizations. This function is often referred to as the external audit. Most organizations of moderately large size have an internal audit function. In the private sector, the internal audit function normally reports to the audit committee of the board of directors. In some cases, the audit department reports to the chief executive officer, the chief operational officer, or the chief financial officer. The last two arrangements are generally considered poor. Internal audit should report, at least functionally, to the highest level of management possible to maximize their independence relative to all other staff and line functions in an organization.

The audit function in government is equally complex and variable. The legislative branch normally has an audit function that performs the equivalent of external audits for all line agencies reporting to the executive branch. The executive branch may have its own audit function, or individual agencies may have their own audit functions that in turn can be assigned on a regional basis. If audit functions are organized into subfunctions, these tend to align with geographic regions rather than with specialized functions such as payroll auditing, manufacturing auditing, or marketing auditing.

The audit function determines the degree of compliance with practices, standards, and policies of both the organization and government. Audit determines the adequacy of controls, management performance, accounting integrity, and verification of assets and liabilities. Auditing has traditionally been staffed with general accountants who function primarily in financial matters.

Electronic Data Processing. Electronic data processing (automatic data processing in government) is normally a service function providing computer services to the rest of the organization. In a service bureau or time-sharing company, EDP would be the line-service activity. However, a part of it would still provide services for the business function of the organization. Although the EDP function normally reports to the financial side of the organization, it may be part of the engineering or production section of an organization. This function is sometimes provided entirely by an outside EDP service vendor or under a facilities management contract. In large organizations the EDP service may be split among several functions in the organization.

Alternative Reporting Relationships

Many organizations that use computers need to examine where security should fit into the overall structure. In the traditional organization, computer security might report only functionally to the EDP organization, might be a part of the EDP organization, or might report to or be a part of the protection or plant security function. In smaller organizations that cannot support a full-time position in computer security, the question becomes what manager should assume computer security responsibilities as part of his other responsibilities.

There are several advantages in placing the computer security function in the EDP department. In contrast to police concepts that have influenced the development of protection services or plant security, today, systems analysis concepts are being used to develop computer security. Therefore, EDP technologists more readily accept and use the newest technology in security.

Except for some physical access controls, computer security is closely associated with information sciences technology. Even physical access, when enforced with computer-controlled mechanisms, is associated with computer technology. Therefore, the demands imposed by the highly complex technology favors the development of security among the technical staff who have this kind of background. Computer security also requires significant restraints to be imposed on data processing personnel. Safeguards might be more easily imposed and accepted if the security function were under the same management as the personnel who are constrained by it.

As part of the protection services of the entire organization, computer security provides greater independence and objectivity than it does as part of the EDP organization. It also allows for greater consistency in interfacing computer security with security in the rest of the organization; it allows for a stronger identity with traditional security technology and experience. With the pervasiveness of EDP throughout an organization, elements of EDP activities often take place outside the EDP organization; therefore, computer security as a part of the protection function for the whole organization can impose the necessary constraints over all EDP functions and related functions.

As stated earlier, personalities and strength of individual managers generally resolve these issues. A strong EDP manager, where all EDP functions are concentrated in one organization, and where EDP management seems particularly concerned and dedicated to the safe use of computers in the enterprise, are factors that support the placement of computer security in the EDP organization. On the other hand, a strong protection services manager who is keeping pace with technological advances and is willing to expand the scope of traditional security to include specialists with EDP technology background, would put the computer security function in protective services.

Another possibility is to place security responsibilities in both functions, so that the security function in EDP would be responsible for the more technological aspects of security such as the hardware, software programming, and operations staffs, while security in the protective services function would cover physical security and other aspects amenable to manual or procedural treatment. A split approach is also possible, in which computer security reports administratively to protection services but functionally to EDP management.

Most arguments favor the placement of computer security in the EDP organization. At some future time when computer security may be a more routine and accepted constraint and cost and plant security specialists are more familiar with computer technology, it may be feasible to place security with protective functions.

Advancing technology's new concepts can also complicate the question of organizing computer security. Large data base management systems have introduced the concept of the data base administrator. The data base administrator has significant security and confidentiality responsibilities for the data bases under his responsibility. Another new concept is the information protection officer at the staff vice-president level who has the responsibility for information protection across the entire organization. This function recognizes the widespread use of computers throughout the organization and allows for a systems analysis approach to information in the variety of forms and communication modes in which it is found in modern organizations. The information protection officer is concerned with security through all phases and forms of data, whether in computer systems or on paper. He can deal with inconsistency in protecting information. Information can be highly protected when stored in computer systems but highly vulnerable in readable from when transmitted manually by messengers or discarded in trash bins in public areas.

An idealized organization optimized for computer security might include a security staff in the EDP organization, physical computer security specialists in the protection organization, data base managers with security responsibilities, and a vice-president for information protection. In smaller organizations these functions would be assumed by managers of other functions, but security would be formalized to guarantee that a proper part of their energies and attention would be directed to security. Security will be effective only when the accountability for security is explicitly assigned to all managers and at least part of their performance is judged on the basis of the effectiveness of security.

In one particular case, protective services, primarily in the form of a uniformed guard function, were the responsibility of the operational vice president of a medium-sized organization. He hired a computer security expert because computer services was the primary business of the organization. The computer security expert was then given all responsibility for the guard forces. This arrangement did not work very well because the guard force was only peripherally related to the computer security function, and the computer security expert's attentions spread too widely into management of the guard force, of which he had no experience. It was the hope of a number of people in the organization that the guard force management would be separated from and run independently of the computer security function.

Another example shows that EDP management might not understand the concepts of security. In this case, management decided to perform an evaluation, planning effort, and implementation of more formal computer security. The plan was to establish a team consisting of employees from all of the EDP functions including operations, programming, data entry, systems analysis, and in addition, a representative from the auditing staff. Together, these people were to address the subject of security throughout the EDP organization. The auditor called a halt to the planned activity on the basis of a gross violation of the basic security tenet of separation of responsibility. This activity would have had a computer operator participating in the evaluation, planning, and implementation of security in data entry and programming functions, a computer programmer involved in planning, evaluation, and development of security in the computer room, and so forth. When the auditor pointed out this problem, EDP management changed their plans. The alternative and acceptable method was to appoint an auditor and one manager in the EDP function to be responsible for the evaluation, planning, and implementation of security. They were to be assisted in each specific area by an employee in that area. However, each of these employees was to function only in his own area and not be aware of security activities in any of the other areas. The auditor and EDP manager were responsible for the overall security and concerned themselves with developing a consistent approach to security across functional lines and at the interfaces between functions.

Another type of problem arose when an ex-military officer unfamiliar with data processing was hired to be the manager of computer security in a computing organization. First he installed a CO_2 fire suppression system without any personnel warning mechanisms. When he was informed of this inadequacy, he redesigned the system so that it would be actuated by a large lever with a brass ball on the end of it placed directly above the computer console operator. The operator's job was to pull the lever and release the CO_2 only after he was sure that the entire computer facility had been evacuated. Unfortunately, part of the computer room could not be seen from the console. When this problem was pointed out, the manager installed military gas masks in the area not visible to the computer operator. (It should have been pointed out to him that gas masks are ineffective in the CO_2 environment, where the danger is not from poisonous gas but from lack of oxygen.) The EDP security manager was finally fired when management discovered that he had ordered twenty-millimeter cannons to be installed at the front entrance of the EDP building, which faced a university campus thought to be in some danger of riot attacks.

Organization of EDP Audit

The location of EDP audit in an organization is as important as the placement of computer security. It is only briefly discussed here since the issue is thoroughly addressed in auditing literature (SAC 1977). The two alternatives are to place EDP audit in the audit function (in the inspector general's office in government) or to have EDP audit report to EDP management. EDP audit should normally be responsible for auditing the performance and adequacy of the computer security functions. Therefore, placing it in the same organization or at least on a parallel basis will not allow adequate independence. Some have argued that EDP audit is essentially a service organization for audit, its primary function being the preparation of reports from the computer systems for the use of financial auditors. Therefore, EDP audit would fit into the EDP organization as another part of a service activity. In some organizations the traditional audit function is staffed with people who have little understanding of or interest in the EDP function; therefore, organizing EDP audit within the audit organization is difficult.

Another alternative in large organizations is to develop EDP audit as part of the EDP organization as well as developing an EDP audit function in the auditing organization. This kind of assignment is based on the concept of internal audit and external audit. This arrangement has been introduced in one large bank holding company, whose EDP organization functions as an independent company while audit also functions as an independent parallel company, each selling its services to the other companies in the banking conglomerate.

Part of the character and image of a company or government agency derives from its unique organizational structure compared with the common structures identified in Figures 6-1 and 6-2. Therefore, the establishment of a standard organization structure is difficult and would find little application. Management contemplating how to organize EDP security and EDP audit should examine organizations similar to their own and should try to thoroughly understand the functions of security and audit before making organizational decisions.

Management should be guided by the following principles and conditions:

- Independence must be maintained between the auditor and the auditee.
- Independence must be maintained in reporting audit results to top management.
- The amount of auditing to be done, based on the size and compexity of the organization and liquidity, value, and turnover of the assets, should determine the number of auditors needed and how to separate or specialize audit responsibilities.
- The chief auditor must be aware of how and to what extent that EDP is changing audit requirements and audit tools, techniques, and subjects.
- Auditors must understand computer technology, and audit special-

ists are needed who match the levels of capabilities and knowledge of the EDP staff.

- Audit must be organized in parallel but independent ways that match the rest of the organization. EDP audit in particular must be organized to respond to the degree of centralization and distribution of the EDP functions.

Organizing the Computer Security Function

The computer security function should be staffed with computer technologists who have had experience with computer programming and operation. Personnel may be systems analysts, programmers interested in planning or standards, quality assurance or software testing specialists, or senior computer operators. Since computer security is such a new subject, there are few trained or experienced specialists, and they command high salaries. At the present stage of development it may be advisable to train and transfer staff internally than to hire specialists from outside.

Computer security is such a diverse subject that it must be staffed with specialists in various aspects of technology and security functions as the department grows. If it is placed in the EDP organization, which is the ideal location, other factors such as manager strengths being equal, then it should report to a planning, standards and procedures group as it does in the U.S. Department of Agriculture. On the other hand, to give it a strong start and to emphasize security, it could be made a separate group or department reporting directly to top EDP management.

EDP top management must emphasize that organizing a computer security activity does not relieve managers, supervisors, and staff from their responsibilities for security. They must be reminded that security is a line-management responsibility along with hiring and firing. The security activity assists line managers in carrying out their responsibilities.

The computer security activity should begin with the collection and review of relevant audit reports and existing organization and EDP department standards, policies, and procedures. A library of literature and periodicals should be started, and contact should be made with others in the field through professional societies and conferences. Specialists should regularly attend seminars on computer security and computer technology.

The first actions of a computer security activity are to perform a brief security review to identify obvious major vulnerabilities requiring and amenable to immediate attention. These vulnerabilities should then be acted upon to reduce their immediate severity. This action has the beneficial effect of demonstrating the action-oriented nature of the staff and providing early visibility which in itself is an important passive deterrent.

It is also wise to form a computer security management review committee with representatives from audit, protection, insurance, and personnel, as well as from EDP management. The committee, which might be chaired by the chief financial officer or other top manager, would review all plans, provide guidance, and approve major actions.

Security Information Files

The computer security activity should develop a set of operational files covering the following subjects:

- **Audit and other security related reports.** The file should be organized chronologically by source of reports. A cross-index by security topic could also be developed.

- **Operational journals.** Chronological records of security-related computer system performance, accesses, and exception reports. Copies of reports of checkpoint restarts, missing tapes and output, lost input, remote data file backup delivery records, programmer test activity reports, production runs made from test libraries, new production systems implemented and moved from test status, personnel actions, and unscheduled maintenance reports. Password and key assignment records.

- **Loss experience.** Reports on all computer and data-related loss incidents and investigations from throughout the organization should be filed chronologically by case with cross-indexes by topics such as accidental and intentional acts, types of assets, organizational and physical locations, alleged perpetrator names, dispositions, size of losses, and modi operandi. Forms for collecting this information are provided in Chapter 10.

- **External matters.** News clippings and other external reports of security-related events outside the organization that might have internal effects. This should include computer-related crimes, disasters, and other losses; international and national terrorist activities; local terrorist events and civil disturbances; civil defense and local law enforcement; fire; health actions and plans; and reports from and about local utility companies.

- **Computer related assets.** Current files should be kept of all assets including computer programs, data files, equipment, supplies and facilities.

- **Floor plans of all facilities.**
- **Organization charts.**

- **Maintenance records of all safeguards and controls.**
- **Personnel summary files.** These should include numbers of employees grouped according to skills, knowledge, and access; turnover rates; accountability assignments for assets; and security-related job descriptions.

Some of these files are discussed in Chapters 11 and 12. Also restriction of use and protection of the files must be established relative to their sensitivity. Some files may be sensitive enough to store in a locked safe or vault. The key operational files should also be backed up with remotely stored copies.

Some typical reports generated by a computer system that are useful for security are as follows:

- **Computer Operator Console Log.** Chronological listing of computer system events and operator actions. Identification of tape reels and disk packs mounted, systems programs used; assignment of job numbers to particular users, commencement and termination of specific jobs, and use of system resources such as a line printer. Directs impromptu operator actions; most comprehensive listing of computer operation events.
- **Machine Room Access Log.** Chronological description of all persons gaining access to the machine room. If visitors are admitted, their escorts are also identified. Identification card/badge readers are often used to record this information.
- **Processing Schedule (Run Book).** Explicit schedule showing the time at which specific jobs should be run. Lists files to be used for the identified jobs; files are specified by tape number and date created. Applications and systems programs to be executed are delineated by program identifiers and accounts to be charged. Files may or may not be stored on magnetic tape reels.
- **Daily Detail List.** In-depth report of users accessing the system, the log-on and log-off times of these users, their priority codes, and accounting data relating to computer system resources consumed. Accounting data includes CPU time, I/O activity, and connect time. Errors and warnings concerning accounting data, such as an invalid job order number, appear here.
- **Computer Utilization Summary.** Extracts data from Daily Detail List to perform statistical analyses. Provides a breakdown of ways in which computer was used: hours on-line, amount of time the processor was idle, I/O activity, etcetera. May be presented by user, job order, application program, project, or division. Helpful in the detection of unauthorized use of system resources.

- **Computer Utilization Accounting Control Report.** Relates statistical data set forth in Computer Utilization Summary to accounting charges made during this period. Shows total dollar accounting units for CPU time, I/O activity, and the like.

- **Valid Job Order List.** Describes job orders that are currently recognized and to which jobs may be charged. Jobs may originate within the organization or through a telecommunications network; accounts to which either may be charged are listed here.

- **Accounting Code Error Listing.** Sets forth time, user, and other circumstantial details of errors in job order codes, user IDs, and the like. An aid in the detection of browsing and searches for accounts to which unauthorized activities may be charged.

- **Computer Utilization Summary by Priority Code.** Description of ranks assigned to tasks that determine the precedence in which jobs receive system resources. Broken down by projects, divisions, locations, or users. Shows disproportionate uses of system resources.

- **Terminal Usage Report.** Details usage, as measured by connect time, for specific terminals. May contain the times at which a terminal was in use.

- **Computer Storage Summary.** Provides a measure of on-line storage used by specific job orders. May also contain information on off-line tape reels and disk packs associated with a job order.

The primary activities of the computer security specialist are presented in Section III.

Chapter 7
Computer Security
and the Law

The increasing impact of laws and regulations on computer security should be addressed by attorneys and individuals responsible for computer security in their organizations so that computer security specialists can rely on competent counsel in developing a computer security program. Some recent legislation related to computer security and its possible effects are presented below.

The Privacy Act of 1974 and the 1979 Office of Management and Budget Circular A-71 impose computer security requirements on federal government agencies. A computer crime law may be passed by Congress in the near future as the result of the pioneering efforts of Senator Abraham Ribicoff, whose 1979 bill (S240) has been greatly improved in committee. At the time of this writing, ten states have passed computer crime laws: Arizona, California, Colorado, Florida, Illinois, Michigan, New Mexico, North Carolina, Rhode Island, and Utah. A number of states have also enacted privacy legislation governing the confidentiality of personal information. Other, more specific laws cover credit reporting businesses, insurance, health records, gambling, and the use of lie detector devices. Regulations include specific rules such as those from the Securities and Exchange Commission enforcing the Foreign Corrupt Practices Act and implicit regulations such as those embodied in the computer security manual used by the Controller of the Currency in the examination of banks. A selection of relevant laws and the current Ribicoff Computer Crime bill are presented in Appendixes C and D.

Other countries are not as advanced in the development of computer security-related laws except in the area of privacy. A 1979 computer crime involving the theft of computer services in Canada has brought into question the applicability of Canadian criminal law to some computer-related crimes. The communication of data across national borders is a major issue, which the U.K. government has addressed by requiring that it be supplied with the capability and keys necessary for decryption of all encrypted data sent across U.K. borders. Laws and international agreements arising from the transnational data flow issues will also affect computer and data communications security.

Privacy

The Privacy Act of 1974 (Public Law No. 90-579) imposes controls on the data banks containing personal information in federal agencies and among federal contractors. It also established the Privacy Protection Study Commission that has completed its mission and published a series of reports now being used by Congress as the basis for new legislation in the federal and private sectors.

The National Bureau of Standards, the Office of Management and Budget, and a number of other government agencies have spent considerable time and resources on the key security-related word in the act, which appears in Section E, Agency Requirements, Subsection 10: "Establish *appropriate* administrative, technical, and physical safeguards to ensure the security and confidentiality of records and to protect against any anticipated threats and hazards." The meaning intended for "appropriate" appears in the words "against any anticipated threats or hazards." The goal of computer security today is to identify these anticipated threats or hazards and to determine appropriate safeguards.

The violation of privacy by compromising personal information is only one of the many problems to be solved. The motivation to develop computer security on the basis of a need for confidentiality of personal information frequently results in suboptimization. Most computer systems contain more sensitive information than personal data. Therefore, personal information should be considered as only one of many types of assets in electronic data processing requiring protection.

Foreign Corrupt Practices Act

The Foreign Corrupt Practices Act of 1977, which applies to most corporations, corporate managers, and directors, establishes personal liability for noncompliance and sanctions up to $10,000 in fines and up to five years' imprisonment. It also imposes fines on corporations for noncompliance and permits civil suits from stockholders. The first key provision requires that a corporation "make and keep books, records and accounts which, in reasonable detail, accurately and fairly reflect the transactions and dispositions of the assets of the issuer." Computer security is required to assure the safekeeping of computer-stored data representing these records. In addition, security requires the same kinds of information for the prevention and detection of crime and error and recovery capabilities.

The second key provision states that a corporation must "devise and maintain a system of internal accounting controls sufficient to provide reasonable assurances that transactions are properly authorized, transactions are properly recorded, access to assets is properly controlled, and assets and assets records are periodically compared." To be in compliance, a system of cost-effective internal controls must exist in application systems and computer operating systems. These form a major part of the safeguards needed for computer security. Cost-effectiveness requires periodic risk assessments and an ongoing computer security program to assure the implementation of controls to the degree necessary, as indicated by the risks. The law also implies the need for action by management in establishing adequate funding and staffing of computer security programs.

The act is currently having a major impact on auditors, especially certified public accounting firms. However, it will have even more direct effect on computer security specialists in the implementation of security programs. Computer security specialists, along with other members of management, are personally liable under this law.

Compliance actions for senior managers and directors include the establishment of policies and procedures to safeguard assets against loss and produce reliable financial records. They must understand recordkeeping and internal accounting control functions and become aware of control deficiencies. Finally, they must allocate resources for system audits to investigate, report, and correct deficiencies and monitor compliance with established policies, procedures, and the law.

Operating managers must comply with the law by implementing corporate policies and procedures, review and document system control deficiencies, and implement adequate controls to correct them. They must design or acquire and implement new systems with adequate controls and work with internal and external auditors and consultants to help ensure compliance. They must identify and report factors required for assessing proposed controls relative to cost benefits and practicality and must inform staff of the purposes and need for controls.

Auditors must monitor complicance with existing policies and procedures and examine and report control deficiencies for existing and planned systems. They must examine and report on errors and irregularities and on financial representations. They should recommend measures to improve controls, participate in establishing guidelines, and establish ongoing education and training programs for internal auditors.

State Computer Crime Laws

Most of the computer crime laws (Appendix D) existing in 1979 in the ten states listed above are based on the original 1978 Ribicoff Computer Crime Bill (S1766), which was poorly drafted, especially in sections containing technical definitions. Florida was the first state to enact a computer crime law based on the Ribicoff bill. Its law covers acts for theft of and damage to computer equipment, supplies, programs, and data. It also covers willful, unauthorized access to computers and denial of services to users. The offenses to programs and data apply whether or not the property is stored inside a computer. It applies to programs and data contained in listings, tapes, discs, cards, and other off-line or on-line media. The law does not require the media of storage to be a material object; consequently, electronic pulses would be considered acceptable representations of programs or data and would be subject to the law. This broad definition will facilitate the finding of theft when a program is taken over a telephone line. Because the word "unauthorized" is not defined by the law and because access is defined so poorly, the intended prohibition against theft of computer services is not clear.

Florida appears to have no specific theft-of-services statute, in that applicability of both the new law and the prior property theft law is unclear. Obtaining a conviction for theft of services such as computer time may remain difficult in Florida. A particular advantage of the Florida law is that computer programs or data stored other than in the computer qualify as property within the meaning of the law. This aspect of the law will aid in the prosecution of thefts, disclosures, alterations, and destruction that occur to computer products but were not covered in prior law.

The Colorado computer crime law is modeled on the Florida law but is narrower in coverage because data and programs must be "contained in the computer" to be the subject of the provisions for damage, alteration, or destruction. Further, it appears that theft or fraud involving property that includes electronically represented data and "software" must be accomplished by use of a computer to fall within the proscriptions of the law. Although Colorado's technical definitions are somewhat more precise than those of other computer crime legislation, "software" and "hardware" are not clearly defined. In the dynamic technology of computers it is important when applying any computer crime law to read the definitions carefully because they differ from law to law, and statutory definitions differ from common usage in the computer field as well. In addition, there is no sanction for denial of computer services unless the denial is part of a scheme to defraud.

Other state laws bearing on computer security cover subjects such as the use of electronic forms of information for crimes involving automatic banking devices, electronic funds transfer systems, and credit cards. Other laws cover theft by deceit, forgery, criminal mischief, interference with use, violation of trade secrets, and privacy invasions, as outlined earlier. The California Computer Crime Law is one of the most effective laws because its technical definitions are sound and it uses the word "malicious" to delimit the notion of unauthorized acts.

Federal Criminal Law

A federal computer crime law was not yet enacted as of 1979. However, forty sections of Title 18 of the United States Code, provisions of the Electronic Funds Transfer Act (Title XX of the Financial Institutions Regulatory and Interest Rate Control Act of 1978) and provisions of the Privacy Act of 1974 are applicable to federal prosecutions of computer abuse. Other applicable federal laws include the Federal Copyright Act, theft, miscellaneous theft and theft-related offenses, abuse of federal channels of communication, national security offenses, trespass and burglary, deceptive practices, property damage, and other miscellaneous provisions such as derivative crimes and conspiracy.

Senator Ribicoff's Federal Computer Systems Protection Bill (S240), as reported out of the U.S. Senate Subcommittee on Criminal Justice in late 1979, was a much-improved version of the original bill. This bill would apply to acts perpetrated in, by, or against the U.S. Government, financial institutions, and their contractors. It would also apply to acts involving any organization that has a computer that is used in or that uses facilities of interstate commerce. Intrastate use of computers would come under state and local criminal laws.

The first offense is: "Whoever uses, or attempts to use, a computer with intent to execute a scheme or artifice to defraud, or to obtain property by false or fraudulent pretenses, representations, or promises, or to embezzle, steal, or knowingly convert to his use or the use of another, the property of another. . . ." The penalties would be 2½ times the amount of gain or $50,-000, whichever is higher, and/or up to five years in prison. The words "attempts to use" are probably sufficient to cover acts that had not yet involved a computer but the intent of which was clear. For example, it should apply to a programmer caught inserting instructions in a program that, if executed in a computer, would result in a fraud.

The second offense is: "Whoever intentionally and without authorization damages a computer. . . ." The penalties would be a fine not more than $50,000 and/or five years in prison. The phrasing of this section is problematic because the offense will be different for each potential victim and will depend on how he defines authorization. It also might include acts by which the victim derives benefits from intentional, unauthorized damage. For example, a technician may find it necessary to damage a malfunctioning process-control computer to save the life of a heart patient in a life support system or to save a dam in a flood control system. Legislative experts indicate, however, that acts to preserve life and property would normally be excluded.

The broad scope of the bill and further problems are embodied in its definitions.

> "Computer" means a device that performs logical, arithmetic, and storage functions by electronic manipulation, and includes any property and communication facility directly related to or operating in conjunction with such a device; but does not include an automatic typewriter or typesetter, or any computer designed and manufactured for, and which is used for routine personal, family or household purposes including a portable, hand-held electronic calculator. . . . "Property" means anything of value, and includes tangible and intangible personal property, information in the form of electronically processed, produced or stored data or any electronic data processing representation thereof, and services. . . .

The exclusions in the definition of a computer are not effective, correct, or practical and should be stricken. the terms "automated typewriter or typesetter" and "portable hand-held electronic calculator" are not precisely defined, have many changing meanings, and include many computers which the bill was originally meant to include and should include. Devices should not be excluded when the real purpose may be to exclude certain uses. Devices change rapidly as technology advances. Whatever an automated typewriter is today will be different tomorrow. Today it could mean a typewriter with ribbon cartridge, automatic erasure, interconnection to a computer (a computer terminal), or a computer output printer incapable of use as an input device or as a typewriter. Tomorrow it could mean a voice-actuated typewriter.

In the reference to calculators, the adjectives "portable" and "hand-held" are redundant. In addition, some modern calculators are programmable and as powerful as a minicomputer with limited storage; future models might be comparable to some of the largest computers in use today and might be able to store a vast quantity of data. They should not be excluded.

The exclusion of "any computer designed and manufactured for, and which is used exclusively for routine personal, family, or household purposes" might be reasonable with one exception. The word "routine" is not appropriate because it suggests that new or innovative nonroutine personal, family, or household purposes would not be excluded and should be. Therefore, maintenance of a Christmas card mailing list would be excluded, but how routine would a new mathematical method of calculating female menstrual periods be? That would probably not be routine at first, but after coming into common use, it would become routine.

We should leave it to the courts to decide what is a computer and what is a significant violation within the technology of the times. If the intent is to exclude letter, report, literary, news, or educational writing by computer, then those uses could be excluded under "use" definition, but devices or uses that could also be involved in heinous crimes should be included.

Minor problems of definition should also be corrected. The ambiguous and dated phrase "by electronic manipulation" is inappropriate in a technological definition. Future computers may not be electronic, and manipulation may not adequately describe the functioning of electronic circuits and execution of computer programs. The definition is adequate without this phrase.

It is hoped that future legislation will take these technological issues into account. The inadequacies of this bill are understandable in view of the growing technical complexity in crime, but they should not be readmitted in future legislation. Computer security specialists will have to deal with these issues when formulating policies, procedures, and safeguards, and when serving as expert witnesses in the courts.

Susan H. Nycum, author of part of the above material, offers a more detailed discussion of the laws identified here in the "Criminal Justice Resource Manual on Computer Crime" produced by SRI International for the U.S. Department of Justice, LEAA (Parker and Nycum 1980).

Impact of Laws on Computer Security

Adequate computer security is becoming a requirement imposed by law and regulation. At the same time, increasing numbers of laws are limiting the use of various safeguards such as privacy laws that limit background investigation of people to be placed in positions of trust, laws that prohibit use of lie detectors, and laws that preserve rights of employees. Computer security will always have to be balanced with the welfare, rights, and freedom of data processing employees in positions of trust, and of people served by computers. Managers and computer security specialists are becoming personally responsible and liable under new laws and regulations. The adequacy of levels of security in the use of computers will be judged independently by CPAs, regulatory agencies, and the courts.

Generally accepted practices will have the force of legal standards. For example, if a funds transfer fraud could be inhibited by use of data encryption devices, the victim might face a consequential damages stockholder suit, because encryption is used by most other potential victims of similar fraud. Such events will force many organizations to use safeguards whether the risks warrant them or not. In fact, risk assessments must take into account the consequential damages factor, for it may be a more significant factor than the direct loss from an actualized threat.

Computer crime legislation includes unauthorized acts as crimes and thus provides management with significant motivation to specify the exact nature and limits of authorized and unauthorized acts in and around computer systems. This legislation should also encourage the establishment of codes of conduct and greater emphasis on ethics in the computer field (Parker 1979). Suggested codes have been included in Appendixes A and B.

Future laws may establish the licensing of data processing people in positions of trust or even the licensing of computer systems to engage in specific types of data processing. In addition, new laws and regulations may require that safeguards be built into commercially available computer products and commercial computer programs in ways similar to those required for safety devices in automobile products.

Organizations using computers should employ adequate safeguards and controls for their own welfare, independent of any rules or regulations. This action would help to reduce the need for laws and regulations. Computer users should help to formulate legislation in order to assure that it will be practical and effective for the purposes intended.

SECTION III
COMPUTER SECURITY PROGRAM

Chapter 8
Getting Started

Methodology Overview

In developing a program of adequate protection, organizations that use computers should begin with a computer security review. A review is also necessary for the ongoing protection of an organization and should be conducted periodically.

The purpose of a security review is to identify, quantify, and rank vulnerabilities for appropriate allocation of security resources and selection of safeguards to reduce risk of loss to an acceptable level. A security program to reduce risk that includes a security review is described here in nine steps based on a threat scenario and risk analysis methodology. Each step is briefly identified and described in this introductory section. Detailed treatment of each step is described following this introductory section. A threat scenario and risk analysis methodology is recommended for the thorough evaluation, planning, and implementation of a computer security program.

1. A task force may be formed consisting of representatives from functions that relate to computer security. An alternative approach is to develop a staff of computer security specialists augmented with

individuals having whatever additional expertise is needed. Another option is to contract with an outside consulting service to assist with whichever alternative is chosen. The task force or staff is charged with performing the review and presenting an evaluation and implementation plan to management at the conclusion of the review.

2. The scope of responsibility and the information activities to be covered by the review must be identified. This provides the scope of the charter of the effort.

3. The first task is to identify the organization's intellectual and physical assets that require protection. An assets model and inventory file identifying all assets are developed at this stage. A measurement of possible losses or, alternatively, a ranking of assets by importance is completed (see Chapter 9, Identification and Valuation of Assets).

4. The second task is to determine the threats to the organization and to the assets. A file of loss experience is established to gain helpful information from past losses. A threat model is used to aid in the identification and recording of all significant threats. A measurement of expected frequency of acts, an exposure potential by occupations, or, alternatively, a ranking of threats by seriousness is completed (see Chapter 10, Identification of Threats).

5. A risk assessment is performed to identify vulnerabilities relative to current safeguards in place by matching threats, assets, and existing safeguards to measure or rank the resulting vulnerabilities. This assessment is based on quantitative measurement methods or qualitative ranking methods with the help of risk assessment formulas, occupational exposure indexes, and vulnerability scenarios (see Chapter 11, Risk Assessment).

6. Published literature, check lists, and experience of other organizations are used to identify all possible safeguards relative to the deficiencies identified in the risk assessment. All candidate safeguards are then evaluated on the basis of a set of safeguard principles. The best safeguards in each threat situation are selected, ranked, and scenario tested for their impacts (see Chapter 12, Safeguards Identification, Selection, and Implementation).

7. Recommendations are made for the implementation of safeguards and the ongoing computer security program.

8. The recommendations are presented to management in ways to gain their approval and gain authorization to implement the safeguards and the program.

9. Line management implements or advances the computer security program.

The basic strategies used in this methodology are risk avoidance, scenarios and exposure indexes, risk analysis, and safeguard principles to produce both quantitative and qualitative approaches to improved computer security. The level of detail is the most difficult aspect of a review to establish and control. Several reviews of varying levels of detail and scope may be conducted sequentially. A review based on identifying assets, threats, and vulnerabilities may be conducted in general terms and gather little or no data but cover the widest scope of assets to be protected. The results in terms of subjective ranking of vulnerabilities and potential losses may be adequate at the first-level review to answer the most general questions of allocation of security resources. Most important safeguard needs will be obvious, such as physical access control to the key areas, a badge system, password control at terminals, and fire detection and suppression systems. This first-level review conducted without data gathering is called assessment by reason.

Second-level reviews can be conducted within each area of assets, threats, EDP activities, or computer applications. Data on asset values and actualized threats probabilities can be gathered on a broad scale of low, medium, and high, and risks can be ranked in terms of threat probability and potential loss relative to existing safeguards in values of high/high, high/medium, medium/high, medium/medium, medium/low, low/high, low/medium, and low/low. Fuzzy set theory can also be used to divide the scale into more than three units and add a reasonableness or confidence variable for each measure (Hoffman, Michelman, and Clements 1978). This type of review, conducted only when questions about allocation of security resources warrant it, is called a graded assessment.

Finally, third-level reviews called numerical assessments can be conducted in limited areas of concern where risks and cost of safeguards may be particularly high, as in a funds transfer computer application. Such reviews may also be done when questions as to the correctness or quality of a graded or reasoned assessment arise. Numerical assessments use methods such as the Courtney risk assessment described in Chapter 11.

Gathering data by any of the assessment methods should normally be done through the managers responsible for each asset. They are accountable for the security of assets in their charge and will probably have the most information about them. On the other hand, they usually need assistance in identifying potential threats, especially external threats. The threat model in Chapter 10 and the exposure and scenario analyses and questionnaire described in Chapter 11 are most helpful in this regard.

Whatever level of review is chosen—reasoned, graded, or numerical assessments—the methodology consists of the same basic steps described in this section and in Chapters 8 –12.

A number of security review and risk assessment methods have been proposed and a few are in limited use. The U.S. National Bureau of Standards (NBS) has studied them to determine the basis for establishing future federal standards. One methodology based on Courtney risk assessment (described in Chapter 11) has been published by NBS (NBS 1979). A method of relative assessment has been developed by SRI International (Nielsen et al. 1978). Other methods, developed in great detail with data forms, questionnaires, and computer aids, include Securate (Hoffman, Michelman, and Clements 1978), RAMP (Jacobson 1979), U.S. Department of Agriculture and Department of Justice methods, Peat, Marwick and Mitchell proprietary method, National Computer Centre method in the United Kingdom (Wong 1977), SAFE Checklist method (Krauss 1972) and others. There may be great potential in new decision analysis techniques that provide a means of combining subjective and objective data in decision models in useful ways.

The security program suggested in this section is not presented in specific detail. Various alternative techniques are suggested, and many of the methods mentioned above may be substituted. No single methodology has been judged better than another, and there has been only limited experience in using them. The purpose of this section is to provide a basic framework, principles, and examples consistent with the current state of the art and experience.

Task Force Organization

The task force should be headed by the information security manager or a qualified person temporarily assigned to this responsibility. The individual chosen should have computer technology and operations expertise, knowledge and understanding of the organization, and a personality suited to the work. He will probably be dealing with some managers who are hostile to constraints of security. Therefore, he needs the respect and trust of top management and all functions he will be delving into. He also needs leadership ability to effectively direct an interdisciplinary team and use outside consultants. The leader usually comes from the data processing department, but he must possess an independence and objectivity in dealing with all relevant functions in the organization. The leader should not be in an audit function, because the auditors must be in a position to evaluate the effectiveness of the security task force as well as its results. Members of the task force may be auditors, however, as long as they are not the individuals assigned to review the task force or its products in their audit capacities.

The task force staff should be composed of representatives of functions within the organization that relate to or have a need for information security. The following functions can be included:

- Computer operations
- Data entry
- Computer job scheduling
- Magnetic media library
- Computer hardware maintenance
- Computer facilities planning and maintenance
- Systems programming maintenance
- Systems programming development
- EDP quality assurance
- EDP standards

- Application programming
- Computer user departments
- Information system expeditors
- Data base administrator
- Facilities management
- The protection or security department
- The insurance department
- The legal staff
- Government and public relations
- Personnel department
- Fire department

Each individual representing a functional area requiring computer security must function in the task force in isolation from representatives of all other functions requiring security. This assures a separation of responsibility and maintains the principle of privilege or need to know. For example, it would be unwise to have a programmer studying operations security. In addition, each individual must be able to devote significant time to the task force. This commitment requires fixed schedules of work for the task force and well-planned and coordinated meetings, especially to maintain necessary separations of responsibility. The task force must receive management commitment to function for the necessary period of time to complete the study. The study may take several days, several weeks, or several months, depending upon the scope of the assignment, the size of the information processing functions, and the specified detail of the review.

Scope of the Security Review

The task force must be responsible for the review of information security, not merely data security or computer system security. Information security encompasses the flow of information throughout the organization, starting with the point at which data are generated before they enter computer readable form and enter the computer up to and including the final destination of all output from the computer system in all computer readable and human readable forms. Any study having smaller scope will lead to serious suboptimization situations and inconsistencies in the protection of an organization that uses EDP.

In establishing the physical dimensions of the scope of the study, geographic locations of data sources, users, computer facilities, and telecommunications must be included. In general the scope should include geographical and physical areas of all information activities, all parts of the organization related to information flow, all computer and terminal locations, the paths of information flow, insurance protection, protection and health services, personnel, audit, legal department, data processing users, and the fire department within the organization and the publicly provided services. It should include interviews with the local law enforcement, fire fighting, civil defense, and prosecutorial agencies. Other specialized agencies may also be included. For example, in California it is advisable to contact the U.S. Geological Survey in Menlo Park to evaluate the potential threat of earthquakes. Because of the scope of the task force, schedules and deliverable products for each participant should be documented and approved by his management.

The members of the task force should have sufficient expertise in and knowledge of all aspects of their parts of the study. Task force members should also be people who have the respect and trust of parts of the organization they are to study. Computer security implies the possibility of constraints, reduction of performance, and possible degradation of services in sensitive functions. Therefore, it may be seen as a threat to some parts of the organization, and members of the task force must have tact and understanding of these implications and provide assurances that safeguards will not unilaterally be recommended or imposed without the understanding and review of those affected by them. For security to be effective, it must be sold, not imposed except as a last resort.

The scope and charter of the task force must be consistent with the objectives and disposition of recommendations after delivery. Will the product be a one-time report, an addition to the organization standards, or a series of reports issued periodically? Will the task force be disbanded, become a permanent function, be absorbed by another function, or become permanent in a different form? Each member of the task force should be made aware and assured of his role and options in his future at the end of the study. Reassurances will help avoid any reluctance to serve or disgruntlement during the study.

Project Planning

The project should be carefully planned with its scope and goals clearly in mind. A hypothetical sixteen-week project is scheduled in a Gantt chart in Figure 8-1. Each line item is described on page 114.

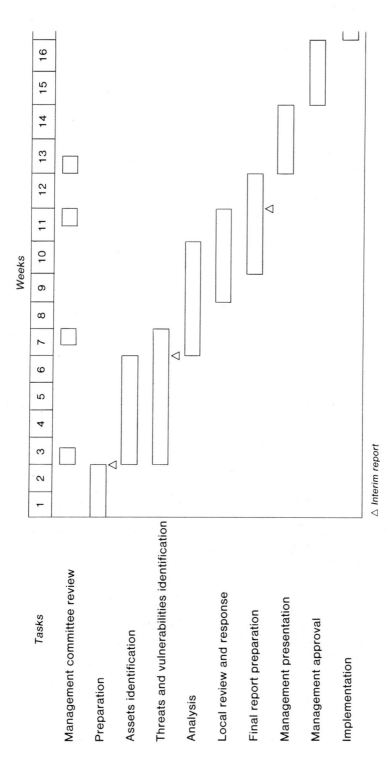

△ Interim report

FIGURE 8-1 Typical Review Project Gantt Chart

113

The management review committee meets periodically to review progress and deal with problems. The objective is to avoid unpleasant surprises as the project progresses.

A preparation and startup phase is essential to orient the participants and bring them up to speed. Managers and supervisors to be interviewed must be contacted and schedules should be made. Questionnaires and interview guides must be developed.

The assets, threats, and vulnerabilities identification efforts can be run simultaneously by taking about one fourth of the scheduled time. These efforts are described in detail in Chapters 9 and 10.

Analysis takes about one-fourth of the scheduled time overlapping with the identification phase. Analysis is described in Chapters 11 and 12.

A period in which analysis and report preparation overlap is needed for review and response from managers and supervisors who will be affected by the final results. This provides a means of gaining their support, avoiding surprises, testing conclusions and receiving exception memos from those who disagree with final conclusions. These memos should be included in the appendix of the final report.

Final report preparation is difficult and often disliked by participants. Writing assignments should be explicit and based on field notes, interim reports, and analysis. An attempt should be made to isolate participants who prefer to talk rather than write. They tend to slow down the process. Allow ample time for typing, editing, proofing, and report production. A word processing computer system is ideal for pulling together pieces of the report when there are several authors. Finally, it usually takes one talented writer from among the participants to organize the final report, integrate the pieces, edit, and produce the final report.

The oral presentation to management and approval for implementation of recommendations are followed by unspecified implementation time that may proceed indefinitely. Periodic implementation reviews are essential to assure adherence to the recommendations or explicit and intentional deviations from them. These last tasks are described in Chapter 12.

Participants should be encouraged to take field notes and transcribe them into readable task reports to be used in the analysis and final report writing. Interim progress reports are needed for briefing the management review committee. All task force documents must be kept at least as secure as the security recommended for all assets in the documents. Although project costs are too variable to provide any explicit guidelines, a budget and budget controls are essential for a successful effort.

Chapter 9
Identification and Valuation of Assets

Each threat, vulnerability, and safeguard recommended must be related to one or more of the assets requiring protection. Failure to identify and evaluate assets results in the fortress syndrome, which occurs when extensive, more elaborate security is installed than may be necessary for the existing amount, form, location, and types of assets requiring protection.

It is also possible that some assets generally thought to need protection, after careful consideration, may not require protection at all, or may need less protection than was initially thought. In one case, for example, a pharmaceutical company started extensive plans to increase the security of proprietary drugs data stored in its computer system. A marketing study concluded, however, that the data even in the hands of their competitor would do them no harm. The company then offered copies of the data for sale to the industry for a small enough price so that obtaining the data in any unauthorized ways would not be worthwhile. This action significantly reduced the resources necessary for security.

Risk Avoidance by Removal of Assets

In identifying assets within the scope of the security review, the avoidance of some risks should be accomplished by possibly excluding assets from the review, determining their value to be inconsequential, or removing them from potential or actualized threat exposure. An asset may be excluded if its protection is better handled by another part of an organization equipped to protect it. For example, a microfilm activity that is not directly associated with EDP could be excluded.

Secondly, it may be discovered that the value of an asset or one form of an asset is inconsequential to its custodian or owner, or there may be no known potential threats associated with it. Computer users often save obsolete data files or old unusable computer media such as worn-out tapes or warped punch cards. These can be declared inconsequential in value. It may also be discovered that computer output reports, while of great value to an industrial espionage agent, are unused by authorized recipients. Therefore, eliminating the reports avoids risk.

This second type of avoidance is not feasible unless a true value assessment of the asset is obtained from the custodian, user, or owner. Getting this information may require considerable effort since many people are obsessive savers and are unwilling to give up an unused asset. Such individuals should be made to strongly justify retention of assets of questionable value. Their efforts should be reviewed by higher authorities or by those presumed to be the beneficiaries of retention.

Finally, an asset might be removed from exposure to a potential or actualized threat to avoid risk. For example, it may be found that sensitive data files can be removed from on-line computer access during many periods of time when potential threats are present, such as during system hardware maintenance or time-sharing by unknown individuals. Magnetic tapes can be degaussed (erased by placing in a strong magnetic field) immediately after their data contents are no longer needed, and such tapes carry no risk in storage. A computer system could be removed from a high crime or flood area. This does not reduce the value of the asset but removes it from some risks.

Removal of an asset in the event of an actualized threat before the loss occurs is also possible in some cases. For example, some cryptographic devices are designed to be tamper-resistant, but if intrusion attempts are detected, the secret key is immediately destroyed and encryption is stopped. Detection of attempts to compromise a terminal password system can trigger the erasure or encryption of sensitive on-line files, and thus remove them from risk. While these are safeguard techniques to be identified later in the security review, they can be used as arguments for excluding at this stage certain identified assets, forms of assets, or assets of no consequence at specified times.

Identification of Assets

All assets requiring protection should be identified and recorded in an active ongoing file that will be updated as the nature and types of assets, and assets themselves, change. Documentation is a common procedure for physical assets but should be extended to data and programs as well.

Several problems must be avoided in identifying assets. The first is incompleteness. All assets related to EDP and information flow throughout the organization must be identified, and all forms of each asset, their locations, and accountability for them must be established. An asset in the form of a data file stored on magnetic tape in a tape library may be identified, but the same data may also be stored in other forms and places, for example, on tape in a remote stored backup facility, on paper stored in a desk or file cabinet, in meters or gauges on machinery or in transmission lines. An aid to assure the comprehensive collection of the identities of all assets is presented in Figure 9-1. This assets model identifies the name of each asset, its various forms, locations, and persons accountable for its safekeeping. Under each heading is a set of descriptors that may be used as checklists to assure com-

ASSETS MODEL

Assets	Form	Location	Accountability
People	Immoveable property	Remote	ADP Employees
Facilities	Moveable property	Vicinity	Employees
Supplies	Electrical pulses	External environment	Vendors
Hardware	Magnetic patterns	Internal environment	Outsiders
Systems programs	States	Adjacent environment	
Application programs	Punch cards/tape	Immediate environment	
Data	Printed paper	Telecommunications equipment/circuits	
Information	Negotiable instruments	Peripherals	
Negotiable assets	Nonnegotiable instruments	Computer	
Property	Usable		
Services	Accessible		
Safeguards	Occupations		
Other	Roles		
	Other		

FIGURE 9-1

prehensive identification. Note, however, that the descriptors may not completely cover all assets.

When the task force has completed this model, a number of submodels should be developed from the master model, each of which identifies those assets and forms of assets to be found in each part of the organization. The submodels should then be distributed to management in each of the identified parts of the organization asking them to identify additional assets, new forms, and locations, or to cross off nonexistent assets. In order to carry out the need-to-know principle, it is important that each part of the organization be given a list of only those assets under its jurisdiction. One part of the organization need not know the assets identified by another part of the organization. Note that this approach should also be taken in assigning tasks to the members of the task force. Only the leadership of the task force should be responsible for compiling the complete sets of submodels into the master model.

Listing assets can be a major task even without the valuation of data. After a detailed list of assets has been compiled using the assets model in Figure 9-1, the individual assets may be combined into groups based on computer application, form, location, or type. For example, at a basic level assets might be classified under one of the following major headings:

**Internal and on-line in
the computer system**

- Data
- Application programs
- System programs
- Computer equipment and supplies
- System services

**External to the
computer system**

- Data
- Application programs
- System programs
- Staff
- Facilities and utilities

This classification will be used in the exposure analysis method in Chapter 11.

The Most Important Asset

In seminars on computer security, participants are frequently asked to identify the most important asset requiring protection. Some of them make several guesses before they reach the correct answer, even though it is obviously "people." When this most important asset is identified in a security review, results can be startlingly different. For example, the primary security-related reason for staffing a computer room with more than one operator is not to provide separation of duties and dual control, but to ensure safety of the operator.

Another example illustrating the same point concerns the use of fire extinguishers. Most people mistakenly believe that the primary purpose of a fire extinguisher in a computer room is to put out a fire. Computer operators should be instructed that their own lives are more important than anything else in a computer room. If they notice any flames or smoke, they should immediately leave the area of danger. They should not attempt to extinguish the fire. Once personnel are safe, then action can be taken to deal with the fire. Therefore, a fire extinguisher's primary purpose is to be used by an operator to clear a safe path for his escape, not to put out a fire.

In planning security, the safety of people is so important and so specialized compared with inanimate assets that it should be treated separately. At the same time, the safety of people must be considered in every computer security issue including assets identification, threats identification, vulnerabilities, risk analysis, security resources allocation, and selection of safeguards. For the most part, this task should be handled by the health and safety experts in an organization with the assistance of the computer security specialist. A body of knowledge and literature on industrial health and safety already exists, and computer technology does not require sufficiently specialized treatment to warrant attention here. Therefore in spite of its importance, this subject is not treated extensively in this book. ·

Another often overlooked asset is the set of all safeguards. Safeguards are valuable and important assets subject to loss from attacks by perpetrators attempting to gain other assets or to cause other losses. Therefore, safeguards require protection.

Valuation of Assets

When each part of the organization is asked to identify the assets, forms, locations, and responsibility for them, it should also be asked for additional information concerning each asset. Figure 9-2 provides an idealized form showing the additional information needed. There are several values that may be attached to each asset and several metrics that may be used for value. First, an asset will have a particular value to the owner and a different value to other people or organizations who covet it. Figure 9-2 identifies the nine possible types of losses that could be associated with each asset. Note the importance of separating accidental from intentional loss (see Chapter 4). For each type of loss, there may be up to four estimated values: the aver-

Asset Name/Form and Location	Type of Loss									Denial of Use for Days									
	Accidental				Intentional					1/4	1/2	1	2	3	4	5	10	15	20
	Disclosure	Modification	Destruction	Use	Disclosure	Modification	Destruction	Use											

FIGURE 9-2 Assets Loss Estimate Form

age or expected loss and maximum loss to the owner and the average or expected and maximum gain to the perpetrator of any unauthorized acts associated with the asset.

Various units of value or metrics for valuation of assets may be used. The common metric is monetary, which is generally used for data that represent money where the threat is direct financial theft or fraud. A monetary metric is also useful when there is a way to price assets in known markets such as software packages, mailing lists, and used computer or peripheral equipment. Loss from software or data unavailability is measurable if business interruption is measurable in dollars lost. Asset loss may also have been evaluated for insurance purposes and may be found in such records. Most data, if lost in computer readable form, are reconstructable from human readable forms, and the cost of this effort is possible to establish.

A service bureau or time-sharing service usually takes great care to avoid learning the meaning of its customers' data. They usually limit their liability to the cost of reproducing the data from a backup source, but if a copy of the data is stolen, the service company usually accepts no liability. However, it may lose future revenue from an unhappy customer.

Other assets are difficult to measure in absolute terms but can be measured in relative ways. The value of data can be measured as a fraction or percentage of total budget, assets, or worth of a business in relative fashion. Assets may also be ranked by sensitivity or importance to an organization in relative ways. Another method of assigning values to assets in relative ways is to give nondenominational tokens to the evaluator. For example, he may be given 100 tokens to valuate a particular set of assets. The number of tokens assigned to a particular asset constitutes that asset's value. When potential threats or exposures are assigned to assets, a ranking by degrees of seriousness of loss can be established. This ranking can be a superior method to using a money metric because of the variable implications evaluators may place on money.

It must be remembered that the purpose of assets evaluation is to aid in the allocation of protective resources. Therefore, it only needs to be carried to the refinement needed for this purpose. Varying amounts of information will be called for, as determined by the size of the study and the detail of the investigation. The least amount of detail calls for listing the assets only as they are stated in Figure 9-1.

It may be asking too much of line management to detail all values that are implied in filling out the form in Figure 9-2. If monetary value estimates are to be obtained, then the information requested might be limited to one or another of the possible values indicated in this figure. The task force must decide how it is going to conduct the study and use the results before requiring large amounts of information and effort on the part of people supplying the information. Credibility and respect for the task force may de-

TABLE 9-1

Scale for Assets Valuation in Dollars

v	VALUE IN DOLLARS
1	10
2	100
3	1000
–	
–	
–	
7	10,000,000
etc.	

cline significantly if individuals are asked for excessive information and effort. The minimum amount of information necessary to adequately carry out the study must be determined. If the study is to include a numerical risk analysis, then significant amounts of specific values of assets will be required. If the study is to include only a reasoned risk analysis, then only a ranking of the relative sensitivity and importance of assets will be needed.

If dollar values of assets are to be identified, the danger is that too much effort will be expended in trying to evaluate them with more precision than is required. One suggestion recommended in the risk assessment procedure suggested by Robert Courtney of IBM (Courtney 1977), which is described in detail in Chapter 10, is to establish values by a logarithmic scale as illustrated in Table 9-1. Thus value in dollars $V = 10^v$. Individuals requested to fill out value data can then be instructed to use only the dollar values in the table or the value of "v" as estimates.

Another important procedure by which to gain reasonable information about the value of assets is to obtain a consensus from several individuals using a simple Delphi technique, which will obtain value estimates from each individual. The estimates are compiled without identifying the individuals. Subsequently, the compiled estimates are submitted to all the individuals who are asked to revise their own estimate on the basis of the compiled value estimates.

The Delphi Technique

The Delphi technique developed by the Rand Corporation is a convenient and often valid means of determining a consensus on the value of assets. It can be carried out in the following steps:

1. Enlist the aid of appropriate individuals who are familiar with the assets to be evaluated.

2. Ask each individual to give his estimates and basis for them in private without aid or discussion with others.

3. Inform each individual of the estimates and basis provided by the others. Do this without identifying individuals.

4. Ask each individual to revise his estimate on the basis of other individuals' estimates.

5. If a consensus on estimates in a narrow enough range is not achieved, hold a meeting of the individuals or a sample of them to allow discussions and debate to further narrow the range of estimates to an acceptable degree.

Several iterations of this procedure might be performed to gain a closer consensus of the asset values. Again, this should only be done if the task force intends to produce detailed and precise final results.

Other Asset Considerations

It should be remembered that a particular asset in one form may have different values than the same asset in another form. In identifying the assets using the aid in Figure 9-2, each form of a single asset that has a different value should be listed. For example, a company personnel telephone directory in booklet form may have a much smaller value to the perpetrator of an unauthorized act than the same information on a magnetic tape, or the same information that might be distributed throughout the records of a much larger file containing additional information not needed by the perpetrator. The difference will be the effort made by the unauthorized user of the information to put it into a form for required use.

The value of many assets is time dependent. For example, stock market information may be of great value during the hours in which a security is traded in only a single day. The data could be totally useless by the following day. If the owner of an asset is denied use of that asset, then the time over which he is denied use will change the value of the asset to him and to the perpetrator. Figure 9-2 provides columns to indicate the losses in relation to the amount of time of unavailability of the asset.

In one case, for example, a power failure caused a large computer system to be without power for one hour. It required 33 hours after power was restored to restore the equipment to correct functioning condition. During the 34 hours of system unavailability, more than 15,000 employees failed to receive directions for their production work; therefore, they had to guess how many parts of different kinds should be produced. When the computer system was reactivated, the current state of parts production was input to the computer. These data deviated significantly from input expected by the application programs. Therefore, significant amounts of erroneous output data were produced and created further confusion in the production of the parts. Several months passed before all erroneous data were purged from the system and parts production was back on a correct schedule. Although the direct loss of the value of the computing capability was minimal, the total production losses were approximately a million dollars. A thorough asset identification and evaluation must include these types of possibilities. The secondary effects of asset loss can be far greater than the initial loss.

A scenario analysis method and exposure analysis method described in Chapter 11 will help to determine the total and expected potential losses of assets. If this next step determines materially different asset values, then the task force must return to the assets step in order to reevaluate those assets. After the study is completed, it will be important to periodically update the assets inventory file produced during this step to make sure that the value of the effort conducted in the study will not be lost in later studies and continuing security evaluation.

Chapter 10
Identification of Threats

In Chapter 9, we focused on one aspect of threats; that is, the identification of the type of loss associated with each asset. In this chapter, the sources and the full nature of threats will be evaluated in two ways, by experience and by modeling. Either or both methods may be used. First, however, we should consider removing threats as a form of risk avoidance.

Risk Avoidance by Removal of Threats

In identifying potential threats of losses within the scope of the security review, the avoidance of risk should be attempted first. Risk can be avoided by finding that a suspected threat does not exist, by finding that an actualized threat could not result in a loss, or by eliminating the threat.

In the identification of threats it is necessary to identify all sources of possible loss, no matter how remote the possibilities, and remove from consideration those that do not represent a threat. Note that a threat should not be removed from consideration at this stage merely because the probability of actualization is low, but only if it is essentially zero. For example, if there has never been an earthquake from natural causes and there are no reasons to believe one could occur, it should be removed from consideration. If there are no trade secret data processed by the computer, than the threat of industrial espionage can be eliminated from consideration.

Risk can also be avoided by finding that an actualized threat could not result in a loss. For example, check kiting is a common banking fraud that relies on float time involved in processing and clearing checks, but it cannot succeed under electronic funds transfer systems, which reduce the float time to no more than a few seconds and thereby eliminate the possibility of loss for the bank. In another example, water from a sprinkler system may inundate a computer central processor but not permanently damage the computer circuitry. This inundation does not avoid the risk of interruption, but avoids the risk of permanent computer damage. The second example shows the importance of identifying the risks that have been avoided and those that have not.

Finally, risk can also be avoided by eliminating the potential threat. Before trying to reduce the probability of actualization of a threat, consider how the threat may be eliminated. Threats can be eliminated by removing the asset from exposure, as outlined in Chapter 9, or by various other means. For example, employees who represent threats through errors or intentional acts might be eliminated by automating their work. Automatic teller machines eliminate the threat of real-time errors and fraud by human tellers. A potential threat of computer room damage could be eliminated by moving dangerous chemicals out of the building. Note that installation of a sump pump in the computer room does not eliminate the threat; it only reduces the probability of damage and does not avoid a risk.

Internal Loss Experience

Experience is a sound basis for identifying threats. The first step in identifying threats should be to identify threats that have resulted in losses. A file of all loss incidents throughout the organization should be maintained. Traditionally such a file has been maintained by the protection or plant security department or by the auditors. If such a file is already available, then it should be searched for all incidents that are related to the computer security study. A separate file of these cases should be established, or cases discovered should be indexed in the master files.

Many loss experience files are poorly maintained and thus are not useful for analysis. Furthermore, many of these files are sorted chronologically and usually are not useful in this form. An adequate means of collecting loss experiences for this file should be instituted and made uniform and convenient. Figure 10-1 illustrates a form found to be effective for one organization; it has been generalized to fit various organizations. Such a form should be available to management throughout the organization, who should be instructed when, how, and under what circumstances the form should be filled out and submitted.

The file should be kept and administered by a part of the organization sufficiently motivated to perform this task. Possible departments include insurance, protection or security, or the auditor. The file will probably contain highly sensitive information and therefore must be kept in a secure manner. It might be advisable to use code numbers to identify individul perpetrators, victims, and witnesses in the report, and to maintain in a more secure fashion than the file itself a master index matching names and numbers.

The file should also include a report form shown in Figure 10-2, which should be filled out by the security or audit organization that performs the investigation and recovery of loss. Several of these forms may have to be completed for a case as the investigation and recovery steps take place. The final disposition of each case should be recorded to complete the file. It is also useful to collect other documents and evidence associated with each case. Such materials can include testimonies of witnesses, legal documents, newspaper clippings, and evidence of the incident. Physical evidence too bulky to store in the file should be stored in another suitable, secure facility that is code numbered to indicate the associated case.

The file should be ordered and indexed in ways that will make it most useful for future use. (See the discussion of files in Chapter 6.) The most useful indexes contain alphabetized lists of names of perpetrators, occupations of perpetrators, names of witnesses, names of departments in which the incidents occurred, dates of cases, names and types of assets involved, dollar losses, names of investigators, types of sanctions applied, dispositions of cases whether solved or unsolved, assets recovered or unrecovered, and mistakenly reported incidents that never occurred.

External Loss Experience

As noted earlier, valuable information can be gained by studying the experience of others. The Computer Abuse Project at SRI International (Parker 1976a) is one source of information on known external losses. The research file now contains more than 700 reported cases of abuse, which is defined as any intentional act associated with computer technology in which a victim suffered or could have suffered a loss, and in which one or more perpetrators made or could have made a gain. Table 10-1 shows the annual distribution by type and totals of known losses. This table, of course, represents only a

Notice of Loss

For lost or missing assets or unauthorized acts or attempted acts, follow instructions in Policies and Procedures Manual.

Company (Private)
For each loss, distribute copies of this completed form to:

1. Originator
2. Protection Services
3. Auditor
4. Loss Area Manager

(Please print or type only)

Control Number (Leave Blank)

Date form completed: _____

Date and time of discovery: _____

Originator's Name	Dept.	Location	Telephone	Location of Act	Original Location of Assets

Date(s) of acts: _____

Initial notification to: _____

_____ via _____

_____ via _____

by: _____

Witnesses or source of information: _____

Type of Assets	Recovery	Value of Original Loss:
	Partial/ Total	$ _____

Less than:

$ 100
1,000
10,000
100,000
More

Monetary ....
Equipment ....
Facilities ....
Supplies ....
Services ....
Information/
Documents ....
Personal ....
Other ....

Description _____

Statements of (1) alleged event(s), (2) discovery, and (3) counteraction(s):

_____

_____

(Continued on reverse side)

Possible person(s) involved (Include person(s) last known to handle missing item(s) and those accountable):

Name: Title or Functions: Location: Phone:

_____

_____

_____

(Continued on reverse side)

Signature of or for Authorizer

_____   Date of authorization: _____

FIGURE 10-1   Notice of Loss Form

129

Loss Investigation Report

Follow instructions in Policies and Procedures Manual.
Respect and Protect the rights of all persons and organizations.

Company (Private)
For authorized use only
Distribute copies to:
1. Originator   3. Day file
2. Case file   4. Other _____

Control Number

Case Name

Date form completed _____

Date of investigation _____

Notice of Loss Form Completion date: _____

Person(s) contacted / areas observed / assets examined

Identify	Dept.	Telephone	Location of contact or observation	Purpose

(Continued on reverse side)

Investigator: _____ Others present: _____

Action(s) recommended: _____

_____

_____

Findings: _____

_____

_____

_____

_____

_____

(Continued on reverse side)

_____ _____

Signature of Investigator Signature of Authorizer

_____

Date: _____

FIGURE 10-2 Loss Investigation Report

131

TABLE 10-1

Reported Computer Abuse Cases and Losses
Incidence and Loss by Type of Crime (Yearly)

YEAR	TYPE 1 PHYSICAL DESTRUCTION			TYPE 2 INTELLECTUAL PROPERTY DECEPTION AND TAKING		
	No. of Cases;[1] % of Total	Known Losses for Type 1[2]	Av. Loss Per Case Type 1[2,3]	No. of Cases;[1] % of Total	Known Losses for Type 2[2]	Av. Loss Per Case Type 2[2,3]
1958	— —	—	—	— —	—	—
1959	— —	—	—	— —	—	—
1962	2 0	—	—	— —	—	—
1963	1 50	2,000	2,000	— —	—	—
1964	1 17	—	—	2 33	2,500	2,500
1965	— —	—	—	1 13	—	—
1966	1 33	<1	<1	— —	—	—
1967	2 50	<1	<1	— —	—	—
1968	1 8	—	—	3 25	7,203	3,602
1969	4 20	2,000	2,000	8 40	1,003	334
1970	8 21	3,600	900	6 16	6,843	1,369
1971	7 12	—	—	20 34	9,844	1,641
1972	17 23	11,148	2,230	19 26	180	30
1973	10 13	4	2	26 35	26,782	2,435
1974	7 10	2,010	1,005	20 27	2,197	439
1975	5 6	115	58	21 25	91,670	13,096
1976	5 8	1,110	370	19 32	49,465	7,066
1977	14 16	2,252	322	16 18	17,946	2,991
1978	10 24	2,523	841	13 31	300	50
1979	2 10	—	—	11 55	—	—
TOTAL	97 14%	26,761	836	185 28%	215,932	3,322

1. Cases: Total known cases of this type in year, whether or not loss is known.
2. Known Losses: In thousands of dollars.
3. Average Loss: Average for cases where loss is known.

small sample of likely incidence and losses. The decline in number of cases in the most recent years can be attributed to the time lag between occurrence and reporting of cases—cases are still being discovered that took place several years ago. Information on external losses has been found to be valuable in justifying security expenditures to top management, especially when top management is reminded that individual managers and members of boards of directors can be personally prosecuted and successfully sued for failure to deal properly with major fraud in the corporation. Management in government agencies has a similar responsibility.

Results of the Computer Abuse Project are becoming directly helpful to increasing numbers of computer security specialists. For example, the project indicates that collusion is more prevalent in reported computer abuse than in overall white-collar crime. As discussed in Chapter 3, half of the computer-related cases involve collusion of two to sixty-five people each. Collusion is probably high in these cases because the acts require more skills in, knowledge of, and access to the technical environment of computers than

Table 10-1 (Continued)

TYPE 3 FINANCIAL DECEPTION AND TAKING				TYPE 4 UNAUTHORIZED USE OF SERVICES				ALL TYPES		
No. of Cases;[1] % of Total		Known Losses for Type 3[2]	Av. Loss Per Case Type 3[2,3]	No. of Cases;[1] % of Total		Known Losses for Type 4[2]	Av. Loss Per Case Type 4[2,3]	Total Cases	Total Known Losses[2]	Average Loss[2,3]
1	0	<1	<1	—	—	—	—	1		
1	0	278	278	—	—	—	—	1	278	277
—	—	—	—	—	—	—	—	2	—	—
1	50	81	81	—	—	—	—	2	2,081	1,040
3	50	100	100	—	—	—	—	6	2,600	1,300
4	50	126	63	3	38	—	—	8	126	63
2	67	28	14	—	—	—	—	3	28	9
—	—	—	—	2	50	10	10	4	10	5
6	50	5,251	1,313	2	17	—	—	12	12,454	2,075
4	20	6	2	4	20	2	2	20	3,011	376
13	34	8,910	810	11	29	—	—	38	19,353	967
24	41	5,943	540	8	14	351	175	59	16,137	849
19	26	3,090	257	18	25	107	21	73	14,524	518
28	37	206,274	11,460	11	15	7	1	74	233,066	6,474
34	47	3,952	158	12	16	3	3	73	8,162	247
49	58	6,513	176	9	11	14	5	84	98,312	2,006
30	51	2,026	78	5	8	—	—	59	52,601	1,461
44	51	47,501	1,319	13	15	154	77	87	67,853	1,330
17	40	12,384	826	2	5	—	—	42	15,207	633
4	20	200	200	3	15	—	—	20	200	200
284	42%	302,661	1,462	103	15%	646	32	668	546,001	1,685

have previous manual systems. The incidence of collusion should have an influence on the choice of safeguards and computer security strategy. For example, isolation of programmer and computer operator technical staffs from the people involved in data entry and output usage is well advised. Most known collusion cases have involved a technical person who worked with people around the manual data-handling periphery of computer systems who can convert technical acts into economic gain (Parker 1976a).

The kinds and ranking of vulnerabilities based on identification and counting of vulnerabilities in the reported computer abuse case file produced the results shown in Table 10-2. It is obvious that among the reported cases the greatest vulnerabilities by far are physical access and the manual handling of input data. Most people are unaware of the true nature of computer abuse because unusual cases are the ones most widely reported in the public and trade media. Most computer abuse cases consist of mundane and simple "data diddling" (see Appendix E1.). Computer security planning and implementation should take this factor into account.

TABLE 10-2
Areas of Vulnerabilities

RANK		PERCENT
1	Physical access to facilities	25
2	Handling of input data	23
3	Logical access to assets	15
4	Business ethics	8
5	Handling of output data	8
6	Access to application programs	7
7	Handling of machine-readable data	7
8	Access to systems proarams	3
9	Backup/recovery	2
10	Data communications	1

The classical computer abuse case that best illustrates the more common data diddling problem (except for presence of collusion) occurred in a railroad company several years ago. (This case is used as a scenario in Chapter 11.) A timekeeping clerk submitted hours-worked forms for about 300 workers to the accounting department. The forms identified workers by their names and by their identification numbers. The clerk discovered that all manually performed controls were based on names, for clerks and auditors did not recognize workers by their identification numbers. He also noticed that the names and numbers were read into the computer timekeeping and payroll system, but only the numbers were used for identification in the computer. This use of numbers included even retrieving employee names and addresses for printing on the payroll checks.

The timekeeping clerk merely filled out false overtime forms under names of employees who frequently worked overtime, but he put his own identification number on the forms. There was no manual checking of numbers, and the computer produced checks for the clerk. This went on for several years until he was caught by accident when an auditor noticed an unusually high annual income on the clerk's W-2 income tax form. A little investigation exposed the activity, the clerk admitted what he had done, and he was transferred to another department with the promise that he would not reveal what he had done to anyone else. It was too much trouble to change the system to prevent future occurrences.

Many new reported computer abuse cases involve terminals, minicomputers, and microcomputers. In a recent case, a burglar stole a microcomputer from a home and returned the next night. He had forgotten to take the floppy disk with all the programs on it. When he was caught, he was asked why he had stolen the computer. He answered that he needed it for a burglar alarm system he was building.

There is no comprehensive collection and analysis of computer-related errors and omissions. Therefore, the only data come from individual organizations that from time to time collect and sometimes report their experiences.

A Threat Model

The most difficult part of threat analysis is to assure that all significant threats have been identified. Figure 10-3 presents a threat model that may be used to help assure more complete and orderly identification of threats. This model shows that a threat cannot be represented only by potential loss, acts, or sources, but is composed of all these factors.

Identify Sources of Threat

The task force should start by identifying all subpopulations of people who might represent sources of threats because of their skills, knowledge, and access. Job descriptions of all employees, personnel files, customer lists, vendor lists, creditor lists, and the loss experience file are sources of information for this task. However, subpopulations cannot be determined entirely on the basis of the skills, knowledge, and access required for their jobs and indicated in their job descriptions. An individual in a particlar job may possess important skills, knowledge, and access that are not directly related to his job function. For example, many computer operators are young people aspiring to become computer programmers or to enter some other profession. Therefore, the sources of threats should be ordered according to the skills, knowledge, access, and resources of people rather than their current job functions.

It is important to include all subpopulations that could intentionally or accidentally cause losses to the organization. These people might include advocates or dissidents who might gain from causing losses to the organization. Anti-establishment and political organizations, workers on strike at other organizations and disgruntled with their particular industry, and professional criminals should all be considered. Other people who might cause an organization losses are airplane pilots flying over and crashing airplanes into important organization facilities, individuals using public dial-up telephones that could gain access to the organization's on-line computer, newspaper and other public media reporters who could publicly reveal sensitive information or inaccurate or false information, and the children and other relatives of people within the subpopulations identified in the threat identification process.

The last major item under sources is natural forces. In order to make the threat model consistent for both people and natural forces, natural forces

THREAT MODEL

Sources	Motives	Acts	Results	Losses
ADP Employees	Incompetence	Overt	Disclosure	None
Employees	Human failure	Covert	Modification	Monetary
Vendors	Irrational behavior	Descriptive	Destruction	Denial of use/possession
Outsiders	Personal problems	Single event	Use of services	Denial of exclusive use/possession
Natural forces	Personal gain	Multiple events		Denial of access
	Professional crime	Continuous		Personal values
	Business gain	Physical		Health/life
	Economic advocacy	Logical		Privacy
	Political advocacy	Local/remote access		Other
	Social advocacy	Real-time		
	Religious advocacy	Nonreal-time		
		Collusion		
		Testing		
		Other		

FIGURE 10-3

can be treated in the same way as people sources. For example, one source of threat is fire, and fire can be thought of as having certain capabilities that are the equivalent of acts, results, and losses associated with people.

The hazards related to natural forces are so numerous that it is impossible to compile a comprehensive list. Basic categories include extreme temperature, gas, liquids, living organisms, projectiles, earth movements, and electromagnetic discharge. Fire is included under the category of extreme temperature, explosions under gas (rapidly expanding gas), and smoke and dust under gas, even though these are solids suspended in gas. Frozen liquids are classified under liquids. Light energy in the form of laser beams and atomic radiation are included under the electromagnetic category. Taking these few liberties with physical sciences to combine items that are associated with similar safeguards, the list in Table 10-3 on the following page was constructed.

Some of the natural forces in Table 10-3 may seem ridiculous or farfetched, but it is better to include such items and later reject them as unlikely than to have overlooked an obscure but important source of threat.

Identify Motives

Motives should be identified next. Some motives will probably be noted during identification of sources. Many psychologists believe that it is useless to develop taxonomies of reasons for causing losses or seeking to make unauthorized gains. In general, this reservation applies to specific motives arising from poor marital relations, financial indebtedness, or an antisocial goal. Motives at a more general level can be identified, and knowing them would be particularly useful for purposes of finding deterrents during the development of safeguards. Some categories of general motives are listed in the threat model depicted in Figure 10-3.

A study of motives in bank embezzlement cases conducted by the FBI concluded that the most common reason for bank embezzlement was the desire to do a favor for a customer. The next most common reason for embezzlement was the need to solve a personal business problem, and the third most common reason, which represented less than 19 percent of all cases, was a desire to live beyond one's means (wine, women, and song, or gambling or keeping up with one's peers).

Identify Acts, Results, and Losses

The acts, results, and losses can all be identified by considering the skills, knowledge, and access of the sources of threats. The motives and the assets identified in the previous step are also helpful. Listing acts requires a great deal of imagination. Reviewing the file of loss experience and the liter-

TABLE 10-3
Natural Forces

EXTREME TEMPERATURE	GAS	LIQUIDS
Hot weather	War gases	Water, rain, flood, ice,
Cold weather	Commercial chemical vapors	snow, sleet
Spontaneous Fire	Humid air	Chemical solvents
	Steam	Fuels
	Wind, tornado, hurricane	Plastics
	Explosion	
	Smoke, dust	

LIVING ORGANISMS	PROJECTILES	EARTH MOVEMENTS
Rodents	Bullets	Earth collapses
Insects	Rockets, missiles	Mud slides, lava
Bacteria	Shrapnel	Liquefaction
Viruses	Surface vehicles	Shaking, waves
	Airborne vehicles	Cracking, separations
	Thrown objects	Shearing
	Meteorites	

ELECTROMAGNETIC DISCHARGES
Electric power surges and blackouts
Lightning, static electricity
Microwaves
Magnetism
Lasers
Atomic radiation
Cosmic rays

ature on computer crime (Parker 1976b; Whiteside 1978) and technical papers on security will be of assistance. Putting oneself in the position of the perpetrator and his environment and envisioning what he would do is helpful. Bear in mind that most acts will be relatively simple and mundane rather than complicated or exotic. A perpetrator would find it more desirable to change data before input than to write a program to change data in the computer.

On the other hand, elaborate, sophisticated acts must also be considered for; although their frequency is low, losses can be very large. Some common acts of this type are described in Appendix E.

As the threat model in Figure 10-3 shows, only four basic results of unauthorized acts are possible. Disclosure, one of the four results, must be interpreted in its broadest sense to include taking an original and taking a copy, as well as revealing secrets.

Note that criminal terms such as theft, fraud, embezzlement, and larceny are not used in context of this threat model. Such terms are often ambiguous because they have different meanings among legal jurisdictions. Strictly speaking, these terms apply to only acts of persons convicted of violation of criminal law. A security specialist using these terms might be subject to false arrest or intimidation charges or might alienate an otherwise cooperative suspect by using crime-associated terms.

Losses described in the threat model in Figure 10-3 should not be taken as an exhaustive list but merely as the range of possibilities. The assets model in Figure 9-1 will be an aid in identifying losses. In fact, the loss column of the threat model should closely match the first column of the assets model, since losses always occur among identifiable assets. The first column of sources in the threat model should also be closely related to the last column of accountability in the assets model, since many sources of threats are people in positions of trust (accountable for assets). These two models are circularly related for a wide range of losses (assets) and sources of threats (people accountable for assets). At this stage it is important to be as comprehensive as possible. Do not intentionally leave out a threat because it appears that further steps in the study will eliminate it.

Develop Submodels

After the threat model is completed it should be divided into submodels according to threats in each part of the organization. The submodels can then be submitted to management in each appropriate part of the organization for review and addition of new threats. Do not allow any deletions of threats at this stage. Opportunity for that will come at a later stage of the study. Additional sources of threats may be found in the current literature on computer security. A list of this current literature is provided in the References of this book.

Other sources of threat can be identified from the study and collection of newspaper and other public media clippings if used cautiously with other supporting data. Alert security and audit organizations should be collecting this kind of material as part of their work. In addition, a number of underground newspapers and other media are available. The FBI, postal inspectors, local police, and district attorneys' offices should be contacted to obtain this kind of source material. Such organizations, including the fire department and insurance companies, may be able to assist generally in the identification of threats, especially in the local geographic area within the scope of the study. Other organizations in the same or similar business and geographically close organizations may also be contacted to learn about their experience of threats that might affect the organization under study. Participation in local chapters of the American Society for Industrial Security (ASIS), Institute of Internal Auditors (IIA), EDP Auditors Association, National Crime Prevention Association, and community anti-crime groups is also useful in this regard.

The ranking and expected frequency of actualized threats will be treated in the next chapter. Note that this can only be done by taking into account the existing safeguards. An intelligent enemy will anticipate strengths and weaknesses of security, and this will affect the likelihood and frequency of actualized threats. The evaluation of threats in the context of safeguards is often called vulnerability analysis. This complex topic is included in the discussion of risk assessment in Chapter 11.

Chapter 11
Risk Assessment

Risk assessment is a greatly misused and misunderstood "buzzword" in computer security. The term is used to identify highly structured methods requiring probability and dollar value of assets calculations at one extreme, and action plans based on a few observations and interviews at the other extreme. Risk is defined as the product of the amount that may be lost and the probability of losing it. This product is the basis of the first method of assessing risk described in this chapter. The second is a subjective aid for conducting risk assessment by means of scenarios. The third method of risk assessment is based on an exposure index, an alternative to probability of loss. The use of questionnaires is also described as an aid in gathering data for assessment. Finally, a composite of methods is described as the most practical way of measuring and ranking vulnerabilities. Other methods, such as one based on fuzzy set theory (Hoffman, Michelman, and Clements 1978), are described in computer security literature.

Courtney Risk Assessment

A quantitative method of numerical risk assessment recommended by Robert Courtney of IBM (Courtney 1977) is one approach to safeguarding. It is based on estimates of the expected frequency and amount of loss from each

TABLE 11-1
Frequency of Threats

P = 0 if practically never
1 if once in one thousand years
2 if once in one hundred years
3 if once in ten years (taken to be one thousand days)
4 if once a year
5 if once a month (ten times a year)
6 if twice a week (one hundred times a year)
7 if three times a day (one thousand times a year)

particular actualized threat. The expected frequency of threats occurring per year P is calculated (in most cases approximately) by the formula $P = 10^{(p-4)}$ where p is assigned one of the values in Table 11-1.

It can be seen that P takes on the value of the number of loss events expected to take place per year. For example, if an event is expected to happen once in ten years, then $p = 3$ and $P = 10^{(3-4)} = 1/10$th or once in ten years. If a loss event is expected to happen about once each month, then $p = 5$ and $P = 10^{(5-4)} = 10$. Combining this numerical method of calculating frequency of threats with the explicit calculations of the dollar loss per event identified as $V = 10^v$ in Chapter 9, then E, the expected loss per year based on frequency and size of the loss, is given by

$$E = P \times V = 10^v \times 10^{(p-4)} = 10^{(v+p-4)}.$$

For example, if a fraud involving a checking account system in a bank is expected to occur once in ten years and a loss could be \$100,000, then $p = 3$, $v = 5$ and expected loss per year is $E = 10^{(5+3-4)} = \$10,000$.

An alternative equation is $E = 1/3 \times 10^{(p+v-3)}$ for approximating annual loss from values for v and p given in Table 11-2.

It is imporant to note that this method of calculating expected annual loss is a powerful aid for making decisions concerning the amount of resources to invest in safeguards to reduce the expected loss. To carry this process out, however, amounts of information are needed to produce reasonable loss values of assets and expected frequency of the occurrence of incidents involving each asset. Dollar loss data covering several years of high frequency loss experience would be an ideal data base to use in the formulas to calculate expected annual losses. When these data are not available, this method becomes less valuable. Quantitative risk assessment by applying metrics and consensus techniques as described above may provide useful information, but the resulting numbers may be deceiving because of the high degree of guesswork in producing the substantiating data. Because

TABLE 11-2
Alternative Frequency and Loss Values

v	LOSS	p	APPROXIMATE FREQUENCY
0	0	0	Practically never
1	10	1	Once in 300 years
2	100	2	Once in 30 years
3	1,000	3	Once in 3 years
4	10,000	4	Once in 100 days
5	100,000	5	Once in 10 days
6	1,000,000	6	Once per day
7	10,000,000	7	Ten times per day
8	100,000,000		

this method entails so much work it should be used for only the most sensitive information-processing applications that involve a high potential loss. For more practical and general purposes, it may be more practical to simply rank the seriousness of threats and sensitivity of assets by means of qualitative grades or reasoned risk assessment.

Organizations have been known to produce elaborate risk assessments and to generate vast amounts of data by the numerical method, only to find that they could have identified sensitive assets and possible losses in more simple ways for their purposes. The decision to use an elaborate metric method of risk assessment should be based on the following considerations.

1. Are there obvious vulnerabilities and known acceptable safeguards to reduce them?

2. Act on these vulnerabilities first on the basis that this will have to be done no matter what studies may be necessary. In other words, close and lock the barn doors before worrying about the rat holes.

3. Identify all assets, as suggested in Chapter 9. What metrics, tokens, or dollars can be used for valuation? Can the assets be classified in groups delineated in relation to a unique set of threats for each group (for example, all physical assets in a particular room or all data files subject to on-line terminal access)? How many groups might result from this? Would the values placed on each group be valid? For purposes of setting security priorities and allocating security resources, can the groups of assets be ranked in terms of relative value rather than absolute value?

4. Identify all threats to the degree possible. What confidence is there that all types of threats have been identified, and do the identified threats sound reasonable relative to the organization and the expe-

rience or concerns of others? Can believable threat scenarios be developed? Can the threats be grouped to apply to the groups of assets identified in step 3? Can the groups of threats be ranked by relative expected frequency of occurrence? What is the level of confidence in the ranking?

5. Pair off the groups of threats and groups of assets to identify vulnerabilities. Identify and evaluate existing controls protecting assets from threats. Rank the vulnerabilities in the following order (graded risk assessment):

> Highest frequency and highest loss per incident
>
> Moderate frequency and highest loss per incident
>
> Highest frequency and moderate loss per incident
>
> Lowest frequency and highest loss per incident
>
> Lowest frequency and lowest loss per incident

Make minor adjustments in the ordering of vulnerabilities so that approximations of loss per incident are ordered from highest to lowest. For example, threats of very high frequency and moderate loss might be higher than threats of moderate frequency and highest loss. Are there any inconsistencies or questionable ranking? Are there vulnerabilities of questionable risk and high cost for increased protection? These are the key questions because the answers can be used to decide whether a more detailed analysis requiring a numerical risk assessment must be performed.

6. If this ranking of vulnerabilities and possible new safeguards identified from checklists and other sources is satisfactory for current purposes, proceed to select safeguards for implementation as suggested in Chapter 12, starting with the greatest vulnerability and proceed according to strategies in Chapter 4.

A detailed quantitative risk assessment can be costly and take a considerable period of time. The experience of the computer security staff, the state of computer security, the commitment of management to advance security beyond current levels, requirements that may be imposed by law, regulation or pressures from external auditors are all factors to consider. In general, a comprehensive numerical risk assessment should not be undertaken by a large data processing facility unless it has already given extensive attention to security, unless it plans an ongoing security program, and unless it employs at least one full-time computer security specialist who has had some experience and has the confidence of the EDP staff and users. If these basic commitments are not met, the risk assessment could result in wasted and inefficient efforts, more detailed and voluminous data than can be effectively used, and questionable results based on a mix of subjective and objective unreliable data.

The application of analytical methods to computer security is in its infancy. Much experimentation, experience with different methods, and stronger consensus on the best methods are needed.

Exposure Analysis

In many cases it is exceedingly difficult to determine meaningful probabilities of losses from acts performed by people for use in risk assessment formulas. In some cases there is enough recorded experience of errors (for example, data keying errors) and incidence of intentionally caused losses (for example, credit card fraud) to use actuarial methods. In most cases, however, data are not available and guessing does not produce enough consistent results to induce confidence.

An alternative to producing probabilities of losses is to determine exposures to losses on the basis of numbers of people who could accidentally or intentionally cause losses. This method has the advantage of eliminating most guesswork and consensus determination, the need to separate accidental from intentional acts, and the need for motive or competence considerations. One possible disadvantage of this method, however, is that the results are in a relative or index form rather than in absolute form of expected loss in dollars. On the other hand, this form could be an advantage since expression of expected loss in absolute terms such as dollars may be deceiving.

Guesswork is eliminated because the results are based on actual counts of all people categorized by skills, knowledge, and access to identified assets. Confidence in the results may be reduced in some cases where identification of all people according to these capabilities is not practical. Counting people within the organization is more straightforward than, for example, counting all people who could sabotage a computer facility from outside. Therefore, this method tends to produce better results for acts committed from known positions of trust than for others, but most known losses have been caused by the former.

The need to separate accidental from intentional acts in considering the results of modification, destruction, disclosure, and use is eliminated in this method since exposure to loss does not take into account how the loss might occur, but only the possibility of loss based on the number of people who could cause it, for whatever reason. This analysis does not depend on motive or competence, although later refinements could include these considerations by the application of weighting factors.

In a computer environment, four basic sources of exposure to loss from people can be established:

1. **People with physical access to assets who have the capabilities to perform physical acts.**—Physical acts include destructive attacks on equipment, data and programs, false data entry into computer systems through normal manual input methods, and scavenging for information available in physical form (such as computer output listings, punch cards, reels of tape, and disk packs). Skills needed are minimal. They include physical strength, persuasion in dealing with people and (possibly) keyboard operation ability. Knowledge is required of the target and its environment and the operational procedures of the EDP staff.

2. **People with access who have operational capabilities.**—Transactional acts include impersonation (assuming the identity and privilege of another person) and piggybacking to obtain the same privilege of another person having access rights to a system. Such actions may be performed physically or logically, through the use of terminal and utility programs to modify, copy, or delete data stored in computer media. Skills required include terminal and computer operation knowledge, persuasion in dealing with people, and impersonation of others. Knowledge of interactive and physical access protocols, data file organization, or utility program operation in a particular computer system would also be required.

3. **People with access who have programming capabilities.**—These people have more sophisticated skills and knowledge than people in the first two categories. Various programming techniques can be used such as Trojan Horse attacks, trap doors, asynchronous processing attacks, salami techniques (such as round-down accumulation), data leakage, and logic bombs; in addition, the computer can be used as a tool for the simulation and modeling of crimes. These methods can be used in application programs, operating systems and data communications. Skills required include programming and systems analysis. Detailed knowledge is needed of particular application, system, and communication programs. Knowledge of simulation and modeling methods would also be an asset.

4. **People with access who have electronic engineering capabilities.**—This class includes wiretapping and electronic hardware modifications to produce the same results as software modification and use. Individuals would have to be skilled in electronic fabrication, circuit diagram reading, and the use of electronic tools. Knowledge is needed of electronic engineering, digital logic design, and electronic details of specific computers.

TABLE 11-3

Occupations as Sources of Exposure

OCCUPATION	PHYSICAL	OPERA-TIONAL	PROGRAM-MING	ELEC-TRONIC
User transaction and data entry operator	x	x		
Computer operator	x	x		
Peripheral equipment operator	x	x		
Job set-up clerk	x	x		
Data entry and update clerk	x	x		
Tape librarian	x			
User tape librarian	x			
Systems programmer	x	x	x	
Application programmer	x	x	x	
User programmer	x	x	x	
Terminal engineer	x	x		x
Computer systems engineer	x	x	x	x
Communications engineer/operator	x	x		x
Facilities engineer	x	x		
Operations manager	x	x		
Data base administrator	x	x		
Programming manager	x	x	x	
Security specialist	x	x	x	x
EDP auditor	x	x	x	x

EDP occupations identified according to these sources of exposure are presented in Table 11-3.

This categorization of occupations suggests that risk assessment can be approached by identifying and counting these people by their skills, knowledge, and access. Occupations provide a convenient way of labeling categories. The people to be considered need not be just employees but may include anyone in a position of trust who has sufficient skills, knowledge, and access to represent potential threats to EDP assets. These ideas were expressed for the first time in a study and report prepared by SRI International for the Federal Deposit Insurance Corporation entitled "A Guide to EDP and EFTS Security Based on Occupations" (Parker and Dewey 1978) and a report on "ADP Occupational Vulnerabilities" prepared for another federal agency (Parker and Madden 1978).

This study uses generic EDP occupations. The results of a vulnerability analysis associated with five possible acts against eight forms of assets, and

TABLE 11-4

Occupational Vulnerability Analysis

VULNERABILITIES: PHYSICAL · OPERATIONAL · PROGRAMMABLE · ELECTRONIC	OCCUPATIONS	VULNERABLE ASSETS BY ACTS[a] — Internal Data			Internal Application Programs		
		M	DE	DI	M	DE	DI
	Tape librarian						
	User tape librarian						
	User trans. & data entry operator	2	2	2		1	1
	Computer operator	1	5	5		5	5
	Peripheral equipment operator						
	Job set-up clerk						
	Data entry & update clerk	3	3	3		4	4
	Facilities engineer						
	Operations manager	1	5	5		5	5
	Data base administrator	3	3	3			
	Systems programmer		5	5		5	5
	Applications programmer	1	1	1	2	2	2
	User programmer	1	1	1	2	2	2
	Programming manager	1	1	1	4	4	4
	Communications engineer/ operator		5	5			
	Terminal engineer						
	Computer systems engineer						
	Security officer	5	5	5	5	5	5
	EDP auditor	5	5	5	5	5	5

[a]Acts		Exposure Scale	
M—Modification	T—Taking	blank	no effect
DE—Destruction	DN—Denial of use	1	up to 20%
DI—Disclosure		2	up to 40%
		3	up to 60%
		4	up to 80%
		5	up to 100%

general types of safeguards are presented for each occupation as an example. The ranges of exposed assets have been subjectively assigned to each occupation; occupations have been ranked in five levels according to degree of exposure as a derivation from the example.

Two difficulties with previous computer security threat analysis methods have been the lack of completeness and consistency. Completeness refers to the assurance that all vulnerabilities associated with an asset are considered in security evaluation and planning. Consistency refers to the

TABLE 11-4 (Continued)

Internal System Programs			External Data			External Application Programs			External System Programs			Computer Equipment & Supplies			System Service	
M	DE	DI	M	DE	DI	M	DE	DI	M	DE	DI	M	DE	T	T	DN
				4	4		3	3		3	3		1	1		
				2	2		1	1					1	1		
			2	2	2		1	1					1	1		
	5	5	1	3	3								5	5	5	5
				3	3		4	4		1	1		2	2		
				3	3		4	4					1	1	5	
	5	5	3	3	3		4	4		1	5		1	1		
												1	5	5		5
	5	5	1	3	3		4	4		1	5		5	5	5	5
			3	3	3								1	1		
5	5	5							5	1	5		1	1	5	5
						2	2	2					1	1		
						2	2	2					1	1		
						4	4	4					1	1		
												2	2	2		
												1	1	1		
												5	5	5		
2	2	2										5	5	5		
5	5	5	3	3	3	4	4	4	5	5	5	5	5	5	5	5
5	5	5	5	5	5	5	5	5	5	5	5	5	5	5	5	5

amount of safeguarding appropriate to the potential loss from all vulnerabilities. The method in this study minimizes these two difficulties in the area of personnel threats.

The development of this method started with the selection of a set of occupations in data processing. The occupation choices and descriptions were made consistent with the IBM Manual, "Organizing the Data Processing Activity" (GC20-1622-2). No attempt was made to eliminate duplication of a particular function in two occupations, for example, the computer operator and the peripheral equipment operator both handle tapes and disk packs. Each occupation includes managers who have the same capabilities and manage people in the same occupation.

Generation of the occupational vulnerability analysis depicted in Table 11-4, was completed next. The vulnerability column headings are a refinement of those developed during an SRI study for the National Bureau of

Standards, "Development of Technical Specifications to Serve as a Basis for Federal Guidelines to Prevent Intentional Computer Misuse." The refinement consisted of separating application programs and system programs when considering their modification, destruction, or disclosure, either internal or external to the system. This separation is important in delineating the sources of vulnerabilities among the designated occupations. Upon completion of the table, it was possible to generate detailed occupation descriptions with confidence that the vulnerabilities were being handled in a consistent manner. The detailed occupations descriptions are presented in Appendix F. Although they were derived in a special study, their applicability is general.

The matrix entries in Table 11-4 are based on an exposure scale of blank (no effect) and numbers one to five indicating the percentage of the asset that an individual could affect:

BLANK	NO EFFECT
1	up to 20% of the asset
2	up to 40% of the asset
3	up to 60% of the asset
4	up to 80% of the asset
5	up to 100% of the asset

An entry of "5" on the line of a particular occupation in the column "Internal Data/Disclosure" indicates that an individual is in a position to disclose almost all data internal to the system. An entry of "2" indicates the ability to affect up to 40 percent of the data in the same way. A blank entry denotes no effect.

Assets in the form of data, application programs, and system programs are designated as internal to a computer system when the central processor has continuous access to them from any attached storage device. Assets are considered external to a computer system when they are in human-readable form or in computer-readable form and where ADP personnel have manual, direct access to them. Computer equipment, supplies, and services complete the range of types of assets.

Three types of acts, and in one case, two, are stated for each form of asset. Modification (M) refers to the intentional addition, deletion, or replacement of the asset. Destruction (DE) means rendering the asset totally useless. Destroying part of a data record, but leaving an identifiable and usable part intact, is considered modification, not destruction. Disclosure (DI) is unauthorized revealing of data or programs by observation, taking, or using. Taking (T) is the unauthorized removal of computer supplies, equipment or use of computer resources. Denial of use (DN) applies to services and resources. In all acts it is assumed that a perpetrator does profit or could profit from his act, and that a victim does experience or could experience a loss from the act.

The matrix entries in Table 11-4 are based on a specific environment in which usual safeguards and controls have been installed in idealized, totally effective ways. Different matrix entries might be assigned for a specific EDP facility on the basis of its actual environment and safeguards in place. For example, in this study, whenever it is possible to limit the access and functioning of an individual, this is done. One reason that the application programmer and the user programmer are assigned a limited exposure level rather than a great exposure level is that the study assumes that these individuals communicate with the system through a programmer terminal or intermediary. They never have access to current production so that independent software verification takes place before their products are put into production. Similarly, it is assumed that the computer systems engineer is never permitted to work on a computer system when any production data or application programs are present.

Some ambiguity exists in the classification of a particular act. For example, a systems programmer might modify a system program internal to the system and successfully deny authorized system service. In this situation, the convention adopted is to classify the violation in the category that had to occur first. Therefore, this example would be classified as an internal modification of a systems program rather than a denial of system service.

Generating the occupation descriptions was straightforward once the table was complete. Appendix F contains nineteen occupation descriptions. However, the classification of safeguards deserves comment. An organization structure from Chapter 3 is used in the occupation descriptions to show the organizational relationships. Note that occupations are described in generic and idealized form in terms of job function, skills, knowledge, and access. In practice, the skills, knowledge, and access of personnel do not match exactly these descriptions of their occupations. It is assumed here that each occupation is limited to only the description provided. For example, a computer operator who has programming skill, knowledge, and access in addition to his operator capabilities must be classified as a programmer as well as a computer operator in the scheme of this report. If he functions in both capacities, then the two occupations presented here must be combined in depicting the individual as a source of exposure to loss, and all vulnerabilities and safeguards in both descriptions apply to the individual.

A practical application of this report to a threat analysis based on occupations requires that the pertinent skills, knowledge, and access of all personnel associated with the use and operation of a computer system can be identified independently of their specific occupations. Identification could be carried out by questionnaires, interviews, and examination of personnel, experience, and education records. Individuals could then be assigned to one or more of the occupational categories identified. The resulting counts of people in each occupation category then represent the degree of exposure to the assets by type of act, as identified in Table 11-4. The occupational categories serve as a convenient means of identifying skills, knowledge, and access in this methodology.

Collusion of two or more individuals is not considered. It is always assumed that each individual performs a single act alone with a single asset. This approach is sufficient for accidental losses. In actual experience, an intentionally caused loss often results from sequences of parallel independent and dependent acts by more than one person involving several assets in several forms.

In Table 11-4 the range of exposure scale entries in a given row tend to be the same for columns in pairs or in triples. The entries for destruction and disclosure of a particular asset are almost always the same, and in many cases, the entry for modification matches the other two. This matching is explained by an individual's ability to destroy or disclose an asset if he is able to gain access or has access to it, and his ability to modify an asset if he has the appropriate knowledge. The duplication suggests that the number of columns might have been reduced, but this was not done since it is important to highlight all possible acts.

It can also be seen that row sums have little meaning unless acts in each column have the same significance of loss. If one were to assign a loss factor, that is, monetary value, to each column, an identifiable exposure to loss index for each row could be produced by summing the matrix elements weighted by the loss factors. The results could be used as relative measures of the degree of vulnerabilities represented by persons in the various occupations. A process of this kind led to the ratings that appear in the risk level section of the occupation descriptions in Appendix F. A listing of occupations by risk level as a result of the study appears in Table 11-5.

Similarly, weighted column sums could be of value. In this case, it appears that the proper row weighting would be the number of persons in each occupation. The resulting column indices would then represent the relative vulnerabilities of assets to the indicated acts by all personnel.

This study could also be extended to include collusion. Approximately one-half of the catalogued computer abuse cases have involved more than one person. The present study offers useful insights into the vulnerabilities of a system to acts by a single individual; the extrapolation to acts by more than one individual is not straightforward. However, it appears that a study considering a set of typical collusion situations might provide additional valuable insights.

In addition, a formal security methodology can be derived from this work, including a framework for weightings in the matrix entries of Table

TABLE 11-5

Risk Level of Occupations Based on Range of Assets Exposure
(Occupations in Alphabetical Order within risk level)

	Page in Appendix F Occupation Description
GREATEST RISK	
EDP Auditor	270
Security Specialist	269
GREAT RISK	
Computer Operator	253
Data Entry and Update Clerk	256
Operations Manager	266
Systems Programmer	259
MODERATE RISK	
Computer Systems Engineer	263
Programming Manager	268
LIMITED RISK	
Application Programmer	260
Communications Engineer/Operator	264
Data Base Administrator	267
Facilities Engineer	265
Peripheral Equipment Operator	264
Tape Librarian	257
User Programmer	261
User Transaction and Data Entry Operator	252
LOW RISK	
Terminal Engineer	262
User Tape Librarian	258

11-4. Such a methodology has been tested on a limited basis to prove its feasibility.

Case Study of an Exposure Analysis

This case concerns a large computer installation for which the allocation of security resources had to be decided. The distribution of resources and prioritization of safeguards had to be established among the major vulnerability areas relative to exposure to loss and generic categories of assets needing protection. (Protection of staff and building facilities were considered separate from this study.)

Five EDP functions were considered:

- Data preparation and control
- Computer operations
- Applications programming and analysis
- Systems programming
- Vendor equipment maintenance

These functions closely match the skills, knowledge, and access of the EDP staff, so that determining the exposure could be accomplished by approximate counts of the number of people working in each functional area. The high rate of annual employee turnover was taken into account by weighting the total staff counts by adding the turnover amount for the previous year to each function count.

Five generic categories of assets were identified:

- **Physical equipment.** Equipment in terms of physical damage, use, or taking.

- **Equipment logic.** Equipment in terms of unauthorized modification of functions performed.

- **External data.** Data in all forms external to the EDP equipment (off-line) subject to modification, destruction, use and disclosure.

- **Internal data.** Data in computer storage (on-line) subject to modification, use, destruction, and disclosure by manual operations and use of utility programs.

- **Programs.** Application and system programs subject to modification (and subsequent data modification, use, destruction, and disclosure), destruction, use, and disclosure.

The data were gathered by structured interviews with the highest and second-level managers in each department. The form in Figure 11-1 was used. In addition, each department was required to submit a report of numbers of employees and turnover during the past year to verify the numbers obtained in the interviews. There was little concern that counts based on job descriptions did not match actual skills and knowledge. For example, some of the computer operators know programming (but they are not allowed to run their own programs on the computer they operate). It was felt that access restrictions limited the impact of this problem.

A matrix was formed in which the five occupation areas were placed on the vertical axis and the five assets losses on the horizontal (see Figure 11-2). The total number of employees and annual turnover are presented in the first and second columns. The sum of these two numbers was used to calculate the fraction of all employees represented by the occupation area. The fraction is shown in the equation at the end of each row.

EXPOSURE FACTS

Department: _____ Manager: _____

Occupation: _____

Skills: _____

_____

Knowledge: _____

_____

Physical Access: _____

_____

Assets Access:
  Internal Data
    Applications _____
    Operating Systems _____
  External Data
    Applications _____
    Operating Systems _____
  Computer Equipment and Supplies _____
  System Service _____

Accountability Items: _____

_____

Vulnerability Class: Physical___ Operational___
                Programming___ Electronic___

Current Number: Employees___ Contract___ Vendor___

Annual Turnover/Work Period: _____

Upgrade Training: _____

_____

FIGURE 11-1

In the first pass, a graded metric was used to identify the capabilities to cause a loss and the size of the potential loss to that particular asset: none (0), low (L), medium (M), and high (H). In some cases, an explanation for

	Personnel		Physical Equipment	Equipment Logic
	No.	Turnover per year	High Relative Loss 100 points	Medium Relative Loss 50 points
Data preparation and Control	1508 79%	750 82%	L/L for data entry multiple in-house backup	L/M: high access but low knowledge
Capability & size of potential loss				
Percent of asset that could be lost			10%	0%
Relative point value of each asset lost			10	0
Computer Operations	137 7%	35* 6%	H/H: total destruction of DP capabilities	O/H: low knowledge and skills
Capability & size of potential loss				
Percent of asset that could be lost			90%	0%
Relative point value			90	0
Applications Programs and Analysis	172 9%	40 8%	L/L: Terminals only	O: low access, skills, knowledge
Capability & size of potential loss				
Percent of asset that could be lost			5%	0%
Relative point value			5	0
Systems Programming	80 4%	5 3%	M/H: limited to access to computer facilities, operators present	M/M: several persons have enough hardware capability
Capability & size of potential loss				
Percent of asset that could be lost			70%	70%
Relative point value			70	35
Vendor maintenance staff	10* 5%	5* 0.5%	H/H	H/H
Capability & size of potential loss				
Percent of asset that could be lost			100%	100%
Relative point value			100	50
TOTAL	1907 100%	2742 100%		

(* = guesses)

FIGURE 11-2   Capabilities to cause loss/potential loss

156

External Data	Internal Data	Programs	TOTAL POINTS (PER OCCUPATION AREA)
Medium Relative Loss 40 points	High Relative Loss 100 points	Medium Relative Loss 80 points	
L/M: high access but low knowledge 10% 4	L/L 0% 0	L/L: key entry of programs 5% 4	82% × 18 = 15
M/H: high access but low knowledge 50% 20	H/H 95% 95	L/M: low knowledge & skills, high access 20% 16	6% × 221 = 13
L/L: low access 5% 2	H/H 95% 95	H/H 90% 72	8% × 174 = 14
L/M 10% 4	H/H 95% 95	H/H 95% 76	3% × 280 = 8
L/M 5% 2	H/H 95% 95	H/H 95% 76	0.5% × 323 = 2

FIGURE 11-2 (Continued)

ratings is given. Next, the same metric was used to evaluate the severity of loss of each asset.

In the second pass, a more precise metric of 0 to 100 percent in steps of 5 percent was used to estimate the percentage of the asset that could be lost from an act by an individual in each occupation area. Next, the relative value of each asset loss was estimated on a scale of 100 points in increments of 10 points.

Then the product of asset loss points at the top of each column times percent of asset loss in each matrix entry was calculated for each occupation area and each asset loss. The products were added across each row to produce the total points of all losses for each occupation area. These are shown in the formulas in the last column. The formulas show the multiplication of the percentage of total employees in each occupation area times the total points for each occupation area.

In retrospect, the numeric values throughout the matrix are compared to the first pass rough estimates to assure consistency throughout. The final numeric results show the exposures to loss of assets based on the numbers of people with different skills, knowledge, and access for each occupation area.

As a result of the study, two priority levels were established: data preparation, computer operations, and application programming in highest priority; and systems programming and vendor maintenance in the second priority. Physical equipment, internal data, and programs were of greatest interest among assets. A cursory examination of safeguards and backup in the low exposure functions/assets combinations indicated no great exposures needing immediate attention. This finding further supported the choice of priorities.

This example of a risk analysis was designed to be only as detailed as necessary to answer the key questions at an early stage in a security program. It would probably be necessary to perform a more detailed risk analysis in each EDP function at the next stage.

Scenario Analysis

Part of the risk assessment method is the identification of vulnerabilities and their implications. The vulnerabilities in numeric risk assessment are identified as the various expected annual loss items that make up the total expected annual loss. The safeguards in place at the time of the assessment are taken into account in calculating probabilities of loss. Where probabilities are unobtainable to a sufficient degree of reliability, exposure analysis can be used. The ultimate goal is to answer specific questions about allocation of security resources and the weakest links to be fixed.

A companion methodology that has been found valuable, even though it is highly subjective, parallels the risk analysis methods but goes a step further as an aid in evaluation and selection of safeguards (which are covered in Chapter 12). Analysis is performed by matching the threats identified by methods described in Chapter 10 to the assets identified by methods described in Chapter 9 through the development of a set of scenarios or stories. Scenarios are merely short stories, each describing a related range of threats, the act that could be performed, and the assets subject to loss. Examples of scenarios based on real loss incidents are provided in Appendix J. The combined assets and threats models described in Chapters 9 and 10 provide a general model for the scenarios. Each scenario will use one or more items from each column of the threat model. A limited security study may require at most two or three one-page scenarios. A very elaborate, in-depth study for a large computing activity may require hundreds of scenarios.

Scenarios provide two significant advantages over analyses based on tabulated data. First, scenarios are valuble for communication purposes. An information security study requires the interaction of people from several different areas of expertise who may have communication difficulties. For example, top management finds it difficult to understand the technical material, commonly presented in tabular form, concerning threats, the identity of assets, and vulnerabilities of computers. When a set of stories depicts the same information, however, top management can easily recognize, understand, and consider the credibility of threats and vulnerabilities that their organization faces. Likewise, auditors, security specialists, insurance specialists, attorneys, data processing specialists, and computer users must be able to communicate and understand the technical aspects of the security of each of their functions and some aspects of the functions they interface with.

Scenarios are also useful because they can be applied or played out theoretically against the organization as an effective means of identifying both security strengths and vulnerabilities and evaluating safeguards. Scenario analysis is basically a formalization of a process that has been inherently used by auditors and security specialists for a long time. This technique involves placing oneself in the role of the source of the threat. For example, if I were a computer programmer with certain skills, knowledge, and access, what would I do in a particular working environment to make unauthorized gain from my position of trust to aid in the solution of my personal business problem? The admonition, "Know your enemy in order to defend yourself from him," is the basis of the threat scenario analysis technique.

While scenarios can be powerful devices in the hands of the intelligent and careful expert, they can be dangerous and cause harm under some circumstances. Scenarios in the wrong hands may encourage wrongdoing by providing offenders with ideas and methods of causing losses. In addition, scenarios could be inadvertently or intentionally revealed to people such as customers of a bank who trust the integrity of the organization. The revealed scenarios, published in a newspaper, for example, may negatively affect these people by encouraging doubts about the safety of dealing with the organization.

If such dangers are perceived, then the scenarios must be treated with great confidentiality. The issue should be brought to the attention of appropriate management before scenarios are developed to assure proper authorization to use them. Scenarios should be revealed only to those managers who evaluate them. They should not be seen by people who represent the sources of threats in the scenarios.

If scenarios present too great a danger, they should be used and seen only by the security task force or should not be used at all. An alternative to the use of scenarios starts with the threats and assets models using reasoned risk analysis. All important combinations of threats and assets subject to the threats can be matched in tabular form. Safeguards and security practices coming between the threats and assets that will protect the organization can be identified. This alternative method requires significant insight and experience. It may not be as effective as the method based on scenarios. It relies primarily on checklists and popular safeguards with possibly resultant inconsistencies and general rather than specific and customized solutions.

The scenario method should proceed as follows. For each major source of threats, write several scenarios that describe how losses might occur relative to the various assets that could be available to the identified sources. For each function in the organization, submit copies of the relevant scenarios to the function managers. These managers should review the scenarios and give their opinions on whether the scenarios are credible and practical. Document the managers' opinions on the practicality and suitability of the scenarios. Discard or revise the scenarios that they reject. This method will provide an initial profile of the security strengths and vulnerabilities.

If the threat in a scenario appears to be adequately prevented with existing safeguards, then attempt to revise the scenario to violate the prevention capabilities and play such scenarios back against the organization to determine their practicality and credibility. When the threats in scenarios are prevented from completion by existing safeguards, the stories should be extended to show how the safeguards would be invoked and the circumstances that would result afterward. This step will probably identify additional threats and vulnerabilities having to do with secondary or aftereffects of invoking safeguards or controls. For example, a safeguard may be invoked to suppress an attack to crash or hang up an operating system but may be expended in the process. A second, similar attack launched soon enough might then be successful.

Finally, a set of credible and practical scenarios will be collected with general agreement that they represent the range of significant vulnerabilities to the important assets of the organization. Next, each scenario should be formally played out in theoretical fashion against the organization, and each strength or vulnerability discovered in the process should be documented. Three findings will result from this effort: a list of current protection; a list of planned protection in which managers indicate that protection mechanisms are in the process of development; and a list of remaining deficiencies. Methods presented in Chapter 12 to identify, select, and implement safeguards can then be used to reduce these remaining deficiencies. The scenarios can be used again to verify the effectiveness of safeguards chosen.

A file of scenarios ordered by functional area in a data processing operation should be maintained along with a chronological record of use. They should be reviewed and updated periodically and whenever significant changes in systems and applications have been made.

Scenario Case Study

A potential threat analysis using scenarios was conducted to determine vulnerabilities in the programming development department of a company. About 80 programmers in the department occupied an office complex on the tenth floor of a public office building and had access to a large IBM computer facility in another building through TSO programmer terminals and a Remote Job Entry Station (RJE). The RJE station was operated by an operator during first shift and operated by programmers when the operator was not present. Production and test program libraries were on-line. Entrance to the programming office complex was by a card key that activated a locked door and a guard inside the door who controlled access for about half of the first shift. Many programmers worked at night and on weekends, and programmer turnover was about 25 percent per year.

Initial interviews with project managers and the management staff indicated that application programmers had access only to their own programs in the test library by password and were unable to access live data files and production programs. Transfer of a program and data files from test to production and from production to test had to be made by an operator at the computer by written request authorized by managers. Management insisted that programmers could not perform unauthorized acts in the production system.

On the basis of experience in many other companies, the security consultants performing the analysis concluded that the programmers probably had unlimited access to the entire system. Further in-depth interviewing of application programmers and systems programmers and their manager and observations during evenings and weekends as well as during first shift produced conflicting results and supported the hypothesis of full access.

The following scenarios were written to describe the suspected vulnerabilities. They were presented to applications programming, systems programming, operations, security, and general managers. Some of the managers who had denied the vulnerabilities changed their positions when confronted with the scenarios that were validated by the systems programming manager and several other knowledgeable people. The identified vulnerabilities coupled with potential loss (also determined at the meeting) were added to the full list of vulnerabilities with appropriate priorities for solution.

Scenario 1 (Programmer Employee, Superzap, Employee Purchase File). A programmer wrote a short program, debugged it using authorized procedures, and stored it in the test library. When the RJE operator was out to lunch, the programmer entered a job through the RJE terminal to run the test program with JCL changes that caused the program to access and change a production file using the Superzap macro. He knew how to use Superzap, a normally restricted macro, because he had received help from a systems programmer at a previous debugging session and observed the systems programmer's use of Superzap. The applications programmer changed the special prices of specific products in a file used to bill and deduct employee purchases from the payroll file. He was able to purchase large numbers of high-priced products for himself and other employees at low prices and change the prices in the file to correct values afterward by using his program.

Scenario 2 (Former Employee, Physical Access, Industrial Espionage). A former employee now working for a competitor observed the comings and goings of a programmer he had known during his previous employment. One evening he waited for the programmer to emerge from the elevator to enter the office complex. The former employee was carrying a stack of magnetic tapes. He greeted the programmer and said he had come back to do some contract programming for the company. The programmer was not suspicious of wrongdoing when he saw his former associate attempting to carry tapes into the office (he wasn't carrying anything out). The programmer used his card key to open the door and held it open for his friend. The former employee was able to make copies of the documentation and listings of a valuable proprietary program package. The copy machine was readily available and programs and documentation were never locked up.

The following scenarios (not associated with the above case) illustrate how the most technical subjects and least technical subjects can be treated without complete stories to document and test specific vulnerabilities.

Scenario 3. (Programmer, PDP-10 Address Wraparound). A user placed a certain supervisor call at the next-to-last word of his virtual address space. The supervisor call returned either to the word immediately following, or the one after that, depending on whether the call was successful or not. To cause the "skip return," supervisor code incremented the program counter by one before returning. In this case, the net result of the normal program-counter advance and the additional increment was that the next instruction to be executed was located at the user's virtual address zero. However, the incrementation forced the program counter to overflow the lower half of the word in which it was stored, and caused one to be placed in the low order position of the upper half of the same word. Unfortunately, that bit is the privileged-mode bit. Control was therefore returned to user code at his virtual location zero—in privileged mode (Popek and Farber 1978).

Scenario 4. (User, TENEX Password/Page-Boundary Error). In the TENEX system, users can gain access to the files in another user's directory by executing the CONNECT command, which requires as an argument the password associated with the directory. The algorithm which checks these passwords did so one character at a time, and reported failure as soon as a mismatch occurred. The candidate password resided in user memory. This structure, together with the fact that it was possible to both sense and cause page faults, led to the undermining of the password check. A malicious user placed the candidate password so that its first character was in the last position of one memory page and the remainder in the next page, and then caused the latter page to be out of memory. (A page fault would occur at the beginning of the check of the second character of the password.) He then issued a CONNECT call. By watching whether an algorithm rejection or a page fault occurred first, and by repeating the test with different characters, it was possible to quickly determine the first character of the correct password. He then merely repeated the process, but with the candidate password successively shifted by one character. In this fashion, he obtained the entire password (Popek and Farber 1978).

Scenario 5. (Timekeeping Clerk, Payroll System). A timekeeping clerk responsible for hours worked for 300 people in his department filled out the data input forms for the timekeeping and payroll system. He noticed that the system processed all data only on the basis of employee numbers, even though employee names were included in the input. Since no one recognized employees by their numbers, he assumed that all verification of data in manual and human-readable form was based on employee names. The clerk took advantage of this dichotomy of controls by filling out data forms for overtime hours using names of workers who frequently work overtime but using his own employee number. Manual verification and system controls did not cause exposure of his activity, and he received several thousand dollars per year without being discovered.

It is obvious that scenarios such as these can form the basis for discussion and analysis of vulnerabilities by key people having various technical knowledge needed to deal with the many vulnerabilities in and around computer systems. When a large number of scenarios are used, classification codes and various evaluation and journaling forms can be designed and used.

Questionnaire Methods

When large amounts of data are required from numerous sources, questionnaire surveys are essential. A significant source of EDP vulnerabilities exists in parts of the organization that supply data and use the computer output. They are commonly identified as users: personnel, accounting, cashier, warehousing, shipping, sales, marketing, audit, and engineering departments. These areas are frequently ignored in computer security studies that are limited to the EDP department. Failure to take them into account can result in the Maginot line syndrome of suboptimizing security relative to the entire enterprise.

This common situation may arise for various reasons. The EDP security specialist or security task force may be directed from a management level that is too low to encompass all user departments, or the security specialist or task force may eliminate the users from the scope of their study because of the massive amount of data needed, range of exposures and vulnerabilities, and mundane and routine nontechnical nature of the safeguards needed that don't interest or challenge the technically oriented specialists. Furthermore, the security staff might find considerable lack of cooperation and hostility among users, many of whom believe that because of the high level of security in the EDP services, they do not have to worry about it in their own areas.

Questionnaire surveys are often the least obnoxious means of collecting data for risk analysis. Effective use of questionnaires is difficult and complex, however, and should be done by experienced experts whenever possible.

The first action is to determine the objectives of the survey, which should be defined formally. Next, the questions that will meet the specified needs must be developed, and the population necessary to answer the questions to produce valid results must be chosen. A number of technical issues must be settled if only a sample is to be used. Normally in this application, a total population will be polled and 100 percent response will be anticipated. This eliminates the need for statistical sample considerations. The questionnaire must be authorized and promulgated by appropriate management for a 100 percent return to be achieved.

The design of the questionnaire is crucial to the success of the survey, but is especially difficult to formulate in a security study because the required results are usually obtained through a combination of subjective opinions and factual data. It is desirable to separate one from the other in designing the questions. Tabulation of answers should be estimated and its meaning analyzed as a first test to determine the applicability of the questions to the goals of the survey.

The second test is to determine the answerability of the questions. It must be determined who will answer, their capability to understand and answer, and their motivation to answer fully and correctly. Respondents may be hostile to the purpose of the survey if its results could mean new constraints and changes in their work functions. The intended use of the results should be carefully explained. The effort required to complete the questionnaire must be estimated for budget planning purposes and in order to be assured the effort will not be excessive from the users' point of view. Do not cover so many issues that the effort and cost of answering the questionnaire and tabulating the results will become excessive. Stick to the subject and original goals.

Pilot testing is essential to determine the adequacy and answerability of the questionnaire. Interviews with respondents to the pilot sample should be carried out to determine their reactions and problems. Some redesign is almost always necessary. In addition, it may be possible to supply information that will aid the answerers and assure that they answer fully and completely. For example, listings of all applications and files owned by each user can be supplied along with the questionnaire.

The time allowed for answering and returning the questionnaires should be practical but not too great. It is better to err by not providing enough time and resorting to time extensions than to specify too much time and thereby allow answerers to procrastinate and lose headway. Respondents may be further motivated if they are told that results of the survey relative to their areas will be given to them. Do not reveal security-related information to those who don't need it or to whom it doesn't apply. Such disclosure would be a serious breach of security.

An example of a questionnaire survey instrument designed by Alan M. Keller at SRI International is presented in Appendix I. It was used successfully in a large bank. The contents explain its purpose.

A Practical Risk Assessment

A combination of some of the methods described in this chapter leads to a practical risk assessment. The results of each step are depicted as columns in Figure 11-3. Each step will be described, starting with the unordered list of vulnerabilities and ending with a list ordered from greatest risk to least risk. The final list contains the detail, where necessary, to form the basis for safeguard selection and justification.

A vulnerability consists of three items:

1. an asset subject to loss, e.g., an employee, a computer terminal, a data file, a program;

2. a potential threat to that asset that could result in modification, destruction, disclosure, disappearance, use, or denial of use; and

3. the state of security in terms of lack of or weak safeguards that would allow the threat to cause a loss to the asset owner or custodian.

The vulnerabilities are shown listed in Figure 11-3 in no particular order except possibly by type of asset or type of threat. The subscript numbers indicate that several vulnerabilities may have the same asset or the same threat, but the state of security is unique and complete for each asset and threat pair.

The next step after identifying and listing the vulnerabilities is to test the reasonableness and believability of the vulnerabilities using scenarios. Some of the vulnerabilities may be discarded, changed, combined, or expanded into several in the process of creating scenarios and reviewing them with the line managers responsible for the areas or functions in which the vulnerabilities are found.

The remaining vulnerabilities are ranked in the empirical ordering step shown in Figure 11-3. This is a subjective or empirical process of obtaining a consensus of the participants in the assessment. The vulnerabilities may be ranked individually or in variously sized groups from greatest risk to least risk. Aids such as questionnaires, simple token distribution among selections, fuzzy set scale, Delphi or discussion methods can be used. Disagreements over ordering can be left for resolution in further steps.

It is not advisable to go further in assessment at this point until additional information is obtained and used, since all previously collected information has been exhausted. The next two steps obtain the information needed to resolve disagreements over ranking vulnerabilities and to provide the necessary additional supporting arguments, beyond scenarios and opinions, to convince management of the validity of the vulnerabilities and their ranking. First, safeguards should be identified that would reduce the risks of

RISK ANALYSIS OF VULNERABILITIES

Vulnerabilities	Scenarios	Empirical Ordering	Possible Safeguards	Quantitative Analysis	Final Ordering
$(A_1T_1S_{11})$	SC_1	Greatest Risk $\{$ (ATS)$_1$	PS_{11}, PS_{12}		(ATS)$_1$
$(A_1T_2S_{12})$		(ATS)$_2$	PS_{21}		(ATS)$_2$
$(A_2T_2S_{22})$	SC_2	(ATS)$_3$	$PS_{31}, PS_{32}, PS_{33}$	E_3	(ATS Ei)i
$(A_3T_3S_{33})$	SC_3	•		$E_3 < Ei$	•
$(A_3T_4S_{34})$		•			•
$(A_3T_1S_{31})$	SC_4	Great Risk $\{$ (ATS)i	PSi1	Ei	(ATS E_3)$_3$
$(A_4T_5S_{45})$	SC_5	(ATS)i+1	•		(ATS)i+1
•	•	•	•		•
•	•	•	•		•
•		•			•
		Least Risk $\{$ (ATS)j	PSj	Ej (PSj cost is high)	(ATS Ej)j

A Assets T Potential threats S State of security SC Scenarios
PS Possible safeguards E Expected loss

FIGURE 11-3

vulnerabilities. This is also a subjective process requiring not quite the rigor of previous steps, because actual safeguard selection is performed after risk assessment (see Chapter 12). The safeguards are identified here only as an aid in determining the extent of quantitative analyses needed in the next step and incidentally as input to safeguard selection. The scenarios are again helpful here to test the effects of possible safeguards on vulnerabilities.

Incidentally, safeguard implementation can even start here for those situations where general agreement requires no further justification or approval. In fact, if there is sufficient confidence in results at this point, further analysis need not be done and the review can be terminated.

The next step is to perform quantitative analysis using the numerical methods described previously in this chapter. Quantitative, numerical risk analysis need be performed for only those few remaining vulnerabilities where there is a risk ranking question and for vulnerabilities where the likely applicable safeguards may be difficult to justify because of cost, lack of effectiveness, or impact on people constrained by them. In the first case the expected annual loss, described in this chapter, would be calculated for vulnerabilities with questioned ranking, and they would be reranked according to size of expected loss. The loss value and data used in its derivation are appended to the vulnerability data in the final ordering (see Figure 11-3).

In the second case the possible safeguards for some vulnerabilities may require more support to justify later recommended actions. For example, a vulnerability may be denial of use of computer services caused by a power failure against which there is inadequate safeguarding or backup. One safeguard against loss is an uninterruptable power supply system that would cost $800,000. Considerable information should be provided to support the safeguard selected to reduce this vulnerability, especially if it is far down in the risk list.

The final ordering and reporting of all supporting information is the last step as indicated in Figure 11-3. This information will be useful for the selection of safeguards and recommendation to management that are the subjects of the next chapter. It can be seen from this combination of security review methods that the practical application of numerical risk assessment lies in its selective application only where justified after all qualitative steps have been taken.

Chapter 12

Safeguards
Identification,
Selection, and
Implementation

Safeguards Identification

Deficiencies in security must be studied and safeguards and security practices to combat them must be identified. Many solutions will be obvious. New ideas can be obtained by referring to the many safeguard checklists available in books and reports on computer security.

Although checklists are not provided in this book—because they are widely available elsewhere—they are a valuable source of new ideas. At the same time, as stated earlier, to rely excessively on checklists and to conclude therefrom that enough security has been applied is dangerous and leads to the Maginot line syndrome. Therefore, the approach taken in this book is to arm the security specialist with a set of principles for selection and implementation of safeguards.

Each safeguard or practice can be inserted in scenarios that demonstrate any deficiencies in its applicability. Usually several solutions are possible. For example, a scenario may show a lack of access control into a sensitive area. Solutions might include any of the following:

- Desensitize the area by removing the asset or function.
- Redesign the locations of entrances and exits.
- Prevent unauthorized persons from reaching entrances (this replaces the deficiency with another in another area).
- Install "authorized admittance only" signs.
- Install locking doors and limit distribution of keys.
- Instruct workers in the area to challenge unauthorized interlopers.
- Install intrusion alarms.
- Install CCTV and remote control locks.
- Post guards at entrances.
- Require wearing of authorized access badges.
- Install mantrap double doors or turnstile with electronic locks.

Scenarios may show the inapplicability of some alternatives. New scenarios illustrating unaccounted-for conditions or results may eliminate others. Discussions with affected managers and workers, personnel management, health and safety experts and security product vendors may further eliminate choices. The remaining possibilities should be documented and indexed to vulnerabilities and possibly to applicable scenarios if they are used. Every acceptable and rejected alternative can be effectively supported with scenarios. The same should be done for all existing and planned safeguards and practices identified.

Safeguards Selection Principles

For various reasons, some safeguards work and others do not. Safeguards are often implemented on an incremental basis, one at a time. A formal basis for the selection and implementation of each safeguard aids in assuring cost-effective, practical computer security. In computer security research, the design of computer operating systems has required the development of principles of communication and relationship among the computer operating system program modules. From this research have come several principles that must be obeyed if a computer operating system is to be secure. It was discovered that these principles had general application to many aspects of computer security, including physical, operational, procedural and computer system security.

These principles have been expanded and formalized here for use by the computer security specialist and auditor. The twenty principles presented here should not be considered complete, however, since new principles are still being discovered. We can say that a safeguard that adheres to these applicable principles will probably be more successful than other safeguards. Some of the principles are mutually exclusive. Total adherence to one principle could possibly violate or partially violate another principle. Here again, the experience and good judgment of the computer security specialist and EDP auditor must come into play.

Cost-Effectiveness.   Safeguards may involve a wide range of costs—from no cost to prohibitive cost. Some even result in cost savings. A risk analysis will determine the potential loss without the safeguards. Since there is no rule of thumb or standard by which to determine how much should be spent for a safeguard given a specific cost risk, the prudent person method could be followed. The prudent person criterion is that even if a loss is sustained, a panel of recognized computer security specialists would agree that sufficient safeguards were in place to protect against the loss. Therefore, the custodian of the assets and those held accountable for the assets should be held blameless. This rule is not particularly satisfying or practical but is symptomatic of the state of the art.

The total cost of a safeguard must be identified, and must include the costs of selection, acquisition of the materials and mechanisms, construction and placement, environment modification, any reduced productivity or performance of work constrained by the safeguard, nontrivial operating cost, maintenance, testing, repair, and replacement. Some of these, such as costs for materials and mechanisms, will be easy to evaluate. Others, such as degradation of performance, may be difficult. For example, the cost of installing floor pullers to lift raised floor panels for emergency use near fire extinguishers can be readily determined, whereas the annual replacement cost will depend on the frequency of "borrowing" and disappearance of the devices, a common occurrence in computer centers.

Many safeguards reduce costs through increased performance and productivity and through reduced rates of error. For example, access control can reduce employee idleness that arises when employees wander into other areas to carry on personal conversations. Check digits can be used to correct input data before entry into the system, after which correction becomes expensive. Indirect cost savings such as reduced insurance premiums should also be accounted for in the overall cost of safeguards. The total cost of a safeguard will normally be a net cost and can sometimes be a negative value, which would indicate a savings.

Minimum Reliance on Real-time Human Intervention.   A safeguard that requires no human operation or intervention during its operation is usually superior to a safeguard with equivalent protective capabilities that requires human involvement. For example, if access to a sensitive work area can be controlled through a simple logical algorithmic process and few or no exceptions are necessary, then an automatic door access mechanism could be superior to stationing a guard at the door. Manual functions are generally the weakest in a safeguard. The human element must be considered not only during the routine functioning of the safeguard but also when safeguards are violated or attacked and need servicing.

Override and Failsafe Defaults. Safeguards that automatically react when attacked or violated usually require some automatic or human override capabilities. Automatic override in case of safeguard failure is usually associated with being failsafe. Every such safeguard must have a shut-down capability. No safeguard should have self-protective capabilities to the extent that some form of human override could not cost-effectively and safely shut it down. No safeguard should endanger human life unless human life is at stake in the violation or attack of a safeguard or of the assets it is protecting.

This principle also includes the concept of failsafe defaults. A default action of a safeguard should result in lack of permission rather than loss of constraints. For example, loss of electrical power should prohibit access through a locked door activated by a card key rather than allow the door to become unlocked. The locked door could also present a dilemma relative to safety. If power fails, it may be indicative of an emergency state in the controlled access area, and the locked door, while allowing exit, would prevent access of people such as firemen who could provide needed assistance. Human access controls and protection from natural disasters most commonly involve this issue. Access controls imply constraints on the movement of people. Since human events and activities are unpredictable, failsafe characteristics of safeguards involving the constraint of people are essential.

For example, elevators are devices that constrain the movement of people. In the event of emergency such as a power failure, however, manual escape from elevators can be achieved. In one instance, programming offices were located on the twelfth floor of a building having public access. The elevator lobby had only two means of exit, the elevator and a locked door actuated by a magnetic card. The elevator lobby contained no communications equipment, and there was no CCTV monitoring of the lobby. The door was glass, and a receptionist normally sat inside the controlled area and thus could observe the lobby and handle any unusual situations. However, the receptionist was away part of the time and her station was not manned. Therefore, it was possible for a person to take the elevator to the twelfth floor, leave the elevator, and become imprisoned for a significant period of time before his condition was discovered. Even if automatic devices for allowing communication or observation had been used, a power failure could still create a serious predicament. There were also no signs in the elevator lobby to indicate what should be done under the various possible circumstances. An override for all possible contingencies should have been provided.

Absence of Design Secrecy. A basic rule in cryptography is to assume that the code breakers will know as much about the cryptographic methods as do the designers. This assures that the protection of encoded data is not based on the secrecy of the encoding method but on the secrecy of each key that is used and on code-breaking complexity. This principle might also be applied to the design of door locks where it is assumed that a breaker will have purchased the same kind of lock and will have thoroughly studied it before his attack. It is common for safe crackers to pose as legitimate purchasers of safes and to spend significant amounts of money purchasing copies of the safes they intend to attack. This principle of not relying on the secrecy of the mechanism of a safeguard but on the complexity and effort to break it should be applied to any safeguard in computer security as well. For example, in the selection of a remote storage area for backup and recovery of data files and computer programs, it should be assumed that an attacker intent on destroying the capability of the data center will know the location of the backup facilities. Safety lies in the invulnerability of the backup facilities to attack.

Application of this principle encourages the changeability of safeguards. For example, the existence of floor limits to determine the cutoff values of financial transactions above which 100 percent audit is performed can be readily established by perpetrators of fraud or embezzlement. However, if the floor limit can be easily changed and the current floor limit made difficult to determine, this safeguard can become more effective. Although the perpetrator may know of the existence of the floor limit and may know how it is used, he will not know the current value. In automated, real-time systems in which the auditing of transactions is also automated, floor limits can be changed frequently. Applications of this principle and the changeability concept can be easily accomplished in various types of door access controls, computer and terminal operations procedures, automatic identification, and computer systems security in intercommunication of programs. Safety lies with the keys or parameters and not necessarily with the secrecy of the method or mechanism of a safeguard (Baran 1964).

Least Privilege (Need to Know). The principle of least privilege or need to know has been commonly employed in national security for many years. It is the concept of providing only the least amount of information to a person or a mechanism for that person or mechanism to carry out necessary functions effectively. When a computer program calls a subroutine to perform a function, frequently data must also be passed to that subroutine.

This procedure commonly involves passing the address of the needed data. The needed data are often embedded in and among other sensitive data. Therefore, the subroutine has access not only to the required data but also to much other sensitive data that are not required. The calling program thus becomes vulnerable because the subprogram must now also be entrusted to the same degree as the calling program. The obvious solution is to impose least privilege and supply the subroutine with only the data that it needs to perform its function but not to provide access to any other data.

Although this principle might be thought to conflict with the principle of absence of design secrecy, that is not the case. The methods and mechanisms of safeguards should be kept as confidential as possible. Their effectiveness, however, should not depend on that confidentiality.

This brings up a common problem in security. Should the presence of safeguards be visible? On one hand, the visibility of safeguards can be an important deterrent. On the other hand, this visibility provides the attacker with vital information concerning the existence and whereabouts of the safeguards. The policy usually recommended is to make safeguards highly visible, and at the same time to maintain the confidentiality of the methods and mechanisms of the safeguards. The presence of many safeguards can be made known without revealing their physical location. On the other hand, if the physical location could be relatively easily determined by the attacker anyway, then there is value in clearly identifying the location or making the location of the safeguard highly visible.

Entrapment. The strategy of entrapment was first put forth in computer science literature. If an organization has limited resources for making a multi-access large-scale computer system secure, and there are more vulnerabilities in the system than can be treated with the limited resources available, the strategy is to make one or a few of the vulnerabilities attractive to the potential violator. These particular vulnerabilities are then heavily instrumented to detect any attempts at compromise on a timely basis. Thus when the perpetrator attempts the attack, he will most likely choose one of these weaknesses and will be detected and stopped.

This strategy has several drawbacks. First, it assumes a rational perpetrator. It assumes that the perpetrator has thoroughly studied a number of possible vulnerabilities through which he might attack. At least one of the vulnerabilities must be chosen for the purpose of entrapment. It must also be assumed that the perpetrator has the same sense of values, the expected skills, knowledge, and access assumed by the security designers. There is no assurance that this is the case.

The second problem is the possible unfairness of enticing an individual to engage in an unauthorized act. If the individual already has the intent and is merely looking for the vulnerability that best matches his needs and skills, then it may be a reasonable strategy. If, however, the individual gains his intent through discovery of attractive vulnerabilities, then this could be termed an irresponsible security strategy. It should be a principle of sound management never to assign an individual a position of trust that exceeds his resistance to temptation. Ideally a manager should know the personality and values of his employees well enough to make such reasonable trust assignments. Intentional efforts at entrapment, if not altogether illegal, would certainly expose management to the possibility of civil suits. Therefore, any potential safeguard should be evaluated in relation to its entrapment possibilities, and any overt entrapment characteristics present should be reason to doubt the desirability of such a safeguard.

Independence of Control and Subject. People who are controlled or constrained by safeguards are called the subjects. The people who make safeguards work effectively are the controllers; the auditors of safeguards independently determine the effectiveness and appropriateness of safeguards for management. This principle concerns the controllers and the subjects. It states that the controllers and subjects should be independent and should come from different populations. Violation of this principle would mean that a person who is meant to be constrained by a safeguard would also be responsible for assuring its effectiveness and making it work. This violation often results in rapid deterioration of safeguards.

Many safeguards impose constraints that are at odds with the job performances of people. The natural tendency of workers is to avoid constraints that interfere with their performance or that make excessive work for them. For example, logging of tapes in and out of a tape library when performed by a tape librarian whose work function and performance are measured by his accuracy of maintaining magnetic tape usage records, will far exceed the performance of computer operators who must log tapes in and out themselves. The logging function is not the primary responsibility and performance measurement of their work. In another example, the requirement of standard protocols for programs calling subprograms is difficult to enforce among programmers if done on a voluntary basis and done without consistent monitoring. It is even worse when the protocol standard adds complexity or extra effort to the programmer's job. If, however, the compiler will not accept a program unless correct protocols are used, then control of the safeguard has been made independent from the people it constrains and it has a greater chance for success.

The concept of maker, checker, signer in banking is another illustration of the principle. One person performs a task requiring a position of trust, a second person checks the performance of the task to determine its correctness, and a third person has the supervisory responsibility of the correct performance and correct checking of the task. Where risk is high, some banks employ the Chinese army technique of employing many people in the same functions.

The separation of responsibilities of control over safeguards can sometimes be impractical, especially in small organizations. Multiple control is an alternative to and sometimes an advantage over total independence. Multiple control calls for a different action by each of two or more people to effect safeguard control. For example, access to a safe-deposit box in a bank vault requires two keys, each in the possession of a different person. The same concept might apply to cryptographic key administration, whereby two halves of a key would each be in the custody of a different person. Dual control is another but sometimes weaker alternative. Each of two or more people have the same safeguard control in contrast to the maker, checker, signer example above.

Universal Application. Exceptions to rules and procedures have probably caused the failure of more safeguards than any other problem. When a safeguard is imposed, it should be imposed uniformly and as completely as possible over the entire domain of the safeguard. The primary values of this principle are simplicity and good order. For example, if a badging system is used for physical access controls to sensitive areas, then it should apply universally to all people entering the area. No one should be allowed in the area without an authorized badge. A mixture of people wearing badges and people not wearing badges soon causes the system to deteriorate, and the value of the safeguard to become lost. In another example, the design of a particular computer system has been judged by many computer security researchers to be secure. However, exceptions to the design taken during implementation for the sake of performance and reduction of development costs, and introduction of errors and lack of human alertness to identify exceptions, have resulted in security vulnerabilities in the delivered products, primarily because they deviate from the design specifications. Compromises of this principle are difficult to avoid in practice. When they are necessary, the exceptions allowed by safeguards should be clearly identified and kept to a minimum.

Compartmentalization and Defensive Depth. This principle has to do with a configuration of a particular safeguard relative to its environment and to other safeguards. Loss experience indicates that perpetrators rarely perform a single act or violate a single safeguard in the attainment of their goals. Often, independent sequences of dependent sequential acts are performed. Therefore, it must be assumed that an attack on a specific safeguard occurs at the beginning of an incident, within the sequence or at the end of a series of acts. Therefore, a safeguard must be evaluated in relation to safeguards that in some sense neighbor it or are in the same environment relative to the protection of the same asset. Since the purpose of security is to defend an asset from loss, the safeguard must be considered in relation to its role in a wide range of possible activities.

Compartmentalization derives from ship design, which specifies built compartments in the hull so that a breach would be localized, would cause minimum damage, and would not spread to other parts of the ship. For example, dampers and exhaust fans are normally placed in various ducts within a building to limit the spread of harmful gases and smoke in case of fire or other types of physical attacks.

Defensive depth is the concept of planning adequate numbers of safeguards that could be serially encountered by a perpetrator working toward a specific target. For example, physical access to the most sensitive computer areas, such as the magnetic tape library or input-output handling area, should require passing through the largest number of access control points in the building housing the data processing function. The violation of one control point should immediately call for alerting and reinforcing all adjacent control points connected to the breached control point. Taking into account this principle can sometimes result in replacing an elaborate, costly safeguard that causes significant restraints and performance degradation by several serially placed safeguards of more simple and less costly nature.

Isolation, Economy, and Least Common Mechanism. While safeguards should be considered in combination with other safeguards, they must also be isolated from other safeguards with as little dependence upon common mechanisms as possible. A computer program that performs a sensitive security function in a computer should be as self-contained and as isolated from other system programs as possible. The number of common subprograms that it shares with other programs should be minimized. As another example, the tape log maintained by a magnetic tape librarian of tape usage during first shift should be isolated from the independent tape logging activities during any other shifts.

The design of a safeguard should also be as simple as possible. The primary reasons for cost reduction and reliability are obvious. In addition, freedom from design and implementation errors and ease of testing and audit are of great importance (Saltzer and Schroeder 1975).

Completeness and Consistency. A safeguard must be completely functional and should meet its specifications before installation and usage. This requires a complete, consistent set of specifications and operating instructions. A safeguard design should be based on why the safeguard should allow actions as well as why it should not allow actions. The specifications should be both "positive" and "negative." That is, they should state exactly what the safeguard is to do (positive) and should also include limitations specifying what the safeguard is not supposed to do (negative), thereby delimiting its application. For example, an underfloor CO_2 fire supression system should be specified relative to the space it is to fill and also the space that gas should not enter.

In one computer installation, a CO_2 underfloor system had been installed but never tested. One day it went off accidentally, and the CO_2, which is heavier than air, seeped down through conduit openings in the base floor and nearly asphyxiated workers on the floor beneath the computer center. In another case, elaborate mantraps were installed at personnel entrances to a newly completed computer center. Although the rate of passage of personnel through the trap was judged to be adequate for normal working activities, the large numbers of people passing through at shift changing times were not anticipated. Three times each day a long line of people waited outside of the building on a busy street as they attempted one at a time to pass through the mantrap to enter the building. This problem was solved by opening the doors and terminating the function of the mantrap during shift change so that large numbers of people could pass through quickly. The problem in this case was that the building access specifications were incomplete, and correction of the problem required inconsistent application of the safeguard.

Instrumentation. No safeguard is complete without instrumentation to monitor on a timely basis its proper functioning, failures, and attacks upon it. A researcher designing secure computer operating systems recently indicated that his interest was in designing safeguards that absolutely prevented compromise. If a safeguard works in a proven, absolute fashion to prevent compromise, then there is no need for instrumentation. This lack of instrumentation is not consistent with the general needs of a computer security program. EDP management must be notified when any safeguard has been attacked, even if there is great confidence that it cannot be violated. Information about attempted attacks is vital in threat analysis, which must be periodically carried out for good security. There is always the possibility of unanticipated events that could neutralize a safeguard. One of the most dangerous conditions in computer security is to have a safeguard that is assumed to be functioning affectively when it is not.

Instrumentation is also valuable in alerting those accountable for the safeguard to its presence as well as to its correct functioning and attacks upon it. The visible output of instrumentation must be in a practical, usable form. If instrumentation output is in printed form, it should not be so voluminous that a person responsible for monitoring it becomes easily fatigued and distracted. If instrumentation produces voluminous data, then the data reduction capabilities of the computer should be used to provide only summary data for human observation. The computer can be used to dump selected detailed data when necessary for further study. A clerk who is handed a three-inch thick printer output report each morning and is told to discover any unusual activities represented in the data in many instances is undertaking a useless and ineffective practice. That is what computers are for—to analyze data. The production of short summary reports can then be effectively reviewed by higher level management.

Acceptance and Tolerance by Personnel.   Safeguards are only as effective as the people who are constrained by them and as the people in control allow them to be. Each new safeguard must be accepted by the people who will be affected by it. A safeguard that is represented as an amusing challenge to those affected by it is a lost cause. People must be convinced that a safeguard is for their own best interest. One advantage of automatic safeguards that function with little real-time intervention is that fewer people must be convinced and motivated to tolerate and accept it.

Management-imposed constraints on a programming staff—for example, a policy to avoid the use of specified programming language features—is not as effective as imposing such constraints through the compiler system of the computer. In their work programmers are accustomed to be constrained by the computer system and tend to accept such constraints more readily, as long as the constraint does not represent a challenge for them to beat. With today's commercial computer systems, there is no safeguard built into a system that ingenious and dedicated programmers who have access to the computer cannot beat without detection. Therefore, universal acceptance by the programming staff and tolerance for the constraints imposed must be achieved before the safeguard's effectiveness can be assured.

An important aid to the acceptance and tolerance of safeguards is the willingness of management personnel to likewise accept and tolerate and be restrained by the same safeguards. Management thus sets a good example and strong incentive for employees to follow suit. At the same time, safeguards should not constrain activities of people beyond a reasonable and accepted tolerance. For example, access control in sensitive work areas requiring employees to challenge the presence of people not authorized to be in the areas usually will fail. Most employees will not challenge others unless highly motivated.

Sustainability.   A safeguard must not only work fully on the day it is installed or adopted, but it must also be working one, two, or three years later at the same level of effectiveness as on the first day. The more automatic a safeguard can be made, the more likely it is to function effectively over time. Safeguards heavily dependent on human activity will always be subject to the possibility of declining performance over time. The most common problem found in security audits is that safeguards specified in policies, procedures, and operating manuals in practice have become almost nonexistent. The effectiveness of safeguards dependent upon significant human performances requires continuing sensitizing and motivational efforts to remain effective.

Auditability. Every safeguard must be testable for the purpose of auditing its performance and compliance with specifications. One of the first events that should occur after implementation of the safeguard is its testing to assure those who will audit it on a continuing basis that it is auditable and that test criteria exist for it. Testing methods and criteria should be part of the design and should appear in the specifications of each safeguard; furthermore, the cost of testing must be included in cost considerations for the safeguard. A CO_2 fire extinguishing system is relatively inexpensive to test, whereas Halon systems can cost several thousand dollars for a single test. It is important that auditors be included in the design and implementation activities for safeguards to assure their auditability. Testing will also help to reveal any unanticipated secondary effects of a safeguard or any weaknesses in it.

In one case, auditors entered a data processing facility and asked to be shown a recovery from remotely stored backup files. The EDP organization prepared to send a vehicle to the remote site to obtain the backup files, programs, and operating instructions. At this point the test was terminated because it was discovered that if all the backup materials were returned to the computing center, there would be no backup capability during the period of the test. This discovery led to the revision of backup procedures, which included the remote storage of two copies of all materials so that when one set is returned to the computing center, a second set will be remotely stored for backup. This kind of experience can be minimized by developing and using scenarios or modeling in the design and specifications of safeguards.

Accountability. There must always be at least one person held accountable for each safeguard. Most often this is the person who is chiefly responsible for the operation of the safeguard and his immediate supervisor. An individual should not be responsible for so many different safeguards that the least privilege and sustainability principles are violated. The individual's job performance must be directly associated with his safeguard accountability performance. The accountability often extends to the assets being protected by the safeguards. The person who has accountability over assets and associated safeguards will have a wider range of responsibilities to achieve consistency in the protection of the assets.

Reaction and Recovery (Gaines 1978). Safeguards should be evaluated according to how they react when activated. They may destroy the asset being protected as well as deny it to the attacker or convey secret information to the attacker. Safeguards may cause a hostile environment that makes recovery difficult or that delays recovery. The triggering of a safeguard may be so violent as to cause panic or terror. For example, dumping Halon into a room as a fire suppressant can be an explosive and nerve-racking experience, and even though the gas might be harmless, it can frighten people. In one case, a fire in a room adjacent to the computer room caused detection devices to be activated and armed the Halon equipment to release in 30 seconds. The computer operators repeatedly overrode the release because they were terrified by the Halon system. It had released accidentally on a previous occasion with unpleasant results, and they did not want it to happen again.

Finally, the timeliness and appropriateness of response should be considered. A safeguard reaction should not reveal information that could be used for further or different attack on a computer system. For example, access to one computer from a terminal requires input of an authorized name and a password. If the name is valid, the password is tested. If the name is not valid, the password is not tested, and the terminal is immediately disconnected. A terminal user can thus tell whether a name is valid whether or not that password is valid, because of the difference in reaction times.

A safeguard should stop a loss or allow capture of a suspect without excessive reaction or negative consequences. An alarm may warn an attacker and allow him to escape. On the other hand, the purpose of a safeguard may be to frighten away a potential intruder. An alarm should not be so violent or pervasive as to cause overreaction and new danger of a different kind of loss.

Residuals and Reset (Holling and Bisbey 1976). Attention must be given to residual conditions and data conditions after a safeguard has been activated; also, attention should be given to the circumstances and needs for resetting or reactivating the safeguard. After a safeguard has performed its function, the assets being protected should remain at least as secure as before. In fact, if a safeguard functions in response to an intrusion, the assets may be in greater danger and additional protection may be called for. Resetting a safeguard that expends itself may take significant time, and assets must be protected by alternate means in the interim. For example, when materials are returned to a computer center from a remote backup facility to restore operations, copies of the material should be preserved in a safe place while recovery proceeds.

Scavenging for residual data can be an effective method for purposes of espionage or theft. Well-designed computer programs erase residual data such as may be left in temporary storage locations (erasure of magnetic tapes usually must be done manually). However, when a safeguard such as a detector causes an abnormal termination of program execution when the value of a variable is exceeded, normal erasure of residual data may not take place. Physical scavenging that can result in collection of discarded, partly finished output reports when a control has caused abnormal halting of a production run is another weakness.

Therefore, safeguards should be evaluated on the basis of postactivation characteristics and circumstances. Use of a safeguard may require extensive additional procedures. If they are not performed, the presence of the safeguard may result in greater vulnerability than was present before its installation.

Manufacturer, Supplier, and Servicer Trustworthiness. If a safeguard is to be trusted, its reliability, integrity, sustainability, and adherence to specifications must be proven. If it is not possible or practical to do all these things, then the manufacturer, supplier, and maintenance service must be trusted. The most impressive example is a cryptographic system. Current products such as the various commercial devices that use the federally approved Data Encryption Standard (DES) are the most popular. IBM developed the basic algorithm that was tested and adopted by the National Bureau of Standards with the assistance of the National Security Agency. None of these three organizations will reveal the methods and results of their tests and state only that the algorithm used with a 56 bit key is adequate for all nonmilitary purposes. Users must trust the three organizations because they themselves cannot sufficiently test the algorithm. Users must trust the manufacturers of the devices because their contents are too complex and protected by tamper-resistant features anyway. The suppliers must also be trusted to deliver the devices in the same state of integrity and the maintenance service trusted to preserve the same level of integrity. Whether the three businesses are independent or form one organization, many unknown people must be trusted.

The best that can be done to determine the trustworthiness of these organizations and their employees is far less than satisfying. The length of time in business with a good reputation is not as important as how long the same management has been in charge, whether recent adversities have occurred, and whether there is a record of good earnings. These factors are still not as important as the individual people employed to provide the products and services. The best strategy is being informed and using all the good business practices that fill many books.

Multiple Functions. A safeguard is almost always selected to serve one security function: deterrence (a code of ethics), prevention (guard at a door), detection (exception reporting), or recovery (remote backup storage). Selection of a safeguard for a particular risk reduction should be based on its primary functional value. However, two safeguards with equal qualities may prove to have unequal qualities when secondary functional qualities are evaluated. For example, most safeguards have some degree of deterrence value. A uniformed guard at a door may have more deterrent value than an electronic lock door actuated by a card key. On the other hand, a well-instrumented electronic lock door may have greater detection value.

A straightforward qualitative method of multiple function evaluation can be developed in the following way. Identify the nature of the potential threats, the risk to be reduced and the principal function of a safeguard. Design a form similar to the one appearing in Figure 12-1. Distribute copies of the form to people most directly involved and affected by the safeguard: computer security specialists, custodians of the assets requiring protection, a sample of responsible people constrained or affected by the safeguards, operators or maintainers of the safeguards, and auditors of the safeguard.

The form requires distribution of 100 tokens among the alternative safeguards for each function. The data can be weighted for each column to emphasize the desired purpose of choosing a safeguard. By adding the rows of weighted numbers, a consensus of the relative values of the safeguards can be derived by principal function and secondary value functions. Safeguards with close total scores can be selected by considering individual scores.

These principles are presented in the chart depicted in Figure 12-2, which can be used as a guide or a checkoff list to assure that all principles are adequately considered in any proposed safeguard. An even more effective method is to identify each principle in the safeguard specifications and state how the safeguard embodies each principle.

Audit Tools and Techniques

EDP auditing is an important activity for computer security. The tools and techniques for auditing must be considered among the safeguards employed. Audit tools and techniques can also be beneficial to the security specialist.

FUNCTIONAL SAFEGUARD EVALUATION

Risk.   Valuable information is manually processed in the computer input/output peripherals operations room. No accounting for materials is done internal to the room. All accounting for input and output is done in the job setup and output distribution rooms and in the computer system. The potential is high that an individual would attempt to enter the room to modify, examine, replace, or stop data, equipment, or reports for expediency or convenience to avoid standard procedures for doing so or for malicious reasons.

Potential threat.   The sources of unauthorized access are those people having access to the area outside of the peripherals room door and having reasons to enter the room: programmers whose data, programs, and reports are being processed, data entry clerks, receivers of output reports, managers and their visitors, off-duty peripheral operators, vendors' personnel. These people are mainly technologists who would more often be attracted to technical challenges than to social or person-to-person challenges.

Instructions.   Distribute 100 tokens in each function column among the safeguard alternatives, applying more points to safeguards having more functional value.

NOTE: The functions have the following meanings:

Deterrence: Discourage from unauthorized entry because of dangerous, difficult or unpleasant circumstances.

Prevention: Keep from unauthorized entry except by extreme methods that would attract notice and cause other safeguard actions.

Detection: Notice of attempted or successful unauthorized entry in a timely manner that would most likely result in inconsequential loss.

Recovery: Aids, conditions, and information that facilitate restoration and replacement of loss.

FIGURE 12-1

	Functions.			
	Deterrence	Prevention	Detection	Recovery
1. "Authorized entry only" signs				
2. Instructions to workers to challenge unauthorized entry				
3. Mechanical key lock door with electrical release operated by a clerk				
4. Combination button locked door				
5. CCTV-monitored, combination button locked door				
6. Guard (with other duties, 3 shifts) with unlocked door				
7. Guard as above with locked, electric release door				
8. Electronic card key lock door with microcomputer monitoring				
9. Turnstile with electronic card key locked door with microcomputer monitoring				
10. Double locked door mantrap with CCTV or direct guard monitoring				

FIGURE 12-1 (Continued)

FIGURE 12-2 Safeguard Principles Compliance

Compliance

Principle	Least Adequate			Most Adequate		Approved
	1	2	3	4	5	
1. Is the cost appropriate for the risk?						
2. Is the reliance on real-time manual activities acceptable?						
3. Is it failsafe and is manual override adequate?						
4. Is effectiveness independent of mechanism secrecy?						
5. Is least privilege involved?						
6. Are any entrapment features fair?						
7. Are control and constrained roles sufficiently independent?						
8. Are exception conditions minimized?						
9. Are backup capabilities adequate in case of failure?						
10. Can it be sufficiently isolated from dependence on other vulnerable functions or conditions?						
11. Are specifications and implementation complete and consistent?						
12. Is there adequate and practical instrumentation and monitoring capability?						
13. Will affected personnel accept and tolerate it?						
14. Can its effectiveness be sustained over sufficient periods of time?						
15. Is it auditable?						
16. Has sufficient accountability been assigned?						
17. Is there sufficient reaction and recovery?						
18. What are the residuals and reset capability?						
19. What is the trustworthiness of the supplies?						

The currently used tools and techniques have been thoroughly documented in a worldwide state-of-the art study conducted by SRI International for the Institute of Internal Auditors and funded by the IBM Corporation. This study's conclusions appeared in a set of three reports, "Systems Auditability and Control," published by the Institute of Internal Auditors (SAC 1977).

Summary descriptions of audit tools and techniques are presented in Appendix G. Effectiveness of these tools and techniques can be measured in one way by the number of occupations of people who could be detected as having caused losses. Occupations as sources of vulnerabilities that may be detected by seventeen EDP audit tools and techniques are presented in Figure 12-3, which depicts EDP audit tools and techniques by occupation applicability. The numbers in the entries indicate the degree of applicability. The tools and techniques related to data integrity apply principally to computer operations staff. Tools and techniques related to computer program integrity apply to software and hardware development and maintenance functions. None apply to security officers and EDP auditors, since they are the users of the tools and techniques.

As seen in Tables 12-1 and 12-2 the number of applicable tools and techniques is greatest for the more technical and professional occupations and least for clerical and technician occupations. The products of the clerical and technical occupations tend to be more directly observable; therefore, more manual detection techniques apply to them.

EDP Controls

Safeguards associated directly with and in a computer system are often called EDP controls. More than 300 of them are identified in detail in the SAC Reports and for this reason are not repeated here, but summaries of them identifying occupations controlled and occupations responsible for their use are presented in Appendix H.

Occupations as sources of vulnerabilities are affected by EDP controls in two ways. An individual in an occupation can be the object of a control which is meant to constrain that individual's activities. Second, an individual in an occupation can be responsible for the operation, implementation, effectiveness, or audit of a control. The occupations and corresponding applicable control types are illustrated in Figure 12-4, which depicts EDP controls by occupation applicability. Each numbered entry in Figure 12-4 indicates how applicable a particular control is to the individual who is the object of that control. There are no corresponding degrees of applicability for individuals in occupations responsible in Figure 12-4 for controls (see Table 12-3). The lists in Tables 12-4 and 12-5 rank occupations and controls by applicability.

EDP Audit Tools and Techniques by Occupation Applicability

Occupations	EDP Audit Tools/Techniques for Detection						
	Test Data Method	Base Case System Evaluation	Integrated Test Facility	Parallel Simulation	Transaction Selection	Embedded Audit Data Collection	Extended Records
Operations							
Transaction Operator					1	2	1
Computer Operator	2	2		1		2	
Peripheral Equipment Operator	2	2		1	1	2	3
Job Set-Up Clerk	2	2				2	
Data Entry & Update Clerk					1	1	1
Communications Operator			3	2	1	1	
Media Librarian							
Software							
System Programmer	1	1	1	1			1
Application Programmer	1	1	1	1			1
Hardware							
Terminal Engineer					1	2	2
System Engineer	3	3	3	1		3	3
Communications Engineer	3	3		1	1	3	3
Facilities Engineer							
Management							
Network Manager	3	3		1	1	3	3
Operations Manager	2	2		1	1	2	3
Data Base Manager					1	1	1
Programming Manager	1	1	1	1			1
Other							
Identification Clerk					1	1	1
Security Officer							
EDP Auditor							

Applicability Codes: 1—Primary
2—Secondary
3—Supportive

FIGURE 12-3

Recommendations

Selection of safeguards and supporting them with scenarios, vulnerabilities ranked by degree of risk and other quantitative data results in the following actions:

1. Existing safeguards

    Accepted   Rejected

    No further actions   Eliminate when appropriate

2. Planned safeguards

    Accepted   Rejected

    Installations encouraged   Stop implementation

Generalized Audit Software	Snapshot	Tracing	Mapping	Control Flow-charting	Job Ac-counting Data Analysis	System Develop-ment Life Cycle	System Ac-ceptance & Control Group	Code Compar-ison	Disaster Testing
3					3				3
3					1			2	1
3					1				1
3					1			1	
3									
3					3				1
3				3	1				1
3	1	1	1	1		1	1	1	
3	1	1	1	1		1	1	1	
3	3	3					3	3	1
3	2	3					1	1	1
3	1	1					1	1	1
									1
3	1	1		2	2				1
3				3	1	1		3	1
3	3			3	3				1
3	1	1	1	1	1	1	1	1	
3					3				1

EDP Audit Tools/Techniques for Detection

FIGURE 12-3 (Continued)

3. New proposed safeguards
   Prioritized list for phased implementation

At this stage various types of useful information have been developed to aid in selecting the order of implementation of recommended safeguards and associated practices. If expected annual losses and frequency of loss events have been calculated, these data may now be used to select the safeguards for implementation. Ranking of assets by sensitivity or ranking of threats can also be used for this purpose in addition to ranking vulnerabilities by degree of risk. However, from a practical point of view the acceptance and enthusiasm of managers in whose functions the safeguards are to be implemented will probably carry the most weight. Therefore, ranking the recommended safeguards by ease of implementation and by least effect or disruption of current practices can be of great value. Top management will

EDP Controls by Occupation Applicability

Occupations	EDP Controls for Detection & Prevention							
	Transaction Origination	Transactions Entry	Data Communication	Computer Processing	Data Storage and Retrieval	Output Processing	Computer Center	Application System Development
Operations								
Transaction Operator	2	1		1		3	1	
Computer Operator		3		1	1	1	1	
Peripheral Equipment Operator		3		1	1	3	1	
Job Set-Up Clerk		1		1	1		1	
Data Entry & Update Clerk	3	2		1	2	2	1	
Communications Operator				2	3	3	1	
Media Librarian			1		1		1	
Software								
System Programmer	R		R	R	R	R	1	3
Application Programmer		R	R	R	R	R		1
Hardware								
Terminal Engineer	1	R	1	2	2	1	1	
System Engineer				R	R	R		
Communications Engineer	3	3	R	1		1	1	
Facilities Engineer							R	
Management								
Network Manager	3	1	R	1	1	1	2	
Operations Manager			3	1	1/R	2	R	
Data Base Manager		1	R	1	R	R	1	
Programming Manager	R		R	R	R	R	1	R
Other								
Identification Clerk	1			1	3	3	1	
Security Officer	R	R	R	R	R	R	R	R
EDP Auditor	R	R	R	R	R	R	R	R

Applicability Codes: 1—Primary
  2—Secondary
  3—Supportive
  R—Responsible for operation or implementation

FIGURE 12-4

TABLE 12-1

Ranking of Occupations by Number of Applicable Tools and Techniques

NUMBER OF APPLICABLE TOOLS AND TECHNIQUES	OCCUPATIONS
14	Applications programmer, programming manager
13	Systems programmer
12	Systems engineer, communications engineer, network manager, operations manager
9	Peripheral operator, terminal engineer
8	Computer operator, communications operator, data base manager
6	Transaction operator, job set-up clerk, identification control clerk
4	Data entry and update clerk
3	Media librarian
1	Facilities engineer
0	Security officer, EDP auditor

TABLE 12-2

Ranking of Tools and Techniques by Number of Occupations Affected

TOOLS AND TECHNIQUES	NUMBER OF OCCUPATIONS AFFECTED
Generalized Audit Software	17
Embedded Audit Data Collection	13
Extended Records	13
Disaster Testing	13
Job Accounting Data Analysis	12
Test Data Method	10
Base Case System Evaluation	10
Parallel Simulation	10
Transaction Selection	10
Code Comparison	9
Snapshot	8
Tracing	7
Control Flowcharting	7
System Acceptance and Control	6
Integrated Test Facility	5
System Development Life Cycle	4
Mapping	3

TABLE 12-3

Responsibility for Controls

NUMBER OF CONTROLS

APPLICABLE	OCCUPATIONS
8	EDP auditor, security officer
7	Programming manager
6	Application programmer
4	Systems programmer
3	Systems engineer
1	Communications engineer, facilities engineer, network manager, operations manager
0	All others

also be interested in this ordering plus a ranking by cost of implementation.

One method of ordering is to place all recommended safeguards in four categories based on cost and urgency, dictated by vulnerabilities ranking by risk as follows:

1. Lowest cost. Greatest urgency.

2. Greatest cost. Greatest urgency.

3. Lowest cost. Lesser urgency.

4. Greatest cost. Lesser urgency.

The implementation of safeguards also requires a plan and organization to carry it out. The safeguards should not be recommended without the means for their implementation. Safeguards and practices should be implemented by those with the greatest expertise and knowledge of the installation environment. This work should be supervised and documented by the appropriate task force members or security specialists. Auditors should monitor this work closely because they will eventually have to inspect and approve the results of the work.

Selling the Recommendations to Management

The recommendations and supporting scenarios should be exposed first to all affected managers at the lower levels before being presented to the managers at the level required for final approval. Avoid surprising anyone.

Don't expect the entire plan to be accepted. It will be easy for management to pick and choose among the recommendations. A great danger at

TABLE 12-4

Ranking of Occupations by
Number of Applicable Controls

Object of Controls

NUMBER OF CONTROLS APPLICABLE	OCCUPATIONS
0	Facilities engineer, security officer, EDP auditor
1	Application programmer, systems engineer, programming manager
2	Systems programmer
3	Media librarian
4	Transaction operator, computer operator, data entry and update clerk, network manager, operations manager
5	Peripheral operator, job setup clerk, terminal engineer, communications engineer, data base manager, identification control clerk
6	Communications operator

this point is that some safeguards may not be accepted, and that there will be inconsistencies in vulnerability reduction. Frequently all safeguards against a particular threat must be accepted for a threat to be effectively reduced. Scenarios play one of their most useful roles in this respect. Recommended safeguards can be associated with scenarios, and presentations to management can be scenario-oriented effectively. Present a threat scenario that has first gained consensus that it is believable. Then present a package of safeguards showing safeguards that must be implemented to reduce the vulnerabilities described in the scenario.

Be prepared to lose on several recommendations. Have an alternative plan ready, or attempt to gain acceptance for later implementation. Recommendations are often more readily accepted soon after a major loss has occurred or a warning has been published in a prestigious publication. These losses are unfortunate, but take advantage of such circumstances.

Implementation and the Ongoing Program

Implementation of recommendations should proceed as resources become available. Implementation will most likely require staff with different talents and positions than those on the task force. Only implement safeguards that will be accepted by management and by those who are constrained yet

TABLE 12-5

Ranking of Controls by
Number of Occupations Affected

CONTROLS	NUMBER OF OCCUPATIONS AFFECTED
Computer Center	13
Computer Processing	12
Output Processing	11
Data Storage and Retrieval	10
Transactions Entry	8
Transactions Origination	6
Data Communication	3
Application System Development	2

are willing to make the safeguards function correctly. Safeguards must be implemented in a sequence that has the effect of reducing vulnerabilities in the order of their severity within each subpopulation of people or forces representing threats. This avoids the Maginot Line syndrome.

Safeguards must be limited to those that can be adequately manned and managed on a continuing basis within anticipated budgets.

Valuable information will be collected and documented in the task force study. An ongoing program that keeps the security review—case file, models and scenarios—up-to-date is essential. As systems change and are upgraded, new studies must be done. They can be done at minimum cost if all security data are up-to-date. These data must be confidentially treated because they could be used with great detriment to the security of the organization.

The Future of Computer Security

The greatest motivation for management to allocate resources for computer security will increasingly be the principle of standard of due care (SDC). This is the principle often applied in negligence suits. It means that prudent protection from loss is based on generally available safeguards accepted and used by others under similar conditions. An executive in a financial institution told me that he did not want to install cryptographic devices in his domestic funds transfer system. However, if the bank across the street installs them, he must follow suit. If he did not install the devices and a loss in any way associated with funds transfer occurred, the risk and consequent damages of a stockholder suit for failure to use standards of due care would be too great.

As various safeguards and security practices become generally accepted under this principle of SDC, the need for risk assessment will be at least partly replaced by justifying security actions based upon what others are doing under similar circumstances. Examples of safeguards already being generally accepted as SDC's are the universal wearing of badges for access control into sensitive areas, cryptographic devices, data file access controls in computer systems, and password use for computer access from terminals. Accepted SDC practices include exclusion of application programmers from computer rooms (system programmers in the future), restricting magnetic tape handling to areas of use and tape libraries, and denial of production computer usage by employees for personal purposes. We will not need a risk assessment to tell us that we need these safeguards and practices.

Computer security reviews will increasingly become or include surveys of other organizations' practices. Risk assessments will also be increasingly used to justify decisions not to install safeguards or security practices used by others. However, advances in computer and communications technology and new forms of losses will continue to provide a security frontier beyond the standards of due care where innovation will rule.

References

1. **Baran, P. 1964.** *Security, secrecy and tamper-free considerations,* RM-3765 PR (Santa Monica, Calif.: Rand Corporation).

2. **Bigelow, R., and Nycum, S. 1976.** *Your Computer and the Law* (Englewood Cliffs, N.J.: Prentice-Hall, Inc.).

3. **Boguslaw, R. 1965.** *The New Utopians* (Englewood Cliffs, N.J.: Prentice-Hall, Inc.).

4. **Courtney, R. H., Jr. 1977.** "Security risk assessment in electronic data processing systems," in *Proceedings NCC* (Arlington, Va.: AFIPS Press), ed. pp. 97–104.

5. **Cressey, D. R. 1971.** *Other People's Money* (Belmont, Calif.: Wadsworth).

6. **Denning, D. E., and Denning, P. J. 1977.** "The limits of data security," in *Abacas* (Arlington, Va.: AFIPS Press), ed. pp. 22–30.

7. **Drucker, P. F. 1969.** *The Age of Continuity* (New York: Harper & Row).

8. **Gaines, S., and Shapiro, N. Z. 1978.** "Some security principles and their application to computer security," *Operating Systems Review,* 12, pp. 19–28.

9. **Gottlieb, C., and Borodin, A. 1973.** *Social Issues in Computing* (New York: Academic Press).

10. **Hoffman, L. J., Michelman, E. H., and Clements, D. 1978.** "SECURATE-security evaluation and analysis using fuzzy metrics," in

Proceedings of the national computer conference (Arlington, Va.: AFIPS Press), pp. 531-40.

11. **Hollingworth, D., and Bisbey, R. L., II 1976.** *Protection from errors in operating systems: Allocation/deallocation residues* (Marina Del Rey, Calif.: Information Sciences Institute, USC).

12. **Hsiao, D. K., Kerr, D. S., and Madnick, S. E. 1979.** *Computer Security*, ACM Monograph Series (New York: Academic Press).

13. **Jacobson, R. 1979.** *RAMP* (New York: International Security Technology).

14. **Krauss, L. I. 1972.** *SAFE* (New York: Amicom, American Management Association).

15. **Lampson, B. W. 1973.** "A note on the confinement problem," in *Communications of the ACM* (New York: Association for Computing Machinery), pp. 613-15.

16. **Martin, J. 1973.** *Security, Accuracy and Privacy in Computer Systems* (Englewood Cliffs, N.J.: Prentice-Hall, Inc.).

17. **National Bureau of Standards 1979.** *Risk Assessment* (Washington, D.C.: U.S. Department of Commerce).

18. **Nielsen, N. R., Ruder, B., Madden, J. D., and Wong, P. J. 1978.** *Computer system integrity, a relative-impact measure of vulnerability* (Menlo Park, Calif.: SRI International).

19. **Parker, D. B. 1976a.** "Computer abuse perpetrators and vulnerabilities of computer systems," in *Proceedings NCC* (Arlington, Va.: AFIPS Press).

20. **Parker, D. B. 1976b.** *Crime by Computer* (New York: Charles Scribner's Sons).

21. **Parker, D. B. 1979.** *Ethical Conflicts in Computer Science and Technology* (Arlington, Va.: AFIPS Press).

22. **Parker, D. B. 1980b.** *What Executives Should Know About Computer Crime,* Law Enforcement Assistance Administration, U.S. Department of Justice (Washington, D.C.: U.S. Government Printing Office).

23. **Parker, D. B., and Dewey, R. 1978a.** *A guide to EDP and EFTS security based on occupations* (Washington, D.C.: Federal Deposit Insurance Corporation), 81 pages.

24. **Parker, D. B., and Madden, J. D. 1978b.** *ADP occupational vulnerabilities* (Menlo Park, Calif.: SRI International).

25. **Parker, D. B., and Nycum, S. 1980a.** *A criminal justice resource manual on computer crime,* Law Enforcement Assistance Administration, U.S. Department of Justice (Washington, D.C.: U.S. Government Printing Office).

26. **Patrick, R. 1974.** *System Review Manual on Security* (Arlington, Va.: AFIPS Press).

27. **Popek, G., and Farber, D. 1978.** "A Model for verification of data security in operating systems," in *ACM Communications* (New York: Association for Computing Machinery), p. 738.

28. **Systems auditability and control (SAC) 1977.** (Altamonte Springs, Fla.: Institute of Internal Auditors).

29. **Saltzer, J. H., and Schroeder, M. D. 1975.** "Protection of information in computer systems," *Compcon Conference Proceedings,* IEEE No. 75CH1050-4.

30. **Whiteside, T. 1978.** *Computer Capers* (New York: Thomas Y. Crowell).

31. **Wong, K. K. 1977.** *Risk Analysis and Control* (Manchester, England: National Computer Centre, and Rochelle, N.Y.: Hayden Book Co.).

Appendices

PRINCIPLES OF BUSINESS CONDUCT

This organization is committed to conducting its affairs at all times in accordance with the law and the highest ethical standards. The reputation which the organization enjoys is based not on a list of detailed rules, but on the example set by management and the character and good judgment of each employee. It is expected that employees at all levels will conduct themselves so that their actions will never embarrass themselves, their families, or the organization. The following principles are stated to furnish general guidance in a variety of situations:

1. Integrity is an essential element of every business transaction; with our employees, with our shareholders, with our suppliers, and with our customers in the accuracy of our advertising, the quality of our products, and the performance of service at the level expected of us.

2. Situations creating a conflict of interest between the organization and an employee or member of an employee's immediate family will not be tolerated. Examples of such conflicts are: (a) significant financial interest in a supplier or competitor; (b) acceptance of entertainment exceeding ordinary social amenities, of money or of gifts from a supplier of merchandise or services to the organization; (c) disclosure of confidential or proprietary information; (d) appropriation or use of organization assets for personal benefit.

3. No employee will knowingly fail to comply with all applicable laws and regulations of federal, state and local governments.

4. As permitted by law the organization will, when appropriate, contribute to candidates and causes which warrant its support. Employees are encouraged to participate in political activities of their choice.

5. Adherence to accounting policies and procedures for the proper recording of all transactions such as sales, price changes, and expenses must be correctly initiated and recorded.

Guidelines cannot possibly cover all circumstances which may arise in the complex affairs of our business. Faced with uncertainty as to appropriate conduct in any situation, each employee should immediately discuss the problem fully and frankly with the supervisor or executive to whom he or she reports.

Appendix B

DATA PROCESSING
ORGANIZATION STANDARDS OF CONDUCT

The data processing organization is entrusted with computer programs, supplies, data, documentation, and facilities that are continuously growing in size and value. We must maintain visible standards of performance, security, and conduct which aid in our efforts to assure the integrity and protection of these assets. Accordingly, the following should be used as a guide in conducting on-the-job activities. The success of this program, however, rests on each member of the data processing organization, maintaining an awareness of the asset value entrusted to her and to him. It must be realized that violation of this trust is grounds for disciplinary action including immediate dismissal.

1. Conduct all activities in such a manner that precludes any form of dishonesty, such as theft, or misappropriation of money, equipment, supplies, documentation, computer programs, or computer time.

2. Avoid any act which compromises one's integrity, such as falsification of records and documents, unauthorized modification of production programs and files, competing in business with the organization, or engaging in any conduct which may affect the company or its reputation. Refuse gratuities from vendors, agencies, or other resources.

3. Avoid any act which may create a dangerous situation, such as carrying a concealed weapon on organization premises, assaulting another individual, or disregard of property, safety, and security standards.

4. Do not use intoxicating liquors, narcotics, or drugs while at work, or report to work while under the influence of same, or in any other way, report in a condition unfit for work.

5. Maintain courteous and professional relations with users, associates, and supervisors. Perform job assignments as requested by supervision or management and do so within conformity to the standards of performance and security. Report any observed violations of conduct or security as soon as possible.

6. Adhere to the no-solicitation rule, and any other employment policy.

7. Protect the confidentiality of sensitive information with regard to competitive position, trade secrets, or assets.

204

8. Exercise sound business practice in the management of company resources, such as personnel, computer usage, outside services, travel, and entertainment.

Should you have a question concerning the above rules and regulations, or if you are ever in doubt about certain conduct being permitted, please contact your supervisor or personnel representative.

FEDERAL COMPUTER CRIME LEGISLATION

As reported out of the Subcommittee on Criminal Justice 11/6/79.

96TH CONGRESS
1ST SESSION

S.240

To amend title 18, United States Code, to make a crime the use, for fraudulent or other illegal purposes, of any computer owned or operated by the United States, certain financial institutions, and entities affecting interstate commerce.

IN THE SENATE OF THE UNITED STATES

January 25 (legislative day, January 15), 1979
Mr. Ribicoff (for himself, Mr. Percy, Mr. Kennedy, Mr. Inouye, Mr. Jackson, Mr. Matsunaga, Mr. Moynihan, Mr. Williams, Mr. Zorinsky, Mr. Domenici, Mr. Stevens, Mr. Chiles, and Mr. Nunn) introduced the following bill; which was read twice and referred to the Committee on the Judiciary.

A Bill

To amend title 18, United States Code, to make a crime the use, for fraudulent or other illegal purposes, of any computer owned or operated by the United States, certain financial institutions, and entities affecting interstate commerce.

Be it enacted by the Senate and House of Representatives of the United States of America in Congress assembled, That this Act may be cited as the "Federal Computer Systems Protection Act of 1979".

Sec. 2. The congress finds that—

   (1) computer-related crime is a growing problem in the Government and in the private sector;

   (2) such crime occurs at great cost to the public since losses for each incident of computer crime tend to be far greater than the losses associated with each incident of other white collar crime;

   (3) the opportunities for computer-related crimes in Federal programs, in financial institutions, and in computers which operate in or use a facility of interstate commerce through the introduction of fraudulent records into a computer system, unauthorized use of computer facilities, alteration or destruction of computerized information files, and stealing of financial instruments, data, or other assets, are great;

(4) computer-related crime directed at computers which operate in or use a facility of interstate commerce has a direct effect on interstate commerce; and

(5) the prosecution of persons engaged in computer-related crime is difficult under current Federal criminal statutes.

Sec. 3. (a) Chapter 47 of title 18, United States Code, is amended by adding at the end thereof the following new section:

§1028. Computer Fraud and Abuse

"**(a)** Whoever uses, or atterapts to use, a computer with intent to execute a scheme or artifice to defraud, or to obtain property by false or fraudulent pretenses, representations, or promises or to embezzle, steal, or knowingly convert to his use or the use of another, the property of another, shall, if the computer:

"**(1)** is owned by, under contract to, or operated for or on behalf of:

"**(A)** the United States Government; or

"**(B)** a financial institution;
and the prohibited conduct directly involves or affects the computer operation for or on behalf of the United States Government or financial institution; or

"**(2)** operates in, or uses a facility of, interstate commerce; be fined not more than two times the amount of the gain directly or indirectly derived from the offense or $50,000, whichever is higher, or imprisoned not more than five years, or both.

"**(b)** Whoever intentionally and without authorization damages a computer described in subsection (a) shall be fined not more than $50,000 or imprisoned not more than five years or both.

"**(c)** Definitions. For the purposes of this section, the term 'computer' means a device that performs logical, arithmetic, and storage functions by electronic manipulation, and includes any property and communication facility directly related to or operating in conjunction with such a device; but does not include an automated typewriter or typesetter, or any computer designed and *manufactured for,* and which is used *exclusively for routine, personal, family, or household purposes including* a portable handheld electronic calculator.

'financial institution' means—

"**(1)** a bank with deposits insured by the Federal Deposit Corporation;

"**(2)** a member of the Federal Reserve including any Federal Reserve Bank;

"**(3)** an institution with accounts insured by the Federal Savings and Loan Insurance Corporation;

"**(4)** a credit union with accounts insured by the National Credit Union Administration;

"**(5)** a member of the Federal home loan bank systems and any home loan bank;

"**(6)** a member or business insured by the Securities Investor Protection Corporation; and

"**(7)** a broker-dealer registered with the Securities and Exchange Commission pursuant to section 15 of the Securities and Exchange Act of 1934.".

" 'property' means anything of value, and includes tangible and intangible personal property, information in the form of electronically processed, produced, or stored data, or any electronic data processing representation thereof, and services;

" 'services' includes computer data processing and storage functions;

" 'United States Government' includes a branch or agency thereof;

" 'use' includes to instruct, communicate with, store data in, or retrieve data from, or otherwise utilize the logical, arithmetic, or memory functions of a computer;

"**(d)** **(1)** In a case in which federal jurisdiction over an offense as described in this section exists concurrently with State or local jurisdiction, the existence of federal jurisdiction does not, in itself, require the exercise of federal jurisdiction, nor does the initial exercise of federal jurisdiction preclude its discontinuation.

(2) In a case in which federal jurisdiction over an offense as described in this section exists or may exist concurrently with State or local jurisdiction, federal law enforcement officers, in determining whether to exercise jurisdiction, should consider—

"**(A)** the relative gravity of the federal offense and the State or local offense;

"**(B)** the relative interest in federal investigation or prosecution;

"(C) the resources available to the federal authorities and the State or local authorities;

"(D) the traditional role of the federal authorities and the State or local authorities with respect to the offense;

"(E) the interests of federalism; and

"(F) any other relevant factor.

(3) The Attorney General shall—

"(A) consult periodically with representatives of State and local governments concerning the exercise of jurisdiction in cases in which federal jurisdiction as described in this section exists or may exist concurrently with State or local jurisdiction;

"(B) provide general direction to federal law enforcement officers concerning the appropriate exercise of such federal jurisdiction;

"(C) report annually to Congress concerning the extent of the exercise of such federal jurisdiction during the proceeding fiscal year; and

"(D) report to Congress, within one year of the effective date of this Act, on the long-term impact upon federal jurisdiction, of this Act and the increasingly pervasive and widespread use of computers in the United States. The Attorney General shall periodically review and update such report.

(4) Except as otherwise prohibited by law, information or material obtained pursuant to the exercise of federal jurisdiction may be made available to State or local law enforcement officers having concurrent jurisdiction, and to State or local authorities otherwise assigned responsibility with regard to the conduct constituting the offense.

(5) An issue relating to the propriety of the exercise of, or of the failure to exercise, federal jurisdiction over an offense as described in this section, or otherwise relating to the compliance, or to the failure to comply, with this section, may not be litigated, and a court may not entertain or resolve such an issue except as may be necessary in the course of granting leave to file a dismissal of an indictment, an information, or a complaint.

Sec. 4. The table of sections of chapter 47 of title 18, United States Code, is amended by adding at the end thereof the following:

"1028. Computer fraud and abuse.".

STATE COMPUTER CRIME LAWS

Arizona

§13-2316. Computer fraud; classification

A. A person commits computer fraud in the first degree by accessing, altering, damaging or destroying without authorization any computer, computer system, computer network, or any part of such computer, system or network, with the intent to devise or execute any scheme or artifice to defraud or deceive, or control property or services by means of false or fraudulent pretenses, representations or promises.

B. A person commits computer fraud in the second degree by intentionally and without authorization accessing, altering, damaging or destroying any computer, computer system or computer network or any computer software, program or data contained in such computer, computer system or computer network.

C. Computer fraud in the first degree is a class 3 felony. Computer fraud in the second degree is a class 6 felony.
Added Laws 1978, Ch. 204, §2, eff. Oct. 1, 1978.

E. For the purposes of § 13-2316:

1. "Access" means to approach, instruct, communicate with, store data in, retrieve data from or otherwise make use of any resources of a computer, computer system or computer network.

2. "Computer" means an electronic device which performs logic, arithmetic or memory functions by the manipulations of electronic or magnetic impulses and includes all input, output, processing, storage, software or communication facilities which are connected or related to such a device in a system or network.

3. "Computer network" means the interconnection of communication lines with a computer through remote terminals or a complex consisting of two or more interconnected computers.

4. "Computer program" means a series of instructions or statements, in a form acceptable to a computer, which permits the functioning of a computer system in a manner designed to provide appropriate products from such computer system.

5. "Computer software" means a set of computer programs, procedures and associated documentation concerned with the operation of a computer system.

6. "Computer system" means a set of related, connected or unconnected computer equipment, devices and software.

7. "Financial instrument" means any check, draft, money order, certificate of deposit, letter of credit, bill of exchange, credit card, marketable security or any other written instrument, as defined by § 13-2001, paragraph 7, which is transferable for value.

8. "Property" means financial instruments, information, including electronically produced data, computer software and programs in either machine or human readable form, and anything of value, tangible or intangible.

9. "Services" includes computer time, data processing and storage functions.

California

Senate Bill No. 66

CHAPTER 858

An act to add Section 502 to the Penal Code, relating to computer crime.

[Approved by Governor September 21, 1979. Filed with Secretary of State September 22, 1979.]

LEGISLATIVE COUNSEL'S DIGEST

SB 66, Cusanovich. Computer crime.

Existing law relative to crimes involving fraud, or unauthorized access to, or damage or destruction of, property does not contain any specific provision relative to computers.

This bill would make it a crime, as specified, to intentionally access or cause to be accessed any computer system, or computer network for the purpose of (1) devising or executing any scheme or artifice to defraud or extort or (2) obtaining money, property or services with false or fraudulent intent, representations, or promises; or to maliciously access, alter, delete, damage, or destroy any computer system, computer network, computer program, or data.

Under existing law, Sections 2231 and 2234 of the Revenue and Taxation Code require the state to reimburse local agencies and school districts for certain costs mandated by the state. Other provisions require the Department of Finance to review statutes disclaiming these costs and provide, in certain cases, for making claims to the State Board of Control for reimbursement.

This bill provides that no appropriation is made by this act pursuant to Section 2231 and 2234 for a specified reason, but recognizes that local agencies and school districts may pursue their other available remedies to seek reimbursement for these costs.

The people of the State of California do enact as follows:

SECTION 1.   Section 502 is added to the Penal Code, to read:
502.   (a) For purposes of this section:

> **(1)** "Access" means to instruct, communicate with, store data in, or retrieve data from a computer system or computer network.
>
> **(2)** "Computer system" means a machine or collection of machines, excluding pocket calculators which are not programmable and capable of being used in conjunction with external files, one or more of which contain computer programs and data, that performs functions, including but not limited to, logic, arithmetic, data storage and retrieval, communication, and control.
>
> **(3)** "Computer network" means an interconnection of two or more computer systems.
>
> **(4)** "Computer program" means an ordered set of instructions or statements, and related data that, when automatically executed in actual or modified form in a computer system, causes it to perform specified functions.
>
> **(5)** "Data" means a representation of information, knowledge, facts, concepts, or instructions, which are being prepared or have been prepared, in a formalized manner, and are intended for use in a computer system or computer network.
>
> **(6)** "Financial instrument" includes, but is not limited to, any check, draft, warrant, money order, note, certificate of deposit, letter of credit, bill of exchange, credit or debit card, transaction authorization mechanism, marketable security, or any computer system representation thereof.
>
> **(7)** "Property" includes, but is not limited to, financial instruments, data, computer programs, documents associated with computer systems and computer programs, or copies thereof, whether tangible or intangible, including both human and computer system readable data, and data while in transit.
>
> **(8)** "Services" includes, but is not limited to, the use of the computer system, computer network, computer programs, or data prepared

for computer use, or data contained within a computer system, or data contained within a computer network.

(b) Any person who intentionally accesses or causes to be accessed any computer system or computer network for the purpose of (1) devising or executing any scheme or artifice to defraud or extort or (2) obtaining money, property, or services with false or fraudulent intent, representations, or promises shall be guilty of a public offense.

(c) Any person who maliciously accesses, alters, deletes, damages, or destroys any computer system, computer network, computer program, or data shall be guilty of a public offense.

(d) Any person who violates the provisions of subdivision (b) or (c) is guilty of a felony and is punishable by a fine not exceeding five thousand dollars ($5,000), or by imprisonment in the state prison for 16 months, or two or three years, or by both such fine and imprisonment, or by a fine not exceeding two thousand five hundred dollars ($2,500), or by imprisonment in the county jail not exceeding one year, or by both such fine and imprisonment.

(e) This section shall not be construed to preclude the applicability of any other provision of the criminal law of this state which applies or may apply to any transaction.

SEC. 2. Notwithstanding Section 2231 or 2234 of the Revenue and Taxation Code, no appropriation is made by this act pursuant to these sections because this act creates a new crime or infraction, eliminates a crime or infraction, or changes the penalty for a crime or infraction. It is recognized, however, that a local agency or school district may pursue any remedies to obtain reimbursement available to it under Chapter 3 (commencing with Section 2201) of Part 4 of Division 1 of that code.

Colorado

Article 5.5

COMPUTER CRIME

18-5.5-101. *Definitions.* As used in this article, unless the context otherwise requires:

(1) To "use" means to instruct, communicate with, store data in, retrieve data from, or otherwise make use of any resources of a computer, computer system, or computer network.

(2) "Computer" means an electronic device which performs logical, arithmetic, or memory functions by the manipulations of electronic or magnetic impulses, and includes all input, output, processing, storage, software, or communication facilities which are connected or related to such a device in a system or network.

(3) "Computer network" means the interconnection of communication lines (including microwave or other means of electronic communication) with a computer through remote terminals, or a complex consisting of two or more interconnected computers.

(4) "Computer program" means a series of instructions or statements, in a form acceptable to a computer, which permits the functioning of a computer system in a manner designed to provide appropriate products from such computer system.

(5) "Computer software" means computer programs, procedures, and associated documentation concerned with the operation of a computer system.

(6) "Computer system" means a set of related, connected or unconnected, computer equipment, devices, and software.

(7) "Financial instrument" means any check, draft, money order, certificate of deposit, letter of credit, bill of exchange, credit card, debit card, or marketable security.

(8) "Property" includes, but is not limited to financial instruments, information, including electronically produced data, and computer software and programs in either machine or human readable form, and any other tangible or intangible item of value.

(9) "Services" includes, but is not limited to, computer time, data processing, and storage functions.

18-5.5-102. *Computer crime.*

(1) Any person who knowingly uses any computer, computer system, computer network, or any part thereof for the purpose of: devising or executing any scheme or artifice to defraud, obtaining money, property, or services by means of false or fraudulent pretenses, representations, or promises, or committing theft, commits computer crime.

(2) Any person who knowingly and without authorization uses, alters, damages, or detroys any computer, computer system, or computer network described in section 18-5.5-101 or any computer software, program, documentation, or data contained in such computer, computer system, or computer network commits computer crime.

(3) If the loss, damage, or thing of value taken in violation of this section is less than fifty dollars, computer crime is a class 3 misdemeanor; if fifty dollars or more but less than two hundred dollars, computer crime is a class 2 misdemeanor; if two hundred dollars or more but less than ten thousand dollars, computer crime is a class 4 felony; if ten thousand dollars or more, computer crime is a class 3 felony.

SECTION 9.   Part 1 of article 8 of title 18, Colorado Revised Statutes 1973, 1978 Repl. Vol., is amended BY THE ADDITION OF A NEW SECTION to read:

18-8-115. *Duty to report a crime.* It is the duty of every corporation or person who has reasonable grounds to believe that a crime has been committed to report promptly the suspected crime to law enforcement authorities. When acting in good faith, such corporation or person shall be immune from any civil liability for such reporting.

Florida

CHAPTER 815.
COMPUTER-RELATED CRIMES [NEW]

815.1 Short title

The provisions of this act shall be known and may be cited as the "Florida Computer Crimes Act."
Added by Laws 1978, c. 78-92, § 1, eff. Aug. 1, 1978.

815.02 Legislative intent

The Legislature finds and declares that:

(1) Computer-related crime is a growing problem in government as well as in the private sector.

(2) Computer-related crime occurs at great cost to the public since losses for each incident of computer crime tend to be far greater than the losses associated with each incident of other white collar crime.

(3) The opportunities for computer-related crimes in financial institutions, government programs, government records, and other business enterprises through the introduction of fraudulent records into a computer system, the unauthorized use of computer facilities, the alteration or destruction of computerized information or files, and the stealing of financial instruments, data, and other assets are great.

(4) While various forms of computer crime might possibly be the subject of criminal charges based on other provisions of law, it is appropriate and desirable that a supplemental and additional statute be provided which proscribes various forms of computer abuse.

Added by Laws 1978, c. 78-92, § 1, eff. Aug. 1, 1978.

815.03 Definitions

As used in this chapter, unless the context clearly indicates otherwise:

(1) "Intellectual property" means data, including programs.

(2) "Computer program" means an ordered set of data representing coded instructions or statements that when executed by a computer cause the computer to process data.

(3) "Computer" means an internally programmed, automatic device that performs data processing.

(4) "Computer software" means a set of computer programs, procedures, and associated documentation concerned with the operation of a computer system.

(5) "Computer system" means a set of related, connected or unconnected, computer equipment, devices, or computer software.

(6) "Computer network" means a set of related, remotely connected devices and communication facilities including more than one computer system with capability to transmit data among them through communication facilities.

(7) "Computer system services" means providing a computer system or computer network to perform useful work.

(8) "Property" means anything of value as defined in s. 812.011 and includes, but is not limited to, financial instruments, information, including electronically produced data and computer software and programs in either machine-readable or human-readable form, and any other tangible or intangible item of value.

(9) "Financial instrument" means any check, draft, money order, certificate of deposit, letter of credit, bill of exchange, credit card, or marketable security.

(10) "Access" means to approach, instruct, communicate with, store data in, retrieve data from, or otherwise make use of any resources of a computer, computer system, or computer network.

Added by Laws 1978, c. 78-92, § 1, eff. Aug. 1, 1978.

815.04 Offenses against intellectual property

(1) Whoever willfully, knowingly, and without authorization modifies data, programs, or supporting documentation residing or existing internal or external to a computer, computer system, or computer network commits an offense against intellectual property.

(2) Whoever willfully, knowingly, and without authorization destroys data, programs, or supporting documentation residing or existing internal or external to a computer, computer system, or computer network commits an offense against intellectual property.

(3) Whoever willfully, knowingly, and without authorization discloses or takes data, programs, or supporting documentation which is a trade secret as defined in s. 812.081 or is confidential as provided by law residing or existing internal or external to a computer, computer system, or computer network commits an offense against intellectual property.

(4)(a) Except as otherwise provided in this subsection, an offense against intellectual property is a felony of the third degree, punishable as provided in s. 775.082, s. 775.083, or s. 775.084.

(b) If the offense is committed for the purpose of devising or executing any scheme or artifice to defraud or to obtain any property, then the offender is guilty of a felony of the second degree, punishable as provided in s. 775.082, s. 775.083, or s. 775.084.

Added by Laws 1978, c. 78-92, § 1, eff. Aug. 1, 1978.

815.05 Offenses against computer equipment or supplies

(1)(a) Whoever willfully, knowingly, and without authorization modifies equipment or supplies used or intended to be used in a computer, computer system, or computer network commits an offense against computer equipment or supplies.

(b) 1. Except as provided in this paragraph, an offense against computer equipment or supplies as provided in paragraph (a) is a misdemeanor of the first degree, punishable as provided in s. 775.082, s. 775.083, or s. 775.084.

2. If the offense is committed for the purpose of devising or executing any scheme or artifice to defraud or to obtain any property, then the offender is guilty of a felony of the third degree, punishable as provided in s. 775.082, s. 775.083, or s. 775.084.

(2)(a) Whoever willfully, knowingly, and without authorization detroys, takes, injures, or damages equipment or supplies used or intended to be used in a computer, computer system, or computer network; or whoever willfully, knowingly, and without authorization destroys, injures, or damages any computer, computer system, or computer network commits an offense against computer equipment or supplies.

(b) 1. Except as provided in this paragraph, an offense against computer equipment or supplies as provided in paragraph (a) is a misdemeanor of the first degree, punishable as provided in s. 775.082, s. 775.083, or s. 775.084.

2. If the damage to such computer equipment or supplies or to the computer, computer system, or computer network is greater than $200 but less than $1,000, then the offender is guilty of a felony of the third degree, punishable as provided in s. 775.082, s. 775.083, or s. 775.084.

3. If the damage to such computer equipment or supplies or to the computer, computer system, or computer network is $1,-000 or greater, or if there is an interruption or impairment of governmental operation or public communication, transportation, or supply of water, gas, or other public service, then the offender is guilty of a felony of the second degree, punishable as provided in s. 775.082, s. 775.083, or s. 775.084.

Added by Laws 1978, c. 78-92, § 1, eff. Aug. 1, 1978.

815.06 Offenses against computer users

(1) Whoever willfully, knowingly, and without authorization accesses or causes to be accessed any computer, computer system, or computer network; or whoever willfully, knowingly, and without authorization denies or causes the denial of computer system services to an authorized user of such computer system services, which, in whole or part, is owned by, under contract to, or operated for, on behalf of, or in conjunction with another commits an offense against computer users.

(2)(a) Except as provided in this subsection, an offense against computer users is a felony of the third degree, punishable as provided in s. 775.082, s. 775.083, or s. 775.084.

(b) If the offense is committed for the purposes of devising or executing any scheme or artifice to defraud or to obtain any property, then the offender is guilty of a felony of the second degree, punishable as provided in s. 775.082, s. 775.083, or s. 775.084.

Added by Laws 1978, c. 78-92, § 1, eff. Aug. 1, 1978.

815.07 This chapter not exclusive

The provisions of this chapter shall not be construed to preclude the applicability of any other provision of the criminal law of this state which presently applies or may in the future apply to any transaction which violates this chapter, unless such provision is inconsistent with the terms of this chapter.

Added by Laws 1978, c. 78-92, § 1, eff. Aug. 1, 1978.

Illinois

Introduced March 21, 1979, by Representatives Waddell—Brady—White, Ryan, Madigan, Friedland, Matijevich, E. M. Barnes, Bianco, Birkinbine, Boucek, Bower, Davis, Epton, Flinn, D. P. Friedrich, Giorgi, Hallock, Hallstrom, Huskey, Dave Jones, Kane, Keane, Kelly, Kempiners, Kent, Klosak, Lechowicz, Macdonald, Mahar, Margalus, Matula, Mautino, McAuliffe, McCourt, Mulcahey, Murphy, Polk, Pullen, Redmond, Reilly, Rigney, Schisler, Schoeberlein, Sharp, Simms, Stanley, E. G. Steele, C. M. Stiehl, Telcser, Van Duyne, Vinson, Vitek, Walsh, Bullock and White.

SYNOPSIS: (Ch. 38, pars. 15-1 and 15-7, new par. 16-9)

Amends the Criminal Code. Makes it a criminal offense to use a computer or alter or destroy computer programs without the consent of the owner of the system. Effective immediately.

LRB8104934KPjw

An act to add Section 16-9 to and to amend Sections 15-1 and 15-7 of the "Criminal Code of 1961", approved July 28, 1961, as amended.

Be it enacted by the People of the State of Illinois, represented in the General Assembly:

Section 1. Sections 15-1 and 15-7 of the "Criminal Code of 1961", approved July 18, 1961, as amended, are amended, and Section 16-9 is added thereto, the added and amended Sections to read as follows:

(Ch. 38, par. 15-1)

Sec. 15-1. Property. As used in this Part C, "property" means anything of value. Property includes real estate, money, commercial instruments, admission of transportation tickets, written instruments representing or embodying rights concerning anything of value, labor, or services, or otherwise of value to the owner; things growing on, affixed to, or found on land, or part of or affixed to any building, electricity, gas and water; birds, animals and fish, which ordinarily are kept in a state of confinement; food and drink; samples, cultures, microorganisms, specimens, records, recordings, documents, blueprints, drawings, maps, and whole or partial copies, descriptions, photographs, *computer programs or data,* prototypes or models thereof, or any other articles, materials, devices, substances and whole or partial copies, descriptions, photographs, prototypes, or models thereof which constitute, represent, evidence, reflect or record a secret scientific, technical, merchandising, production or management information, design, process, procedure, formula, invention, or improvement.

(Ch. 38, par. 15-7)

Sec. 15-7. Obtain. As used in this Part C, "obtain" means:

(a) In relation to property, to bring about a transfer of interest, or possession *or use,* whether to the offender or to another, and

(b) In relation to labor or services, to secure the performance thereof.

(Ch. 38. new par. 16-9)

Sec. 16-9. Unlawful use of a computer.

(a) *As used in this Part C:*

    1. *"Computer" means an internally programmed, general purpose digital device capable of automatically accepting data, processing data and supplying the results of the operation.*

    2. *"Computer system" means a set of related, connected devices, including a computer and other devices, including but not limited to*

data input and output and storage devices, data communications links, and computer programs and data, that make the system capable of performing the special purpose data processing tasks for which it is specified.

    3. *"Computer program" means a series of coded instructions or statements in a form acceptable to a computer, which causes the computer to process data in order to achieve a certain result.*

(b) *A person commits unlawful use of a computer when he:*

    1. *Obtains the use of a computer system, or any part thereof, without the consent of the owner; or*

    2. *alters or destroys computer programs or data without the consent of the owner of the computer system; or*

    3. *Intentionally, knowingly or recklessly obtains use of, alters or destroys a computer system, or any part thereof, as part of a scheme to defraud, obtain money, property or services from the owner of a computer or any third party.*

(c) *Sentence:*

    1. *A person convicted of a violation of subsections (a) (1) or (2) of this Section where the value of the use, alteration, or destruction is $1,000 or less shall be guilty of a petty offense.*

    2. *A person convicted of a violation of subsections (a) (1) or (2) of this Section where the value of the use, alteration or destruction is more than $1,000 shall be guilty of a Class A misdemeanor.*

    3. *A person convicted of a violation of subsection (a) (3) of this Section shall be guilty of a Class 4 felony.*

(d) *This Section shall neither enlarge nor diminish the rights of parties in civil litigation.*

Section 2. This Act takes effect on becoming a law.

Amendment to House Bill 1027

Amendment No. 1. Amend House Bill 1027 on page 1, lines 1 and 2 and line 6, by deleting "Sections 15-1 and 15-7" and inserting in lieu thereof "Section 15-1"; and

on page 1, line 7, by deleting "are" and inserting in lieu thereof "is": and by deleting the unnumbered line after line 28 and lines 29 through 31 on page 1 and lines 1 through 4 on page 2; and

on page 2, by deleting lines 22 through 30 and inserting in lieu thereof the following:

"**1.** *Knowingly obtains the use of a computer system, or any part thereof, without the consent of the owner (as defined in Section 15-2); or*

2. *Knowingly alters or destroys computer programs or data without the consent of the owner (as defined in Section 15-2); or*

3. *Knowingly obtains use of, alters or destroys a computer system, or any part thereof, as part of a deception for the purpose of obtaining money, property or services from the owner of a computer system (as defined in Section 15-2) or any third party.* "; *and*

on page 3, by deleting line 7 and inserting in lieu thereof the following:

"**(3)** *of this Section where the value of the money, property or services obtained is $1,000 or less shall be guilty of a Class A misdemeanor.*

4. *A person convicted of a violation of subsection (b) (3) of this Section where the value of the money, property or services obtained is more than $1,000 shall be guilty of a Class 4 felony.*"

New Mexico

CHAPTER 176

An Act Relating to Computer Use; Amending The Criminal Code to Make Misuse of Computers a Crime.

Be It Enacted By The Legislature of the State of New Mexico:

Section 1. *SHORT TITLE.* This act may be cited as the "Computer Crimes Act".

Section 2. *DEFINITIONS.* As used in the Computer Crimes Act:

A. "access" means to make use of any resources of a computer, computer system or computer network;

B. "computer" means an electronic device which performs logical, arithmetic and memory functions by the manipulation of electronic or magnetic impulses and includes all input, output, processing, storage, software or communication facilities which are connected or related to such a device in a computer system or computer network;

C. "computer network" means the interconnection of communication lines with a computer through remote terminals or a complex consisting of two or more computers and includes interconnected remote terminals;

D. "computer program" means a series of instructions or statements, in a form acceptable to a computer, which permits the functioning of a computer system in a manner designed to provide appropriate products from a computer system;

E. "computer software" means a set of computer programs, procedures and associated documentation concerned with the operation and function of a computer system; and

F. "computer system" means a set of related or interconnected computer equipment, devices and software.

Section 3. COMPUTER FRAUD.

A. Any person who accesses or causes to be accessed any computer, computer system, computer network or any part thereof with the intent to devise or execute any scheme or artifice to defraud is guilty of a fourth degree felony.

B. Any person who accesses or causes to be accessed any computer, computer system, computer network or any part thereof with the intent to obtain, by means of embezzlement or false or fraudulent pretenses, representations or promises, money, property or services where:

(1) the money, property or services have a value of one hundred dollars ($100) or less, is guilty of a petty misdemeanor.

(2) the money, property or services have a value of more than one hundred dollars ($100) but not more than two thousand five hundred dollars ($2,500), is guilty of a fourth degree felony; or

(3) the money, property or services have a value of more than two thousand five hundred dollars ($2,500), is guilty of a third degree felony.

Section 4. UNAUTHORIZED COMPUTER USE. Any person who intentionally, maliciously and without authorization accesses, alters, damages or destroys any computer, computer system, computer network, any part thereof or any information stored therein when:

A. the computer, computer system, computer network, part or information has a value of one hundred dollars ($100) or less is guilty of a petty misdemeanor;

B. the computer, computer system, computer network, part or information has a value of more than one hundred dollars ($100) but not more than two thousand five hundred dollars ($2,500) is guilty of a fourth degree felony; or

C. the computer, computer system, computer network, part or information has a value of more than two thousand five hundred dollars ($2,500) is guilty of a third degree felony.

Michigan

An Act to prohibit access to computers, computer systems, and computer networks for certain fraudulent purposes; to prohibit intentional and unauthorized access, alteration, damage, and destruction of computers, computer systems, computer networks, computer software programs, and data; and to prescribe penalties.

The People of the State of Michigan enact:

Sec. 1. For the purposes of this act, the words and phrases defined in sections 2 and 3 have the meanings ascribed to them in those sections.

Sec. 2.

(1) "Access" means to approach, instruct, communicate with, store data in, retrieve data from, or otherwise use the resources of, a computer, computer system, or computer network.

(2) "Computer" means an electronic device which performs logical, arithmetic, and memory functions by the manipulations of electronic or magnetic impulses, and includes input, output, processing, storage, software, or communication facilities which are connected or related to a device in a system or network.

(3) "Computer network" means the interconnection of communication lines with a computer through remote terminals, or a complex consisting of 2 or more interconnected computers.

(4) "Computer program" means a series of instructions or statements, in a form acceptable to a computer, which permits the functioning of a computer system in a manner designed to provide appropriate products from the computer system.

(5) "Computer software" means a set of computer programs, procedures, and associated documentation concerned with the operation of a computer system.

(6) "Computer system" means a set of related, connected or unconnected, computer equipment, devices, and software.

Sec. 3.

    (1) "Property" includes financial instruments; information, including electronically produced data; computer software and programs in either machine or human readable form; and any other tangible or intangible item of value.

    (2) "Services" includes computer time, data processing, and storage functions.

Sec. 4. A person shall not, for the purpose of devising or executing a scheme or artifice with intent to defraud or for the purpose of obtaining money, property, or a service by means of a false or fraudulent pretense, representation, or promise with intent to, gain access to or cause access to be made to a computer, computer system, or computer network.

Sec. 5. A person shall not intentionally and without authorization gain access to, alter, damage, or destroy a computer, computer system, or computer network, or gain access to, alter, damage, or destroy a computer software program or data contained in a computer, computer system, or computer network.

Sec. 6. A person shall not utilize a computer, computer system, or computer network to commit a violation of section 174 of Act No. 328 of the Public Acts of 1931, as amended, being section 750.174 of the Michigan Compiled Laws, section 279 of Act No. 328 of the Public Acts of 1931, being section 750.279 of the Michigan Compiled Laws, section 356 of Act No. 328 of the Public Acts of 1931, as amended, being section 750.356 of the Michigan Compiled Laws, or section 362 of Act No. 328 of the Public Acts of 1931, as amended, being section 750.362 of the Michigan Compiled Laws.

Sec. 7. A person who violates this act, if the violation involves $100.00 or less, is guilty of a misdemeanor. If the violation involves more than $100.00, the person is guilty of a felony, punishable by imprisonment for not more than 10 years, or a fine of not more than $5,000.00, or both.

North Carolina

    (4) 'computer program' means an ordered set of data that are coded instructions or statements that when executed by a computer cause the computer to process data.

(5) 'computer software' means a set of computer programs, procedures and associated documentation concerned with the operation of a computer system.

(6) 'computer system' means a set of related, connected or unconnected computer equipment and devices.

(7) 'financial statement' includes but is not limited to any check, draft, money order, certificate of deposit, letter of credit, bill of exchange, credit card or marketable security, or any electronic data processing representation thereof.

(8) 'property' includes but is not limited to, financial instruments, information, including electronically processed or produced data, and computer software and programs in either machine or human readable form, and any other tangible or intangible item of value.

(9) 'services' includes, but is not limited to, computer time, data processing and storage functions.

"§ 14-449. *Accessing computers.*

(a) A person is guilty of a felony if he willfully, directly or indirectly, accesses or causes to be accessed any computer, computer system, computer network, or any part thereof, for the purpose of:

(1) devising or executing any scheme or artifice to defraud, or

(2) obtaining property or services for himself or another, by means of false or fraudulent pretenses, representations or promises.

(b) Any person who willfully and without authorization, directly or indirectly, accesses [S-or causes to be accessed] any computer, computer system, computer network, or any part thereof, [S-for any purpose other than those set forth in subsection (a) above,] is guilty of a misdemeanor.

"§ 14-450. *Damaging computers and related materials.* A person is guilty of a felony if he willfully and without authorization, alters, damages or destroys:

(a) a computer, computer system, computer network, or any part thereof, or

(b) any computer software, program or data residing or existing internal or external to a computer, computer system or computer network.

"§ 14-451. *Denial of computer services to an authorized user.* Any person who willfully and without authorization denies or causes the denial of computer system services to an authorized user of such computer system services, is guilty of a misdemeanor.

"§ 14-452. *Extortion.* Any person who verbally or by a written or printed communication, maliciously threatens to commit an act described in G.S. 14-450 with the intent to extort money or any pecuniary advantage, or with the intent to compel any person to do or refrain from doing any act against his will, is guilty of a felony."

Sec. 2. This act shall become effective 90 days after ratification.

Rhode Island

Section 1. Title 11 of the general laws entitled "Criminal Offenses" is hereby amended by adding the following chapter:

"CHAPTER 51

"COMPUTER CRIME

"11-51-1. Definitions. As used in this chapter:

(A) 'Access' means to approach, instruct, communicate with, store data in, retrieve data from, or otherwise make use of any resources of, a computer, computer system, or computer network.

(B) 'Computer' means an electronic device which performs logical, arithmetic, and memory functions by the manipulations of electronic or magnetic impulses, and includes all input, processing, storage, software, or communication facilities which are connected or related to such a device in a system or network.

(C) 'Computer system' means a set of related, connected or unconnected, computer equipment, devices and software.

(D) 'Computer network' means the interconnection of communication lines with a computer through remote terminals, or a complex consisting of two or more interconnected computers.

(E) 'Property' includes, but is not limited to, financial instruments, information, including electronically produced data, and computer software and programs in either machine or human readable form, and any other tangible or intangible item of value.

(F) 'Services' includes, but is not limited to, computer time, data processing, and storage functions.

(G) 'Computer program' means a series of instructions or statements, in a form acceptable to a computer, which permits the functioning of a computer system in a manner designed to provide appropriate products from such computer systems.

(H) 'Computer software' means a set of computer programs, procedures, and associated documentation concerned with the operation of a computer system.

"11-51-2. Access to computer for fraudulent purposes. Whoever directly or indirectly accesses or causes to be accessed any computer, computer system, or computer network for the purpose of (1) devising or executing any scheme or artifice to defraud or (2) obtaining money, property, or services by means of false or fraudulent pretenses, representations, or promises shall be guilty of a felony and shall be subject to the penalties set forth in section 11-51-4.

"11-51-3. Intentional access, alteration, damage or destruction. Whoever intentionally and without authorization, directly or indirectly accesses, alters, damages, or destroys any computer, computer system, computer network, computer software, computer program or data contained in such computer, computer system, computer program or computer network shall be guilty of a felony and shall be subject to the penalties set forth in section 11-51-4.

"11-51-4. Penalties. Any person who is convicted of the offenses set forth in sections 11-51-2 and 11-51-3 shall be fined not more than five thousand dollars ($5,000) or imprisoned for not more than five (5) years, or both.

Sec. 2. This act shall take effect upon passage.

Appendix E

COMPUTER-RELATED CRIME METHODS

This appendix describes twelve computer-related crime methods in which computers play a key role. Although several of the methods are far more complex than the nonexpert will understand in detail, these brief descriptions will aid such people to comprehend sufficiently to interact with technologists who can provide the necessary expertise to deal with them. Most technologically sophisticated computer-related crimes will use one or more of these methods.

Like most aspects of computer technology, a jargon describing the now classical methods of computer-related crime has developed. These are the technical methods for some of the more sophisticated and automated computer-related crimes. The results are modification, disclosure (taking), destruction, and use or denial of use of services, computer equipment, computer programs, or data in computer systems. Depending on the meaning of the data, kinds of services, or purpose of the programs, the acts range over many known types of crime. The methods, possible types of perpetrators, likely evidence of their use, and detection are described below.

1. Data Diddling

This is the simplest, safest, and most common method used in computer-related crime. It involves changing data before or during their input to computers. The changing can be done by anybody associated with or having access to the processes of creating, recording, transporting, encoding, examining, checking, converting, and transforming data that ultimately enter a computer. Examples are forging or counterfeiting documents; exchanging valid computer tapes, cards, or disks with prepared replacements; source entry violations; punching extra holes or plugging holes in cards; and neutralizing or avoiding manual controls.

Data are normally protected by manual methods, and once data are in the computer, they can be automatically validated and verified. Manual controls include maker-checker-signer roles for trusted people with separation of responsibilities or dual responsibilities that force collusion to perpetrate fraudulent acts. Batch control totals can be manually calculated and compared in the computer with matching computer-produced batch control totals. In this method, data are batched into small groups, and data are added together to produce a sum that is the control total. Another common control is the use of check digits or characters imbedded in the data based on various characteristics of each field of data (*exempli gratia*, odd or even number indicators or hash totals). Sequence numbers and time of arrival can be associated with data and checked to ensure that data have not been

229

TABLE E-1
Detection of Data Diddling

POTENTIAL PERPETRATORS	METHODS OF DETECTION	EVIDENCE
Transaction participants	Data comparison	Data documents Source
Data preparers	Document validation	Transactions Computer-read-able
Source data supplies	Manual controls instrumentation analysis	Computer data media Tapes Cards
Nonparticipants with access	Computer validation and verification exception	Disks Storage modules
	Reports analysis	Manual logs, journals, and exception
	Computer output	reports
	Integrity tests	Incorrect computer output

removed or reordered. Large volumes of data can be checked by using utility or special-purpose programs in a computer. Evidence of data diddling is discovered data that do not correctly represent data as found at sources, lack equality with redundant or duplicate data, do not match earlier forms of data by reversing the manual processes that have been carried out, control totals or check digits that do not check nor meet validation and verification tests in the computer.

Potential data diddling perpetrators are employed in different kinds of occupations. Table E-1 summarizes these potential perpetrations, the methods of detecting data diddling, and the sources of evidence.

2. Trojan Horse

The Trojan horse method is the covert placement of computer instructions in a program so that the computer will perform unauthorized functions but usually still will allow the program to perform its intended purposes. This is the most common method in computer program-based frauds and sabotage. Instructions may be placed in production computer programs so that they will be executed in the protected or restricted domain of the program and have access to all of the data files that are assigned for exclusive use of the program. Programs are usually constructed loosely enough to allow space to be found or created for inserting the instructions.

A simplified example of how a Trojan horse works is presented in Figure E-1. Instructions to the computer and their locations in computer storage are listed on the left. On the right are explanations of what the computer does when directed to execute the instructions in sequence by location number. The process can be easily understood by playing the role of the computer and seeing what happens as each instruction is carried out. Think of the storage locations as mailbox addresses and the instructions as the contents of the mailboxes.

It can be seen that when the utility program (Trojan horse)—a basic program available for all computer users—is executed in the special privilege mode by a privileged user, it executes the instructions I previously secretly placed there when I created the program. Privileged mode allows access to all system commands and sections of storage. The result of this is that the legitimate privileged user has unknowingly authorized me—an unauthorized user of privileged instructions—to be a privileged user too because now, each time I log on to the computer at a terminal, the computer makes me—as identified by my password—a privileged user.

Do not be deceived by the simplicity of this example. The programs in the example would contain thousands or at least hundreds of instructions. Each line in the example would translate into an average of approximately five instructions in the form recognized for execution by the computer. The secret code buried in the Trojan horse utility program can be spread out among normal instructions to hide them. Finally, the total Trojan horse could consist of several or many chained programs, each transferring control to the next to perform each function.

There are no practical methods of preventing and detecting Trojan horse methods if the perpetrator is sufficiently clever. A typical business application program can consist of over 100,000 computer instructions and data. The Trojan horse can also be concealed among up to 5 or 6 millions of instructions in the operating system and commonly used utility programs where it waits for execution of the target application program, inserts extra instructions in it for a few milliseconds of execution time, and removes them with no remaining evidence. Even if it is discovered, there is no indication of who may have done it except to narrow the search to those programmers who have the necessary skills, knowledge, and access among employees, former employees, contract programmers, consultants, or employees of the computer or software suppliers. However, the perpetrator may be continuing to benefit from his acts by converting them to economic gain directly or through accomplices. If the conversion to assets can be determined and traced, there is a chance of apprehension using this method.

A suspected Trojan horse might be discovered by comparing a copy of

THE TROJAN HORSE TECHNIQUE
Objective: To obtain the special privilege level for my password.

Programs in Computer Storage
Utility Program for all users

What the Computer Does
Computer executes each instruction in sequence by location number.

Location in storage	Contents of Storage	
1248 1249 . . . 1631	(Normal instructions)	Computer executes utility function for any user, privileged or nonprivileged.
1632	Attempt privileged instruction.	Computer allows execution only if in privileged mode.
1633	If it was executed, go to 1634, otherwise go to 1637.	
1634	Insert the following instruction: "assign highest privilege level to my password," into system LOGON program at location 152	LOGON program instructions are moved down starting with contents of 152 and new instruction is inserted.
1635	Insert: "Go to 1637," at 1632	"Attempt privileged instruction" in location 1632 replaced with "Go to 1637."
1636	Erase contents of 1633 through 1636	Instructions replaced with blanks.
1637 1638 . . .	(Normal instructions)	Computer continues to execute normal utility instructions.

System LOGON Program (before Utility Program is executed)

Location in storage	Contents of Storage	
102 . . . 151	(Normal instructions)	Computer accepts new user at a terminal according to his password.
152	(Normal instruction)	Normal instruction is executed.
153 . . .	(Normal instructions)	Computer continues to execute normal LOGON instructions.

FIGURE E-1

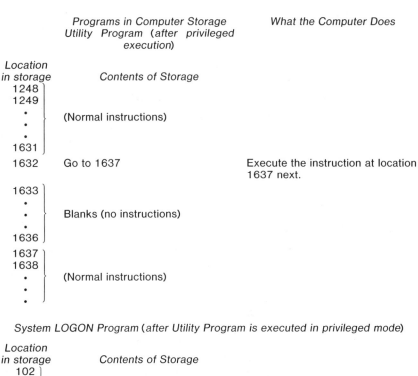

Programs in Computer Storage
Utility Program (after privileged execution)

What the Computer Does

Location in storage	Contents of Storage	What the Computer Does
1248 1249 . . . 1631	(Normal instructions)	
1632	Go to 1637	Execute the instruction at location 1637 next.
1633 . . . 1636	Blanks (no instructions)	
1637 1638 . . .	(Normal instructions)	

System LOGON Program (after Utility Program is executed in privileged mode)

Location in storage	Contents of Storage
102 . . . 151	(Normal instructions)
152	Assign highest privilege level to my password
153 . . .	(Normal instructions all moved down by one location)

FIGURE E-1 (Continued)

the operational program under suspicion with a master or other copy known to be free of unauthorized changes. Backup copies of production programs are routinely kept in safe storage, but smart perpetrators will make duplicate changes in them. Also programs are frequently changed without changing the backup copies, thereby making comparison difficult. Utility programs are usually available to perform comparisons of large programs, but their integrity and the computer system on which they are executed must be assured. This should be done only by qualified and trusted experts.

A Trojan horse might also be detected by testing the suspect program with data and under conditions that might cause the exposure of the purpose of the Trojan horse. However, the probability of success is low unless exact conditions for discovery are known. This may prove the existence of the Trojan horse, but usually will not determine its location. A Trojan horse may also reside in the source language version or only in the object form and may be inserted in the object form each time it is assembled or compiled— *exempli gratia,* as the result of another Trojan horse in the assembler or compiler.

The methods for detecting Trojan horse frauds are summarized in Table E-2. The table also lists the occupations of potential perpetrators and the sources of evidence of Trojan horse crime.

3. Salami Techniques

An automated form of crime involving the theft of small amounts of assets from a large number of sources is identified as a salami technique (taking small slices without noticeably reducing the whole). For example, in a banking system the demand deposit accounting system for checking accounts could be changed (using the Trojan horse method) to randomly reduce a few hundred accounts by 10 cents or 15 cents by transferring the money to a favored account where it can be legitimately withdrawn through normal methods. No controls are violated because the money is not removed from the system of accounts. Instead, a small fraction of it is merely rearranged. The success of the fraud is based on the idea that each checking account customer loses so little that it is of little consequence. Many variations are possible. The assets may be an inventory of products or services as well as money.

TABLE E-2
Detection of Trojan Horse Crimes

POTENTIAL PERPETRATORS	METHODS OF DETECTION	EVIDENCE
Programmers having detailed knowledge of a suspected part of a program and its purpose and access to it	Program code comparison Testing of suspect program	Unexpected results of program execution
	Tracing of possible gain from the act	Foreign code found in a suspect program
Employees Contract programmers Vendor's programmers Users of the computer		

One salami method in a financial system is known as the "round down" fraud. The round down fraud requires a computer system application where large numbers of financial accounts are processed. The processing must involve the multiplication of dollar amounts by numbers—such as in interest rate calculations. This arithmetic results in products that contain fractions of the smallest denomination of currency, such as the cent in the United States. For example, a savings account in a bank may have a balance of $15.86. Applying the 2.6 percent interest rate results in adding $0.41236 ($15.86 × .026) to the balance for a new balance of $16.27236. However, because the balance is to be retained only to the nearest cent, it is rounded down to $16.27, leaving $0.00236. What is to be done with this remainder? The interest calculation for the next account in the program sequence might be the following: $425.34 × 0.026 = $11.05884. this would result in a new balance of $436.39884 that must be rounded up to $436.40, leaving a deficit or negative remainder of $0.00116, usually placed in parenthesis to show its negative value ($0.00116).

The net effect of rounding in both these accounts, rounding down to the calculated cent in the first and adding 1 cent in the second, leaves both accounts accurate to the nearest cent and a remainder of $0.0012 ($0.00236–$0.00116). This remainder is then carried to the next account calculation, and so on. As the calculations continue, if the running or accumulating remainder goes above 1 cent, positive or negative, the last account is adjusted to return the remainder to an amount less than 1 cent. This results in a few accounts receiving 1 cent more or less than the correct rounded values, but the totals for all accounts remain in balance.

This is where the creative computer programmer can engage in some trickery to accumulate for himself a fancy bit of change and still show a balanced set of accounts that defies discovery by the auditor. He merely changes the rules slightly in the program by accumulating the rounded down remainders in his own account rather than distributing them to the other accounts as they build up.

Using a larger number of accounts shows how this is done (Parker 1976b). First, if rounded down correctly, it would be as shown in Table E-3. The interest rate applied to the total of all accounts, $3,294.26, results in a new total balance of $3,379.91 ($3,294.26 × 1.026) and a remainder of $0.00076 when the new total balance is rounded. This is calculated by the program as verification that the arithmetic performed account by account is correct. However, note that several accounts (those marked with an asterisk) have 1 cent more or less than they should have.

Now suppose the programmer writes the program to accumulate the round amounts into his own account, the last account in the list. The calculations will be as shown in Table E-4. The totals are the same as before and the verification shows no tinkering. However, now the new balances of some

TABLE E-3

Example of Rounded Down Accounts

OLD BALANCE	NEW BALANCE	ROUNDED NEW BALANCE	REMAINDER	ACCUMULATING REMAINDER
$ 15.86	$ 16.27236	$ 16.27	$ 0.00236	$ 0.00236
425.34	436.39884	436.40	(0.00116)	0.00120
221.75	227.51550	227.52	(0.00450)	(0.00330)
18.68	19.16568	19.17	(0.00432)	(0.00762)
o 564.44	579.11544	~~579.12~~	(0.00456)	(0.01218)
		579.11		(0.00218)
61.31	62.90406	62.90	0.00406	0.00188
101.32	103.95432	103.95	0.00432	0.00620
o 77.11	79.11486	~~79.11~~	0.00486	0.01106
		79.12		0.00106
457.12	469.00512	469.01	(0.00488)	(0.00382)
111.35	114.24510	114.25	(0.00490)	(0.00872)
o 446.36	457.96536	~~457.97~~	(0.00464)	(0.01336)
		457.96		(0.00336)
88.68	90.98568	90.99	(0.00432)	(0.00768)
o 14.44	14.81544	~~14.82~~	(0.00456)	(0.01224)
		14.81		(0.00224)
83.27	85.43502	85.44	(0.00498)	(0.00722)
127.49	130.80474	130.80	0.00474	(0.00248)
331.32	339.93432	339.93	0.00432	0.00184
37.11	38.07486	38.07	0.00486	0.00670
o 111.31	114.20406	~~114.20~~	0.00406	0.01076
		114.21		0.00076
$3294.26	Total	$3379.91		

accounts are 1 cent less, but none are 1 cent more as in the previous example. Those extra cents have been accumulated and all added to the programmer's account (the last account in the list) rather than to the accounts where the adjusted remainder exceeded 1 cent.

Clearly, if there were 180,000 accounts instead of the 18 accounts in this example, the programmer could have made a tidy profit of $300 ($0.03 × 10,000). This could result in a significant fraud over several years.

There are only two ways that the auditor might discover this fraud. He could check the instructions in the program, or he could recalculate the interest for the programmer's account after the program had been executed by the computer. A clever programmer could easily disguise the instructions causing the fraudulent calculations in the program in a number of ways.

TABLE E-4

Example of Rounded Down Accounts
Converted to Programmer's Account

OLD BALANCE	NEW BALANCE	ROUNDED NEW BALANCE	REMAINDER	ACCUMU-LATING REMAINDER	PRO-GRAMMER'S REMAINDER
$ 15.86	$ 16.27236	$ 16.27	$ 0.00236	$ 0.00000	$0.00236
425.34	436.39884	436.40	(0.00116)	(0.00116)	0.00236
221.75	227.51550	227.52	(0.00450)	(0.00566)	0.00236
18.68	19.16568	19.17	(0.00998)	(0.00998)	0.00236
o 564.44	579.11544	~~579.12~~	(0.00456)	(0.01454)	0.00236
		579.11		(0.00454)	
61.31	62.90406	62.90	0.00406	(0.00454)	0.00642
101.32	103.95432	103.95	0.00432	(0.00454)	0.01074
77.11	79.11486	79.11	0.00486	(0.00454)	0.01560
457.12	469.00512	469.01	(0.00488)	(0.00942)	0.01560
o 111.35	114.24510	~~114.25~~	(0.00490)	(0.01432)	0.01560
		114.24		(0.00432)	
446.36	457.96536	457.97	(0.00464)	(0.00896)	0.01560
o 88.68	90.98568	~~90.99~~	(0.00432)	(0.01328)	0.01560
		90.98		(0.00328)	
14.44	14.81544	14.82	(0.00456)	(0.00784)	0.01560
o 83.27	85.43502	~~85.44~~	(0.00498)	(0.01282)	0.01560
		85.43		(0.00282)	
127.49	130.80474	130.80	0.00474	(0.00282)	0.02034
331.32	339.93432	339.93	0.00432	(0.00282)	0.02466
37.11	38.07486	38.07	0.00486	(0.00282)	0.02952
o 111.31	114.20406	~~114.20~~	0.00406	(0.00282)	0.03358
		114.23		0.00076	0.00000
$3294.26	Total	$3379.91			

However, this would probably be unnecessary because an auditor or anybody else would probably not wade step by step through a program so long as use of the program showed no irregularities.

This program method would show no irregularities unless the programmer's account were audited. It is unlikely that his account—one account among 180,000—would be audited. Besides, the programmer could have opened the account using a fictitious name or the name of an accomplice. He could also occasionally change to other accounts to reduce further the possibility of detection.

Experienced accountants and auditors indicate that the round down fraud technique has been known for many years, even before the use of computers. They say that a good auditor will look for this type of fraud by checking for deviations from the standard accounting method for rounding calculations.

Salami acts are usually not fully discoverable within obtainable expenditures for investigation. Victims have usually lost so little individually that they are unwilling to expend much effort to solve the case. Specialized detection routines can be built into the suspect program, or snapshot storage dump listings could be obtained at crucial times in suspect program production runs. If the salami acts are taking identifiable amounts, these can be traced, but a smart perpetrator will randomly vary the amounts or accounts debited and credited.

The actions and life styles of the few people and their associates who have the skills, knowledge, and access to perform salami acts can be closely watched for aberrations or deviations from normal. This could be successful because real-time actions are usually required to convert the results to obtainable gain. The perpetrator or his accomplice will usually withdraw the money from the accounts in which it accumulates in legitimate ways. Records will show an imbalance between the deposit and withdrawal transactions, but all accounts would have to be balanced relative to all transactions over a significant period of time. This is a monumental and expensive task.

Many financial institutions require employees to use their financial services and make it attractive for them to do so. Employees' accounts are more completely and carefully audited than others. This usually forces the salami perpetrators to open accounts under assumed names or arrange for accomplices to do it. Investigation of suspected salami frauds might be more successful through concentrating on the actions of possible suspects rather than relying on technical methods of discovery.

Table E-5 lists the methods of detecting the use of salami techniques. The table also lists potential perpetrators and source of evidence of the use of the technique.

4. Superzapping

Superzapping derives its name from superzap, a macro utility program used in most IBM computer centers as a systems tool. Any computer center that has a secure computer operating mode needs a "break glass in case of emergency" computer program that will bypass all controls to modify or disclose any of the contents of the computer. Computers sometimes stop, malfunction or enter a state that cannot be overcome by normal recovery or restart procedures. Computers also perform unexpectedly and need attention that normal access methods do not allow. In such cases, a universal access program is needed. This is similar in one way to a master key to be used

TABLE E-5
Detection of Salami Techniques

POTENTIAL PERPETRATORS	METHODS OF DETECTION	EVIDENCE
Financial system programmers	Detail data analysis	Many small financial losses
	Program comparison	Unsupported account buildups
Employees		
Former employees	Transaction audits	Trojan horse code changed or unusual
Contract programmers		
Vendors' programmers	Observation of financial activities of possible suspects	personal financial practices of possible suspects

if all other keys are lost or locked in the enclosure they were meant to open.

Utility programs such as superzap are powerful and dangerous tools in the wrong hands. They are normally used only by systems programmers and computer operators who maintain computer operating systems. They should be kept secure from unauthorized use. However, they are often placed in program libraries where they can be used by any programmer or operator who knows of their presence and how to use them.

A classic example of superzapping resulting in a $128,000 loss occurred in a bank in New Jersey (Parker 1976b). The manager of computer operations was using a superzap program to make changes to account balances to correct errors as directed by management. The regular error correction process was not working correctly because the demand-deposit accounting system had become obsolete and error-ridden as a result of inattention in a computer changeover. The operations manager discovered how easy it was to make changes without the usual controls or journal records, and he made changes transferring money to three friends' accounts. They engaged in the fraud long enough for a customer to find a shortage: quick action in response to the customer's complaint resulted in indictment and conviction of the perpetrators. The use of the superzap program without leaving any evidence of changes to the data files made discovery of the fraud through technical means highly unlikely.

Unauthorized use of superzap programs can result in changes to data files that are normally updated only by production programs. There usually are few, if any, controls that would detect changes in the data files from previous runs. Applications programmers do not anticipate this type of fraud; their universe of concern is limited to the application program and its interaction with data files. Therefore, the detection of fraud will result only when the recipients of regular computer output reports from the production

TABLE E-6

Detection of Superzapping Crime

POTENTIAL PERPETRATORS	METHOD OF DETECTION	EVIDENCE
Programmers with access to superzap programs and computer access to use them	Comparison of files with historical copies	Output report discrepancies
	Discrepancies noted by recipients of output reports	Undocumented transactions
Computer operations staff with applications knowledge		Computer usage or file request journals
	Examination of computer usage journals	

program notify management that a discrepancy seems to have occurred. Computer managers will often conclude that the evidence indicates data entry errors, because it would not be a characteristic computer or program error. Considerable time can be wasted searching in the wrong areas. When it is concluded that unauthorized file changes have occurred independent of the application program associated with the file, a search of all computer usage journals might reveal the use of a superzap program, but this is unlikely if the perpetrator anticipates a search. Occasionally, there may be a record of a request to have the file placed on-line in the computer system if it is not normally in that mode. Otherwise, the changes would have to occur when the production program using the file is being run or just before or after it is run. This is the most likely time of the act.

Detection of the superzap acts may be possible by comparing the current file with father and grandfather copies of the file where no updates exist to account for suspicious changes. Table E-6 summarizes the potential perpetrators, methods of detection, and sources of evidence in superzapping crime.

5. Trap Doors

In the development of large application and computer operating systems, it is the practice of programmers to insert debugging aids that provide breaks in the code for insertion of additional code and intermediate output capabilities. The design of computer operating systems attempts to prevent both access to them and insertion of code or modification of code. Consequently, system programmers will sometimes insert codes that allow compromise of these requirements during the debugging phases of program development and later when the system is being maintained and improved. These facilities are referred to as trap doors. Normally, trap doors are eliminated in the final editing, but sometimes they are overlooked or purposely left in to facilitate ease of making future access and modification. In addition, some unscrupulous programmers may purposely introduce trap doors for later compromising of computer programs. Designers of large, complex programs may also introduce trap doors inadvertently through weaknesses in design logic.

Trap doors may also be introduced in the electronic circuitry of computers. For example, not all of the combinations of codes may be assigned to instructions found in the computer and documented in the programming manuals. When these unspecified commands are used, the circuitry may cause the execution of unanticipated combinations of functions that allow compromise of the computer system.

During the use and maintenance of computer programs and computer circuitry, ingenious programmers invariably discover some of these weaknesses and take advantage of them for useful and innocuous purposes. However, the trap doors may also be used for unauthorized, malicious purposes as well. Functions that can be performed by computer programs and computers that are not in the specifications are often referred to as negative specifications. It is difficult enough for designers and implementers to make programs and computers function according to specifications and to prove that they perform according to specifications. It is currently not possible to prove that a computer system does not perform functions that it is not specified to perform.

Research is continuing on a high-priority basis to develop methods of proving the correctness of computer programs and computers according to complete and consistent specifications. However, it is anticipated that it will be many years before commercially available computers and computer programs can be proved correct. Therefore, trap doors continue to exist, and there is never any guarantee that they have all been found and corrected.

In one computer-related crime, a systems programmer discovered a trap door in a FORTRAN programming language compiler. The trap door allowed the programmer writing in the FORTRAN language to transfer control from his FORTRAN program into a region of storage used for data. This caused the computer to execute computer instructions formed by the data and provided a means of executing program code secretly by inputting data in the form of computer instructions each time the FORTRAN program was run. This occurred in a commercial time-sharing computer service. The systems programmer, in collusion with a user of the time-sharing service, was able to use large amounts of computer time free of charge and obtain data and programs of other time-sharing users. In another case, sev-

TABLE E-7

Detection of Trap Door Crimes

POTENTIAL PERPETRATORS	METHODS OF DETECTION	EVIDENCE
Systems programmers	Exhaustive testing	Computer output reports that indicate that a computer system performs outside of its specifications
Expert application programmers	Comparison of specification to performance	
	Specific testing based on evidence	

eral automative engineers in Detroit discovered a trap door in a commercial time-sharing service in Florida that allowed them to search uninhibitedly for privileged passwords. They discovered the password of the president of the time-sharing company and were able to obtain copies of trade-secret computer programs that they proceeded to use free of charge. In both of these cases the perpetrators were discovered accidentally. It was never determined how many other users were taking advantage of the trap doors.

There is no direct technical method for the discovery of trap doors. However, when the nature of a suspected trap door is sufficiently determined, tests of varying degrees of complexity can be performed to discover hidden functions used for malicious purposes. This requires the expertise of systems programmers and knowledgeable application programmers. Large amounts of computer services and time could be wasted by people without sufficient expertise attempting to discover trap door usage. Investigators should always seek out the most highly qualified experts for the particular computer system or computer application under suspicion.

It is wise for the investigator always to assume that the computer system and computer programs are never sufficiently secure from intentional, technical compromise. However, these intentional acts usually require the expertise of only the very few technologists who have the skills, knowledge, and access to perpetrate them. Table E-7 lists the potential perpetrators, methods of detection, and sources of evidence of the use of the trap door technique.

6. Logic Bombs

A logic bomb is a computer program executed at appropriate or periodic times in a computer system that determines conditions or states of the computer that facilitate the perpetration of an unauthorized, malicious act. For example, in one case, secret computer instructions were inserted (a Tro-

TABLE E-8

Detection of Logic Bombs

POTENTIAL PERPETRATORS	METHODS OF DETECTION	EVIDENCE
Programmers having detailed knowledge of a suspected part of a program and its purpose and access to it	Program code comparisons	Unexpected results of program execution
	Testing of suspect program	Foreign code found in a suspect program
Employees Contract programmers Vendor's programmers Users of the computer	Tracing of possible gain from the act	

jan horse) in the computer operating system where they were executed periodically (Parker 1976b). The instructions would test the year, date, and time of day clock in the computer so that on a specified day of the year 2 years later at 3:00 P.M. the time bomb, a type of logic bomb, would go off and trigger the printout of a confession of a crime on all of the 300 computer terminals on-line at that time and then would cause the system to crash. This was timed so that the perpetrator would be geographically a long distance from the computer and its users. In another case, a payroll system programmer put a logic bomb in the personnel system so that if his name was ever removed from the personnel file, indicating termination of employment, secret code would have caused the entire personnel file to be erased.

A logic bomb can be programmed to trigger an act based on any specified condition or data that may occur or be introduced. Logic bombs are usually placed in the computer system using the Trojan horse technique. Methods to discover logic bombs in a computer system would be the same as for Trojan horses. Table E-8 summarizes the potential perpetrators, methods of detection, and kinds of evidence of logic bombs.

7. Asynchronous Attacks

Asynchronous attack techniques take advantage of the asynchronous functioning of a computer operating system. Most computer operating systems function asynchronously based on the services that must be performed for the various computer programs in execution in the computer system. For example, several jobs may simultaneously call for output reports to be produced. The operating system stores these requests and, as resources become available, performs them in the order in which resources are available to fit the request or according to an overriding priority indication. Therefore, rather than executing requests in the order they are received, the system performs them asynchronously based on resources available.

There are highly sophisticated methods of confusing the operating system to allow it to violate the isolation of one job from another. For example, in a large application program that runs for a long period of time, it is customary for it to have checkpoint restarts. These allow the computer operator to set a switch manually to stop the program at a specified intermediate stopping point from which it may be restarted at a later time in an orderly manner without losing data. This requires the operating system to save the copy of the computer program and data in their current state at the checkpoint. The operating system must also save a number of system parameters that describe the mode and security level of the program at the time of the stop. It might be possible for a programmer or computer operator to gain access to the checkpoint restart copy of the program, data, and system parameters. He could change the system parameters such that on restart the program would function at a higher priority security level or privileged level in the computer and thereby give the program unauthorized access to data, other programs, or the operating system. Note that checkpoint restart actions are usually well documented in the computer console log.

Even more complex methods of attack could be used besides the one described in this simple example. However, the technology is too complex to present here. The investigator should be aware of the possibilities of asynchronous attacks and seek adequate technical assistance if there are suspicious circumstances resulting from the activities of highly sophisticated and trained technologists. Evidence of such attacks would be discernible only from unexplainable deviations from application and system specifications in computer output or characteristics of system performance. Table E-9 lists the potential perpetrators and methods of detecting asynchronous attacks.

TABLE E-9
Detection of Asynchronous Attacks

POTENTIAL PERPETRATORS	METHODS OF DETECTION	EVIDENCE
Sophisticated advanced system programmers	System testing of suspected attack methods	Output that deviates from normally expected output or logs containing characteristics of computer operation
Sophisticated & advanced computer operators	Repeat execution of a job under normal and safe circumstances	

8. Scavenging

Scavenging is a method of obtaining information that may be left in or around a computer system after the execution of a job. Simple physical scavenging could be the searching of trash barrels for copies of discarded computer listings or carbon paper from multiple-part forms. More technical and sophisticated methods of scavenging can be done by searching for residual data left in a computer after job execution.

For example, a computer operating system may not properly erase buffer storage areas used for the temporary storage of input or output data. Some operating systems do not erase magnetic disk or magnetic tape storage media because of the excessive computer time required to do this. Therefore, new data are written over the old data. It may be possible for the next job to be executed to read the old data before they are replaced by new data. This might happen in the following way. If storage was reserved and used by a previous job and then assigned to the next job, the next job would gain access to the same storage, write only a small amount of data into that storage, but then read the entire storage area back out for its own purposes, thus capturing—scavenging—data that were stored by the previous job.

In one case, a time-sharing service in Texas had a number of oil companies as customers. The computer operator noticed that every time one particular customer used computer services his job always requested that a scratch tape (temporary storage tape) be mounted on a tape drive. When the operator mounted the tape, he noticed that the read-tape light always came on before the write-tape light came on, indicating that the user was reading data from a temporary storage tape before he had written anything on it. After numerous incidents of this, the computer operator became curious and reported it to management. Simple investigation revealed that the customer was engaged in industrial espionage, obtaining seismic data stored by various oil companies on the temporary tapes and selling this highly proprietary, valuable data to other oil companies.

The detection of scavenging usually occurs as a result of discovering suspected crimes involving proprietary information that may have come from a computer system and computer media. The information may be traced back to its source that involves computer usage. It is probably more likely that the act was a manual scavenging of information in human-readable form or the theft of magnetic tapes or disks rather than electronic scavenging.

In one case, valuable data were found on continuous forms from a computer output printer (Parker 1976b). Each page of the output had a preprinted sequence number and the name of the paper company. An FBI agent was able to trace the paper back to the paper company. On the basis of the type of forms and sequence numbers, he traced it from there to the com-

---

TABLE E-10

Detection of Scavenging Crimes

POTENTIAL PERPETRATORS	METHOD OF DETECTION	EVIDENCE
Users of the computer system	Tracing of discovered proprietary information back to its source	Computer output media
		Type font characteristics
Persons having access to computer facilities and adjacent areas	Testing of an operating system to discover residual data after execution of a job	Similar information produced in suspected ways in the same form

---

puter center where the paper had been used. The sequence numbers were traceable to a specific printer and time at which the forms were printed. Discovery of the job that produced the reports at that time and the programmer who submitted the job from the computer console log and usage accounting data was straightforward. Table E-10 lists the potential perpetrators. The table also summarizes the methods of detecting and the kinds of evidence typical with scavenging techniques.

9. Data Leakage

A wide range of computer-related crime involves the removal of data or copies of data from a computer system or computer facility (Lampson 1973). This possibility can offer the most dangerous exposure to the perpetrator. His technical act may be well hidden in the computer; however, to convert it to economic gain, he must get the data from the computer system. Output is subject to examination by computer operators and other data processing personnel.

Several techniques can be used to leak data from a computer system. The perpetrator may be able to hide the sensitive data in otherwise innocuous-looking output reports. This could be done by adding to blocks of data. In more sophisticated ways the data could be interspersed with otherwise innocuous data. An even more sophisticated method might be to encode data to look like something different than they are. For example, a computer listing may be formatted so that the secret data are in the form of different lengths of printer lines, number of words or numbers per line, locations of punctuation, and use of code words that can be interspersed and converted into meaningful data. Another method is by controlling and observing the movement of equipment parts, such as the reading and writing of a magnetic tape causing the tape reels to move clockwise and counterclockwise in a pattern representing binary digits 0 and 1. Observation of the movement of the tape reels results in obtaining the data. Similar kinds of output might be accomplished by causing a printer to print and skip lines in a pattern where the noise of the printer, recorded with a cassette tape recorder, might be played back at slow speed to again produce a pattern translatable into binary information.

These are rather exotic methods of data leakage that might be necessary only in high-security, high-risk environments. Otherwise, much simpler manual methods might be used. It has been reported that hidden in the central processors of many computers used in the Vietnam War were miniature radio transmitters capable of broadcasting the contents of the computers to a remote receiver. These were discovered when the computers were returned to the United States from Vietnam.

Investigation of data leakage would probably best be conducted by interrogating data processing personnel who might have observed the movement of sensitive data. It might also be possible to examine computer operating system usage journals to determine if and when data files may have been accessed. Data leakage might be conducted through the use of Trojan horse, logic bomb, and scavenging methods. Possible use of these methods should be investigated when data leakage is suspected. Evidence will most likely be in the same form as evidence of scavenging activities described above. Table E-11 summarizes the detection of crimes resulting from data leakage.

10. Piggybacking and Impersonation

Piggybacking and impersonation can be done physically or electronically. Physical piggybacking is a method for gaining access to controlled access areas when control is accomplished by electronically or mechanically

TABLE E-11
Detection of Crimes From Data Leakage

POTENTIAL PERPETRATORS	METHODS OF DETECTION	EVIDENCE
Computer programmers	Discovery of stolen information	Computer storage media
		Computer output forms
Employees Former employees Contract workers Vendor's employees	Tracing computer storage media back to the computer facility	Type font
		Trojan horse or scavenging evidence

locked doors. Typically, an individual, usually with his hands full of computer-related objects such as tape reels, stands by the locked door. When an authorized individual arrives and opens the door, the piggybacker goes in after or along with him. Turnstiles, mantraps, or a stationed guard are the usual methods of preventing this type of unauthorized access. The turnstyle allows passage of only one individual with a metal key, an electronic or magnetic card key, or combination lock activation. A mantrap is a double-doored closet through which only one person can move with one key action. Success of this method of piggybacking is dependent upon the quality of the access control mechanism and the alertness of authorized persons in resisting cooperation with the perpetrator.

Electronic piggybacking can take place in an on-line computer system where individuals are using terminals, and identification is verified automatically by the computer system. When a terminal has been activated, the computer authorizes access, usually on the basis of a key, secret password, or other passing of required information (protocol). Compromise of the computer can take place when a hidden computer terminal is connected to the same line through the telephone switching equipment and used when the legitimate user is not using his terminal. The computer will not be able to differentiate or recognize the two terminals, but senses only one terminal and one authorized user. Piggybacking can also be accomplished when the user signs off improperly, leaving the terminal in an active state or leaving the computer in a state where it assumes the user is still active.

Impersonation is the process of one person assuming the identity of another. Physical access to computers or computer terminals and electronic access through terminals to a computer require positive identification of an authorized user. The verification of identification is based on some combination of something the user knows, such as a secret password; something the user is—that is, a physiological characteristic, such as finger print, hand geometry, or voice; and something the user possesses, such as a magnetic stripe card or metal key. Anybody with the correct combination of identification characteristics can impersonate another individual.

An example of a clever impersonation occurred when a young man posed as a magazine writer and called on a telephone company, indicating that he was writing an article on the computer system in use by the telephone company (Parker 1976b). He was invited in and given a full and detailed briefing on all of the computer facilities and application systems. As a result of this information, he was able to steal over $1 million worth of telephone equipment from the company. In another case, an individual stole magnetic stripe credit cards that required secret personal identification numbers (PINs) associated with each card for use. He would call the owners of the cards by telephone indicating that he was a bank official, had discovered the theft of the card, and needed to know the secret PIN number to protect

TABLE E-12

Detection of Impersonation Acts

POTENTIAL PERPETRATORS	METHODS OF DETECTION	EVIDENCE
Employees, former employees, vendors' employees	Access observations	Logs, journals, equipment usage meters
	Interviewing witnesses	
		Other physical evidence
Contracted persons	Examination of journals and logs	
Outsiders		
	Specialized computer programs that analyze characteristics of online computer user accesses	

the victim and issue a new card. Victims invariably gave out their secret PINs and the impersonator then used the PINs to withdraw the maximum amount allowed through automatic teller machines that required the cards and numbers for identification.

Electronic door access control systems frequently are run by a minicomputer that produces a log showing accesses and time of accesses for each individual gaining access. Human guards frequently do equivalent journaling through the keeping of logs. Detection of unauthorized access can be accomplished by studying journals and logs and by interviewing people who may have witnessed the unauthorized access. Table E-12 summarizes the methods of detecting computer crime committed by impersonation methods.

11. Wiretapping

There is no verified experience of data communications wiretapping. The potential for wiretapping grows rapidly, however, as more computers are connected to communication facilities and increasing amounts of electronically stored assets are transported from computer to computer over communication circuits. Wiretapping has not become popular as far as is known because of the many easier ways to obtain or modify data.

Wiretapping requires equipment worth at least $200 (available at a Radio Shack store) and a method of recording and printing the information. Recording and printing can usually be done more directly and easily through the computer system or by impersonation through terminals. The perpetrator usually will not know when the particular data he is interested in will be sent. Therefore, he must collect relatively large amounts of data and

TABLE E-13

Detection of Wiretapping

POTENTIAL PERPETRATORS	METHODS OF DETECTION	EVIDENCE
Communications technicians and engineers	Voice wiretapping methods	Voice wiretapping evidence
Communications employees		

search for the specific items of interest. Identification and isolation of the communications circuit can also pose a problem for the perpetrator. Interception of microwave and satellite communications represents even greater difficulty because of the complexity and cost of the equipment to perform the operation. In addition, the perpetrator must determine whether there are active detection facilities built into the communication system.

The best method of protecting data is encryption or secret coding of the data using an encryption key. New, powerful products are now on the market to provide encryption. It is anticipated that most valuable data will be routinely encrypted within the next several years. This probably will greatly reduce the threat of wiretapping.

Wiretapping should be assumed to be the least likely method used in the theft or modification of data. Detection methods and possible evidence will be the same as in the investigation of voice communication wiretapping. Table E-13 summarizes the potential perpetrators, detection and evidence in wiretapping acts.

12. Simulation and Modeling

A computer can be used as a tool or instrument of a crime for planning or control. Complex white-collar crime often requires the use of a computer because of its sophisticated capabilities. An existing process can be simulated on a computer or a planned method for carrying out a crime could be modeled to determine its possible success.

In one case involving a million-dollar manual embezzlement, an accountant owned his own service bureau and simulated his company's accounting and general ledger system on his computer (Parker 1976b). He was able to input correct data and modified data to determine the effects of the embezzlement on the general ledger. He also had the capability to run the simulation in the reverse direction by inputting to the computer the general ledger data he wished to have. He then ran the system in reverse to determine the false entries in accounts payable and accounts receivable that would result in the required general ledger output.

In one phase of an insurance fraud in Los Angeles in 1973, a computer was used to model the company and determine the effects of the sale of large numbers of insurance policies (Parker 1976b). The modeling resulted in the creation of 64,000 fake insurance policies in computer-readable form that were then introduced into the real system and subsequently resold as valid policies to reinsuring companies.

The use of a computer for simulation and modeling normally requires extensive amounts of computer time and computer program development. Investigation should include a search for significant amounts of computer services used by the suspects in complex fraud. This can be done by determining recent business activities of suspects and investigating the customer lists of locally available commercial time-sharing and service bureau companies. If use of the victim's computer is suspected, usage logs may show unexplained amounts of computer time used by the suspects.

Usually a programmer with expertise in simulation and modeling would be required to develop the application needed. In some cases, it was found that the computer programmers had no knowledge that their work was being used for fraudulent purposes. Evidence in the form of computer programs, input data, and output reports would require the attention of a computer programmer expert or systems analyst to determine the nature of the modeling or simulation. Table E-14 lists the potential perpetrators, methods of detection, and kinds of evidence in simulation and modeling techniques.

TABLE E-14
Detection of Simulation and Modeling Techniques

POTENTIAL PERPETRATORS	METHODS OF DETECTION	EVIDENCE
Computer application programmers	Investigation of possible computer usage by suspects	Computer programs Computer program documentation
Simulation and modeling experts		Computer input
Managers in positions to engage in large, complex embezzlement		Computer-produced reports
		Computer usage logs and journals

EDP OCCUPATION DESCRIPTIONS
FOR EXPOSURE ANALYSIS

User Transaction and Data Entry Operator

Function.   Operates a remote terminal, enters transactions, data, and programs, at the direction of user personnel.

Knowledge.   Source document content and format, terminal output content and format, terminal protocol, identification/verification procedure, other procedural controls.

Skills.   Typing and keyboard operation, manual dexterity for equipment operation, basic reading.

Access.   Terminal area, source documents, terminal output, terminal operation instructions, identification/verification materials.

Vulnerability.   The enterprise is vulnerable to both physical and operational violations by this individual. The principal area of vulnerability is violations that involve the modification, destruction, or disclosure of data belonging to the individual's immediate user organization either internal or external to the system. Two secondary areas of vulnerability are the destruction or disclosure of the user organization's application programs either internal or external to the system and the physical destruction or taking of terminal equipment.

Risk Level.   Limited range of assets exposure.

General Safeguards.   The principal safeguards that seek to prevent these internal manipulations of data and application programs are the logical access controls imposed by the EDP Department. Detection safeguards for the same violations are critical action logs of the EDP Department and various audits. Safeguards designed to prevent these external manipulations of data and application programs are the file movement controls of the user department. Detection safeguards for the same violations are audits and surveillance systems. Safeguards against physical manipulation of the terminals are the physical access controls and alarm and surveillance systems of the Security Department.

Conclusions.   This individual is in a key position relative to the immediate user organization's data and programs entering the system and results exiting the system. Modification of data is considered more of a vulnerability than modification of programs since this individual is not apt to understand enough about the programs to do significant modification damage. A serious danger is that data or programs will be destroyed. If this involves the destruction of source documents for which there is no backup, then it is particularly serious. A mitigating factor is that any individual operator will be able to manipulate data and programs only for those application areas that he normally services.

Computer Operator

Function.   Operates a computer from the computer console, alters job schedules and priorities through the console, initiates utility program execution, responds to system error conditions according to documented instructions, mounts magnetic tapes and disk packs, powers up and powers down the system.

Knowledge.   Operating system functions, utility program functions, computer processing workflow, system accounting procedures, console protocol, privileged access procedures, physical access procedures.

Skills.   Typing and console operation, computer equipment operation, reading procedural documentation, reading and interpreting console messages.

Access.   Computer operations area, computer equipment area, files stored in operations area, procedural documentation, privileged access to the computer system.

Vulnerability.   The enterprise is vulnerable to both physical and operational violations from this individual. A general area of vulnerability is violations involving the destruction or disclosure of data, application programs, or systems programs internal to the system in main memory or on tape or disk. Other areas include violations affecting system service such as unauthorized use of services, those involving the physical manipulation of system equipment, and destruction or disclosure of data stored external to the system.

Risk Level.   Great range of assets exposure.

General Safeguards.   The principal prevention safeguards against manipulation of data and programs internal to the system are logical access controls imposed by the EDP Department. Detection safeguards for these same violations are critical action logs not subject to access by the operator, also the responsibility of the EDP Department. These same safeguards are effective against violations having to do with system service. For violations involving manipulation of data external to the system, effective prevention safeguards are file movement controls under the aegis of the Operations Group. Detection safeguards for the same violations are audits and surveillance systems of the Security Department. One must rely on physical access controls and alarm and surveillance systems from the Security Department to thwart physical manipulation of system equipment.

Conclusions.   This individual is in a key position relative to data and programs internal to the system. Although limited to console operations and programs already in the system, in the absence of other controls, a clever individual in this position would be likely to be able to gain access to any data file or program for the purpose of destruction or disclosure. Thus, it is important to have a set of internal controls, the details of which this individual does not know. Other useful measures or safeguards include introducing and examining of a log that records activities at the computer operator console and minimizing possible need for operator intervention in the running of application programs. This individual is also in the position to modify some data; that is, system data, not applications data.

Peripheral Equipment Operator

Function.   Operates all equipment immediately peripheral to the computer system having to do with input/output and file usage including card readers, paper tape readers, MICR readers, optical readers, tape drives, disk drives, sorters, tape cleaners, printers, card punches, paper tape punches, COM devices; loads and unloads removable media including punch cards, tape, disk packs, printer listings; installs expendable supplies on the equipment; sorts and labels output.

Knowledge.   Computer processing work flow, system accounting procedures, media library, physical access procedures.

Skills.   Peripheral equipment operation, reading procedural documentation.

Access.   Peripheral equipment area, job setup area, user output distribution area, input data, output results, procedural documentation, expendable supplies.

Vulnerabilities.   The enterprise is vulnerable to both physical and operational violations from this individual. The principal area of vulnerability is violations involving destruction or disclosure of data, application, and systems programs external to the system but in the general operations area. A secondary vulnerability possibility has to do with destruction or taking of equipment or supplies.

Risk Level.   Limited range of assets exposure.

General Safeguards.   The principal prevention safeguards against external data and program violations are file movement controls that are the responsibility of the Operations Group of the EDP Department. Detection safeguards for these same violations are audits and surveillance systems of the Security Department. Safeguards against physical manipulation of system equipment are physical access controls and alarm and surveillance systems of the Security Department.

Conclusions.   Although this individual will have access to much input data and output results, the physical situation is likely to be such that copying this information for the purpose of disclosure will be difficult. Certainly it will be somewhat easier to destroy such information. Special care should be taken to thwart one particular vulnerability, the individual's access to sensitive forms—such as blank paychecks.

Job Set-Up Clerk

Function.   Assembles jobs including data, programs, and job control information and physically places this material into job queues; requests data from media library; handles procedures for reruns and extraordinary user requests; may also distribute output results.

Knowledge.   Computer processing workflow, system accounting procedures, media library, physical access procedures.

Skills.   Reading job-related documentation, manual capabilities to handle punch cards and magnetic tapes.

Access.   Job setup area, user output distribution area, input data, procedural and data base documentation, may also have access to some media storage and other off-line files.

Vulnerabilities.   The enterprise is vulnerable to both physical and operational violations from this individual. The principal area of vulnerability is violations involving destruction or disclosure of data or application programs, external to the system but in the general operations area. A secondary vulnerability is destruction or taking of media; a tertiary and remote possibility is the taking of system service.

Risk Level.   Limited range of assets exposure.

General Safeguards. The principal prevention safeguards against these external data and program violations are file movement controls that are the responsibility of the Operations Group of the EDP Department. Detection safeguards for these same violations are audits and surveillance systems of the Security Department. Safeguards against physical manipulation of equipment or supplies are physical access controls and alarm and surveillance systems of the Security Department. Safeguards against the unauthorized taking of system service are various logical access controls and critical action logs of the EDP Department.

Conclusions. Although this individual will have access to much input data and many application programs, the physical situation is likely to be such that copying this information for the purpose of disclosure will be difficult. Certainly it will be somewhat easier to destroy such information. As mentioned above, the possibility of the individual taking system service exists but is very remote due to his lack of knowledge as to how the system works.

Data Entry and Update Clerk

Function. Adds, changes, or deletes records in data bases by means of on-line terminal entry, manual updates to punch card decks, or manual entries on data input forms.

Knowledge. Data base concepts; data base languages; data base files, formats, and content; security access controls; terminal protocol; identification/verification procedure; to some extent, computer processing workflow.

Skills. Typing and terminal or keypunch operation, reading procedural documentation.

Access. Terminal area, data source documents, terminal operation instructions, identification/verification materials, on-line files, documentation on data base structure and content, procedural documentation.

Vulnerabilities. The enterprise is vulnerable to physical and operational violations by this individual. The principal area of vulnerability is violations that involve the destruction or disclosure of data, application programs, or systems programs either internal or external to the system. In addition, this individual has the opportunity to modify data either internal or external to the system and to commit violations having to do with destruction and taking of terminal equipment.

Risk Level. Great range of assets exposure.

General Safeguards.   Since this individual is in a position to commit all categories of violations (to some degree) except for modification of programs and equipment, and system service violations, almost all safeguards address these vulnerabilities. For internal manipulation of data and programs, the common prevention safeguards are logical access controls administered by the EDP Department. Detection safeguards for the same kinds of violations are divided between use of critical action logs under the aegis of the EDP Department and various audits. For external manipulation of data and programs of the kind possible by this individual, the common preventive safeguards are data movement controls imposed by the Operations Group of the EDP Department. Detection safeguards for these violations are generally divided between surveillance systems of the Security Department and audits.

Conclusions.   This individual is in a key position relative to data entering the system. Different from many positions, this individual is able to modify the data as well as destroy and disclose. To minimize the risk, it will be important to install a dual control over changes, to divide the change process into a number of stages handled by different individuals, and to maintain a detailed data base change log. The danger of external manipulation of data is somewhat less than that for internal manipulation since it is likely that not all files will be updated by this clerk.

Tape Librarian

Function.   Files, retrieves, and accounts for off-line storage of data and programs on tape and other removable media; provides media to production control and job setup areas; cycles backup files to remote facilities.

Knowledge.   File names and labels, library and job accounting procedures, computer processing workflow, physical access procedures, archived files.

Skills.   Reading procedural documentation, record-keeping and filing.

Access.   Tape library, current and aging program and data files, interface to off-site remote storage facilities and to production control.

Vulnerabilities.   The enterprise is vulnerable to physical violations from this individual. The principal area of vulnerability is violation involving the destruction or disclosure of data or programs stored external to the system on removable media. A secondary area is violations involving the destruction or taking of the media.

Risk Level.   Limited range of assets exposure.

General Safeguards.   Safeguards to prevent unauthorized manipulation of this external data and programs include various kinds of file movement controls imposed by the Operations Group of the EDP Department. Detection safeguards include audits and surveillance systems. Safeguards addressing the problem of physical manipulation of media include various physical access controls and surveillance techniques that are the province of the Security Department.

Conclusions.   Lack of knowledge as to the content of the files being handled limits the likelihood of fraud by this individual. Physical manipulation of the media with the intent to vandalize is more likely.

User Tape Librarian

Function.   Files, retrieves, and accounts for off-line storage of data and application programs on tape and other removable media; provides media to user production control and job setup areas.

Knowledge.   File names and labels, library accounting procedures, physical access procedures.

Skills.   Reading procedural documentation, record-keeping, filing.

Access.   User tape library, program and data files.

Vulnerabilities.   The enterprise is vulnerable to physical violations from this individual. The principal area of vulnerability is violations involving the destruction or disclosure of data or programs stored external to the system on removable media. A secondary area is violations involving the destruction or taking of the media.

Risk Levels.   Low range of assets exposure.

General Safeguards.   Safeguards to prevent unauthorized manipulation of this external data and programs include various kinds of file movement controls imposed by the user department. Detection safeguards include audits and surveillance systems. Safeguards addressing the problem of physical manipulation of media include various physical access controls and surveillance techniques that are the province of the Security Department.

Conclusions.   Lack of knowledge as to the content of the files being handled limits the likelihood of fraud by this individual. Physical manipulation of the media with the intent to vandalize is more likely. Vulnerable assets are limited to those of only one user organization. Backup copies of data and programs in the data processing facility further limit vulnerabilities.

Systems Programmer

Function. Designs, develops, installs, documents, and maintains operating system and utility software, including programming language compilers, loaders, linkage editors, input/output routines, storage management software, program library access and maintenance routines, terminal and communication line handlers, system debugging facilities, system access controls, job scheduling routines, system accounting facilities, interrupt and trap servicing software, sorting and mathematical utility programs.

Knowledge. Operating systems, programming languages, terminal and computer console protocols, identification/verification procedures, computer processing workflow, hardware system architecture, elementary mathematical functions, boolean algebra, number systems, alphanumeric codes.

Skills. Programming and documentation, computer and peripheral equipment operation, reading and analyzing memory dumps and flowcharts, general diagnostic analysis.

Access. System programming area, system documentation, privileged access to the computer and data communciation systems.

Vulnerabilities. The enterprise is vulnerable to physical, operational and programming violations by this individual. A principal area of vulnerability is violations that involve the destruction or disclosure of data, application programs, or systems programs internal to the system in main memory or on tape and disk either by direct, real-time actions or through modification of system software. In addition, this individual is able to modify systems programs internal to the system and to modify, destroy*, or disclose systems programs external to the system. Another major area of vulnerability is violations that make unauthorized use or deny authorized use of system services. A secondary area is violations that involve the destruction or taking of terminal equipment.

Risk Level. Great range of assets exposure.

---

* It should be noted that this threat of destruction of system programs external to the system is not serious since most programs would be backed up with copies on the system.

General Safeguards. Some of the safeguards that are effective in preventing manipulation of data and programs internal to the system are the various logical access controls imposed by the Internal Control Section of the EDP Department. Others are the province of the Personnel and Auditing Departments. Safeguards that are effective for detecting these violations are various logs which are also the responsibility of the Internal Control Section. These same safeguards seem to be best for dealing with the problems of unauthorized use or denial of authorized use of system service. The vulnerability to manipulation of programs external to the system by this individual is addressed by various file movement control safeguards in the Operations Group of the EDP Department and surveillance systems of the Security Department.

Conclusions. This individual is in a position to attempt violations in a number of areas and the categories of safeguards mentioned above are apt to have less than total effectiveness in dealing with a clever systems programmer. Also, all safeguards implemented in software may have limited value since systems programmers are responsible for the design, implementation, and maintenance of such software, and have privileged access to the system.

Application Programmer

Function. Designs, develops, installs, documents, and maintains application programs and systems using a variety of programming languages.

Knowledge. Programming languages, EDP procedures and concepts, terminal protocols, identification/verification procedures, elementary mathematical functions, number systems, alphanumeric codes.

Skills. Programming and documentation, programming terminal operation, reading and analyzing memory dumps and flowcharts, general diagnostic analysis.

Access. Application programming area, application programs and their documentation.

Vulnerabilities. The enterprise is vulnerable to physical, operational, and programming violations by this individual. A principal area of vulnerability is violations that involve the modification, destruction, or disclosure of application programs either internal or external to the system. The individual may also modify, destroy, or disclose the parametric data for his programs. A secondary area of vulnerability is violations that involve the destruction of terminal equipment.

Risk Level.   Limited range of assets exposure.

General Safeguards.   To prevent this individual from manipulating programs and data internal to the system there are safeguards from various sources including the Personnel, Auditing and EDP Departments. Those from the EDP Department are generally of the logical access control type. Programmers must not be allowed access to current data files and production programs while in use. To prevent manipulation of programs external to the system, various file movement control safeguards from the Operations Group of the EDP Department can be used. Safeguards that are effective in detecting internal manipulation are the various logs that are the province of the Internal Control Section of the EDP Department. To detect external manipulation, surveillance safeguards may be used. Safeguards against physical manipulation of the terminals are the access controls and surveillance systems of the Security Department.

Conclusions.   This individual has limited accessibility to areas and facilities that would enable him to attempt violations. Essentially, he has access only to application programs and just the fraction that he is involved with. Conversely, his role with respect to these application programs is such that it is very difficult to be sure that safeguards against his violations will be effective.

User Programmer

Function.   Designs, develops, installs, documents, and maintains application programs and systems using a variety of programming languages.

Knowledge.   Programming languages, EDP procedures and concepts, terminal protocols, identification/verification procedures, elementary mathematical functions, number systems, alphanumeric codes.

Skills.   Programming and documentation, programming terminal operation, reading and analyzing memory dumps and flowcharts, general diagnostic analysis.

Access.   User application programming area, application programs and their documentation.

Vulnerabilities.   The enterprise is vulnerable to physical, operational, and programming violations by the individual. A principal area of vulnerability is violations that involve the modification, destruction, or disclosure of application programs either internal or external to the system. The individual may also modify, destroy, or disclose the parametric data for his programs. A secondary area of vulnerability is violations that involve the destruction or taking of terminal equipment.

Risk Level.   Limited range of assets exposure.

General Safeguards.   To prevent this individual from manipulating programs and data internal to the system, there are safeguards from various sources including the Personnel, Auditing, and EDP Departments. Those from the EDP Department are generally of the logical access control type. To prevent manipulation of programs external to the system, various file movement control safeguards from the user department can be used. Safeguards that are effective in detecting internal manipulation are the various logs that are the province of the Internal Control Section of the EDP Department. To detect external manipulation, surveillance safeguards may be used. Safeguards against physical manipulation of the terminals are the access controls and surveillance systems of the Security Department.

Conclusions.   This individual has limited accessibility to areas and facilities that would enable him to attempt violations. Essentially, he has access only to application programs and just the fraction that he is involved with. Conversely, his role with respect to these application programs is such that it is difficult to be sure that safeguards against his violations will be effective.

Terminal Engineer

Function.   Tests, diagnoses, repairs, replaces, assembles, and disassembles terminals or their components.

Knowledge.   Electronic, mechanical, and communication engineering; digital logic design; physical access procedures; boolean algebra.

Skills.   Operation of terminals and electronic test equipment, reading circuit schematics and diagnostic manuals.

Access.   Terminals and adjacent facilities, network diagram, procedural documentation.

Vulnerabilities.   The enterprise is vulnerable to physical, operational, and engineering violations by this individual. The principal and only area of serious vulnerability is violations that involve the modification, destruction, or taking of terminal equipment.

Risk Level.   Low range of assets exposure.

General Safeguards.   The principal safeguards against physical manipulation of terminals are physical access controls and alarm and surveillance systems under the aegis of the Security Department.

Conclusions. Although allowing a well-trained man access to a terminal would appear to pose a multifaceted threat to system security, the only true vulnerability is to physical manipulation of terminal equipment.

Computer Systems Engineer

Function. Tests, diagnoses, repairs, replaces, assembles, and disassembles computer system hardware and components including computers, terminals, peripheral devices, and communication equipment.

Knowledge. Electronic, mechanical, and communication engineering, programming languages, digital logic design, terminal protocols, physical access procedures, boolean algebra.

Skills. Operation of terminals, computer consoles, peripheral devices, communication equipment, and electronic test equipment, programming and documentation, reading and analyzing memory dumps and flowcharts, reading circuit schematics and diagnostic manuals, general diagnostic analysis.

Access. All equipment and adjacent facilities, some system programs with documentation, documentation for all equipment, procedural documentation.

Vulnerabilities. The enterprise is vulnerable to physical, operational, programming, and engineering violations by this individual. The two principal areas of vulnerability are violations that involve the modification, destruction, or taking of system equipment and those that involve unauthorized use or denial of authorized use of system service. A secondary area is violations that involve modification, destruction, or disclosure of system programs internal to the system.

Risk Level. Moderate range of assets exposure.

General Safeguards. The principal safeguards for both preventing and detecting manipulation of system equipment are the responsibility of the Security Department and consist of physical access controls and alarm and surveillance systems. In the case of violations involving system service, typical prevention safeguards are logical access controls, and detection safeguards are critical use logs. Both are under the aegis of the EDP Department. Controls against misuse of systems programs internal to the system are almost the same as those for system service violations. It is assumed that maintenance work is not permitted while users' data and programs are present in the system.

Conclusions.   This individual poses as great a threat as anyone in the installation to physical abuse of system equipment and manipulation of system service. Although he might appear to have ready access to other sensitive areas as well, it is possible to effect controls to minimize vulnerability in these other areas.

Communications Engineer/Operator

Function.   Tests, diagnoses, repairs, replaces, assembles and disassembles, operates data communications equipment including concentrators, multiplexors, modems, and line switching units. Reconfigures communications network when necessary.

Knowledge.   Electronic and communications engineering, data communication, terminal protocols, identification/verification procedures, physical access procedures, boolean algebra.

Skills.   Operation of terminals, communications equipment and electronic test equipment, reading circuit schematics and diagnostic manuals, reading procedural documentation.

Access.   Communications equipment and adjacent facilities, circuit and network diagrams, procedural documentation.

Vulnerabilities.   The enterprise is vulnerable to physical, operational, and engineering violations by this individual. The principal area of vulnerability is violations that involve the destruction or disclosure of data that is internal to the system and is being transmitted in the communications system. A secondary area is violations that involve the modification, destruction, or taking of terminal or communications equipment.

Risk Level.   Limited range of assets exposure.

General Safeguards.   Principal safeguards for either preventing or detecting manipulation of data internal to the system are imposed by the EDP Department; for prevention, various logical access controls are effective; for detection, critical use logs may be utilized. In addition, safeguards from the Personnel and Auditing Departments will be helpful in preventing this type of violation. The principal safeguards against physical manipulation of terminals and communications equipment are the responsibility of the Security Department and consist of physical access controls, alarm and surveillance systems.

Conclusions. Although this individual is in a position to intercept data for later disclosure, he is not likely to have enough knowledge about the data files to be able to make a judicious selection of material to disclose. The threat from this individual is greater in the area of malicious acts that would serve to disrupt computer processing such as destruction of data files or manipulation of terminal or communications equipment.

Facilities Engineer

Function. Inspects, adjusts, diagnoses, repairs, replaces, assembles, and disassembles equipment supporting computer and terminal equipment, such as power, water, light, heat, and air conditioning equipment.

Knowledge. Electrical and mechanical engineering, physical access procedures.

Skills. Use of test equipment, reading building, circuit and engineering schematics, reading diagnostic manuals.

Access. All building areas, building and support equipment diagrams and documentation.

Vulnerabilities. The enterprise is vulnerable to physical violations by this individual. The two principal areas of vulnerability are violations that involve denial of authorized system service and destruction or taking of system equipment. A minor area is the modification of system support equipment.

Risk Level. Limited range of assets exposure.

General Safeguards. The principal safeguards against the physical manipulation of system equipment and the type of system service denial violation that this individual might perpetrate are physical access controls and alarm and surveillance systems under the aegis of the Security Department.

Conclusions. This individual's authorized access to all areas makes him a prime candidate for malicious acts that would serve to disrupt system operation. Similarly, he has greater opportunity than most individuals to take system and system support equipment. Also, because of his authorized access, it is not likely that prevention safeguards will be very effective in his case.

Operations Manager

Function.   Designs, develops, installs, modifies, documents, maintains, and manages the computer processing workflow system through direction given to operational subordinates. He is also responsible for physical security of system equipment, and data and programs on removable media stored in the operations area. He may be the assigner of terminal and facilities access control passwords.

Knowledge.   Computer processing workflow system, hardware configuration architecture, operations procedures for data files, media storage, job accounting, physical access, and system integration and maintenance, operating system and utility software.

Skills.   Developing and reading flowcharts, principles of operation manuals, and other procedural documentation, performing systems analysis and general diagnostic analysis, management.

Access.   Computer and peripheral equipment facilities, job input/output, scheduling and servicing areas, tape library and its media contents, system documentation and all procedural documentation, data files, application programs, and systems programs internal to the system.

Vulnerabilities.   The enterprise is vulnerable to physical and operational violations by this individual. There are several areas of serious vulnerability to actions by this individual. Primary areas are the destruction or disclosure of data, application programs, or systems programs internal to the system, destruction or taking of system equipment, and unauthorized use or denial of authorized use of system services. In addition, this individual is in a position to destroy or disclose those data files, application programs, and system programs* that are stored in the tape (or media) library, and he can modify parametric data either internal or external to the system.

Risk Level.   Great range of assets exposure.

General Safeguards.   Since this individual is in a position to commit all categories of violations except for modification of programs and system equipment, almost all safeguards address one of these vulnerabilities. Principal prevention safeguards against destruction or disclosure of data or programs internal to the system are logical access controls imposed by the EDP Department while effective detection safeguards are various critical

---

* It should be noted that the threat of destruction of system programs external to the system is not serious since most of these programs would be backed up with copies in the system.

use logs, also the responsibility of the EDP Department. This same set of safeguards is effective against violations having to do with system service. Safeguards against destruction and taking of system equipment are physical access controls and alarm and surveillance systems under the aegis of the Security Department.

Conclusions. As mentioned above, this individual is in a position to attempt many categories of violations. Also, many of the safeguards against his possible violations are the responsibility of the EDP Department, of which he is a key member. Fortunately, with the preferred organization of the EDP Department, there is a System Control Group on the same level as this individual's Operations Group. Almost all safeguards of the EDP Department that are intended to thwart serious violations by this individual are the responsibility of the System Control Group or the EDP Department headquarters.

Data Base Administrator

Function. Responsible for adding, changing, and deleting records in on-line and off-line data bases.

Knowledge. Data base concepts, data base languages, data base files, formats, and content, computer processing workflow, security access controls, terminal protocol, identification/verification procedure.

Skills. Typing and terminal operation, reading procedural documentation, performing general diagnostic analysis.

Access. Terminal area, tape (or media) library in the operations area, on-line files, data source documents, documentation on data base structure and content, procedural documentation.

Vulnerabilities. The enterprise is vulnerable to physical and operational violations by this individual. There are two areas of serious vulnerability to actions by this individual. He has internal and external access to all data that are maintained by the EDP Department and since one of his charters is responsibility for modifying these files, the operation is vulnerable to modification of data as well as to destruction and disclosure. A secondary area of vulnerability is violations that involve destruction or taking of terminal equipment.

Risk Level. Limited range of assets exposure.

General Safeguards. For internal manipulation of data, the common prevention safeguards are logical access controls administered by the EDP

Department. Detection safeguards for the same kind of violations are divided between critical usage logs under the aegis of the EDP Department and a variety of audits. For external manipulation of data of the kind possible by this individual, the common prevention safeguards are data movement controls imposed by the Operations Group of the EDP Department. Detection safeguards for these violations are generally divided between surveillance systems of the Security Department and audits.

Conclusions.   With the proper organization of the EDP Department, this individual will not be administering safeguards that are designed to thwart his violations. The nature of his responsibility, to modify and make corrections to all files, makes detecting his violations particularly difficult.

Programming Manager

Function.   Designs, develops, installs, documents, and maintains application programs through direction given to subordinates.

Knowledge.   Programming languages, EDP procedures and concepts, application subject areas, advanced programming and software engineering techniques, data base design procedure, terminal protocol, identification/verification procedures, computer processing workflow, elementary mathematical functions, number systems, alphanumeric codes.

Skills.   Programming and documentation, terminal operation, reading and analyzing memory dumps and flowcharts, systems and general diagnostic analysis, management.

Access.   Application programming area, application programs and their documentation.

Vulnerabilities.   The enterprise is vulnerable to physical, operational, and programming violations by this individual. A principal area of vulnerability is violations that involve the modification, destruction or disclosure of application programs either internal or external to the system. The individual may also modify, destroy, or disclose parametric data for the programs he is responsible for. A secondary area of vulnerability is violations that involve the destruction or taking of terminal equipment.

Risk Level.   Moderate range of assets exposure.

General Safeguards.   To prevent this individual from manipulating programs and data internal to the system, there are safeguards from various sources including the Personnel, Auditing, and EDP Departments. Those from the EDP Department are generally of the logical access control type.

To prevent manipulation of programs external to the system, various file movement control safeguards from the Operations Group of the EDP Department can be used. Safeguards that are effective in detecting internal manipulation are the various critical usage logs that are the province of the Internal Control Section of the EDP Department. To detect external manipulation, surveillance safeguards may be used. Safeguards against physical manipulation of the terminals are the physical access controls and alarm and surveillance systems of the Security Department.

Conclusions. This individual has limited accessibility to areas and facilities that would enable him to attempt violations. Essentially, he has access only to the application programs generated and maintained by his group. Conversely, his role with respect to the development of these application programs is such that it is very difficult to be sure that safeguards against his actions will be effective.

Security Specialist

Function. Plans, implements, installs, operates, maintains, and evaluates physical, operational, technical, procedural, and personnel-related safeguards and controls.

Knowledge. Security (including identification) concepts, EDP software and hardware technology, industrial security products, procedural, operational, and personnel policies and practices.

Skills. A level of electronic, mechanical, and programming skills sufficient to allow him to conceive and implement suitable safeguards, reading building, circuit, and engineering schematics, reading diagnostic manuals, reading and analyzing memory dumps and flowcharts.

Access. Privileged access to all areas and all systems functions.

Vulnerabilities. The enterprise is vulnerable to all manner of violations by this individual.

Risk Level. Greatest range of assets exposure.

General Safeguards. This individual is in a total position of trust. Since he has complete information on all safeguards, it is unlikely that the safeguards would lead to detection of a clever Security Officer intent on a particular violation.

Conclusions. Because of the impossibility of detecting violations, candidates for this position should be screened with care. In practice, the individual will often have insufficient knowledge and skills to attempt unauthorized acts in some of the violation areas.

EDP Auditor

Function. Performs operational, software, and data file reviews to determine integrity, adequacy, performance, security, and compliance with organizational and generally accepted policies, procedures, and standards; participates in design specification of applications to assure adequacy of controls; performs data processing services for auditors.

Knowledge. Audit techniques, controls, safeguards, system design, software organization, computer applications, facilities security.

Skills. Use of audit tools, programming and documentation, reading technical, operational, and procedural documentation, general diagnostic analysis.

Access. Privileged access to all areas and all system functions.

Vulnerabilities. All manner of violations are possible by this individual.

Risk Level. Greatest range of assets exposure.

General Safeguards. This individual is in a total position of trust. Since he has complete information on all safeguards, it is unlikely that the safeguards would lead to detection of a clever EDP auditor intent on a particular violation.

Conclusions. Because of the impossibility of detecting violations, candidates for this position should be screened with great care. All avenues—screening by external CPA auditors, screening by examiners from regulatory agencies, and peer review of the individual's work and activities—should be used to ascertain that the candidate is competent and trustworthy.

Appendix G

EDP AUDIT TOOLS AND TECHNIQUES

These descriptions of tools and techniques have been abstracted from *Systems Auditability and Control,* published by the Institute of Internal Auditors, Inc. (International Headquarters, 249 Maitland Avenue, Altamonte Springs, Florida 32701), 1977, and prepared by SRI International in consultation with the IIA. The IIA reports give more detailed descriptions of the 17 tools and techniques.

Test Data Method

The test data method verifies processing accuracy of computer application systems by executing these systems using specially prepared sets of input data that produce preestablished results. The method gives internal auditors a procedure for the verification of computer programs and applications. It is a method that can be used by internal auditors with only a modest data processing background when testing specific and limited program functions. It is a good technique to use initially in program verification because tests can be expanded incrementally, providing a learning situation for less experienced internal auditors. Special procedures are not usually required. The test data method is limited to computer processing verification and evaluation and is not an appropriate technique for verification of production data. No evidence is provided concerning the completeness or accuracy of production input data or masterfiles.

Occupations Affected:

Computer operator	Systems engineer
Peripheral operator	Communications engineer
Job setup clerk	Network manager
Systems programmer	Operations manager
Application programmer	Programming manager

Base Case System Evaluation

Base case system evaluation (BCSE) is a technique that applies a standardized body of data (input, parameters, and output) to the testing of a computer application system. This body of data, the base case, is established by user personnel, with internal audit concurrence, as the criterion for correct functioning of the computer application system. This testing process is most widely used as a technique for validation of production computer application systems. One major manufacturing company, however, utilizes the base case approach as a "means to test programs during their development, to demonstrate the successful operation of the system prior to its installation, and to verify its continuing accurate operation during its life." As such, this approach represents a total commitment by corporate management and each user department to the principles and disciplines of BCSE.

Occupations Affected:

Computer operator	Systems engineer
Peripheral operator	Communications engineer
Job setup clerk	Network manager
Systems programmer	Operations manager
Application programmer	Programming manager

Integrated Test Facility

Integrated test facility (ITF) is a technique to review those functions of an automated application that are internal to the computer. Internal auditor's test data are used to compare ITF processing results to precalculated test results. The method is most frequently used to test and verify large computer application systems when it is not practical to separately cycle test data. The ITF technique is used for computer processing verification and evaluation and is of limited value for the verification of production data or data files. Limited evidence is provided concerning the completeness and accuracy of production input data or masterfiles.

Occupations Affected:

Communications operator	Systems engineer
Systems programmer	Programming manager
Application programmer	

Parallel Simulation

Parallel simulation is the use of one or more special computer programs to process "live" data files and simulate normal computer application processing. As opposed to the test data method and the integrated test facility, which process test data through "live" programs, the parallel simulation method processes "live" data through test programs. Parallel simulation programs include only the application logic, calculations, and controls that are relevant to specific audit objectives. As a result, simulation programs are usually much less complex than their application program counterparts. Large segments of major applications that consist of several computer programs can often be simulated for audit purposes with a single parallel simulation program. Parallel simulation permits the internal auditor to independently verify complex and critical application system procedures.

Occupations Affected:

Computer operator	Systems engineer
Peripheral operator	Communications engineer
Communications operator	Network manager
Systems programmer	Operations manager
Application programmer	Programming manager

Transaction Selection

The transaction selection audit technique uses an independent computer program to monitor and select transactions for internal audit review. The method enables the internal auditor to examine and analyze transaction volumes and error rates, and to statistically sample specified transactions. Transaction selection audit software is totally independent of the production computer application system and is generally parameter-controlled. No alteration to the production computer application system is required. This technique is especially suitable for noncontinuous monitoring and sampling of transactions in complex computer application systems.

Occupations Affected:

Transaction operator	Communications engineer
Peripheral operator	Network manager
Data entry & update clerk	Operations manager
Communications operator	Data base manager
Terminal engineer	Identification control clerk

Embedded Audit Data Collection

Embedded audit data collection uses one or more specially programmed data collection modules embedded in the computer application system to select and record data for subsequent analysis and evaluation. The data collection modules are inserted in the computer application system at points determined to be appropriate by the internal auditor. The internal auditor also determines the criteria for selection and recording. After collection, other automated or manual methods may be used to analyze the collected data.

As distinct from other audit methods, this technique uses "in-line" code (i.e., the computer application program performs the audit data collection function at the same time it processes data for normal production purposes). This has two important consequences for the auditor: in-line code ensures the availability of a comprehensive or a very specialized sample of data (strategically placed modules have access to every data element being processed); retrofitting this technique to an existing system is more costly than implementing the audit programming during system development. Because of this, it is preferable for the internal auditor to specify his requirements while the system is being designed.

Occupations Affected:

Transaction operator	Systems engineer
Computer operator	Communications engineer
Peripheral operator	Network manager
Job setup clerk	Operations manager
Data entry & update clerk	Data base manager
Communications operator	Identification control clerk
Terminal engineer	

Extended Records

The extended records technique gathers together by means of a special program or programs all the significant data that have affected the processing of an individual transaction. This includes the accumulation into a single record of results of processing over the time period that the transaction required to complete processing. The extended record includes data from all the computer application systems that contributed to the processing of a transaction. Such extended records are compiled into files that provide a conveniently accessible source for transaction data.

With this technique, the auditor no longer need review several files to determine how a specific transaction was processed. With extended records, data are consolidated from different accounting periods and different computer application systems so that a complete transaction audit trail is physically included in one computer record. This facilitates tests of compliance to organization policies and procedures.

Occupations Affected:

Transaction operator	Communications engineer
Peripheral operator	Network manager
Data entry & update clerk	Operations manager
Systems programmer	Data base manager
Application programmer	Programming manager
Terminal engineer	Identification control clerk
Systems engineer	

Generalized Audit Software

Generalized audit software is the most widely used technique for auditing computer application systems. This technique permits the internal auditor to independently analyze a computer application system file. Most generalized audit software packages, because of their widespread use and long history, are ultra-reliable, highly flexible, and extensively and accurately documented. Generalized audit software programs are currently available that can foot, cross-foot, balance, stratify, select a statistical sample, select transactions, total, compare, and perform calculations on diverse data elements contained within various data files. These extensive abilities are available to the internal auditor to substantively test computer application systems. Generally, this audit method is used to test computer file data; little facility is present to test system logic, other than implicitly by the results that appear in the data files. No explicit compliance testing facility is contained in these programs. Historically, generalized audit software programs operated only in the batch mode. Recently, with the rapid expansion of on-line computer application systems, on-line generalized audit software has become available.

Occupations Affected:

Transaction operator	Terminal engineer
Computer operator	Systems engineer
Peripheral operator	Communications engineer
Job setup clerk	Network manager
Data entry & update clerk	Operations manager
Communications operator	Data base manager
Media librarian	Programming manager
Systems programmer	Identification control clerk
Application programmer	

Snapshot

Both internal auditors and data processing personnel periodically encounter difficulty in reconstructing the computer decision-making process. The cause is a failure to keep together all the data elements involved in that process. Snapshot is a technique that, in effect, takes a picture of the parts of computer memory that contain the data elements involved in a computerized decision-making process at the time the decision is made. The results of the snapshot are printed in report format for reconstructing the decision-making process.

The snapshot audit technique offers the capability of listing all the data that were involved in a specific decision-making process. The technique requires the logic to be preprogrammed in the system. A mechanism, usually a special code in the transaction record, is added for triggering the printing of the data in question for analysis.

The snapshot audit technique helps internal auditors answer questions as to why computer application systems produce questionable results. It provides information to explain why a particular decision was developed by the computer. Snapshot used in conjunction with other audit techniques (e.g., integrated test facility or tracing) provides the determination of what results would occur if a certain type of input entered the data processing system. The snapshot audit technique also can be an invaluable aid to systems and programming personnel in debugging the application system because it can provide snapshots of computer memory as a debugging aid.

Occupations Affected:

Systems programmer	Communications engineer
Application programmer	Network manager
Terminal engineer	Data base manager
Systems engineer	Programming manager

Tracing

A traditional audit technique in a manual environment is to follow the path of a transaction during processing. For example, an auditor picks up an order as it is received into an organization and follows the flow from work station to work station. The internal auditor asks the clerk involved what actions were taken at that particular step in the processing cycle. Understanding the policies and procedures of the organization, the internal auditor can judge whether they are being adequately followed.

By the time the internal auditor has walked through the processing cycle, he or she has a good appreciation of how work flows through the organization. In a data processing environment, it is not possible to follow the part of a transaction through its processing cycle solely by following the paperwork flow. Many of the functions performed by clerks and the movement of hardcopy documents are replaced by electronic processing of data.

Tracing is an audit technique that provides the internal auditor with the ability to perform an electronic walk-through of a data processing application system. The audit objective of tracing is to verify compliance with policies and procedures by substantiating, through examination of the path through a program that a transaction followed, how that transaction was processed. It can be used to verify omissions. Tracing shows what instructions have been executed in a computer program and in which sequence they have been executed. Since the instructions in a computer program represent the steps in processing, the processes that have been executed can be determined from the results of the tracing audit technique. Once an internal auditor knows what instructions in a program have been executed, an analysis can be performed to determine if the processing conformed to organization procedures.

Occupations Affected:

Systems programmer	Communications engineer
Application programmer	Network manager
Terminal engineer	Programming manager
Systems engineer	

Mapping

Mapping is a technique to assess the extent of system testing and to identify specific program logic that has not been tested. Mapping is performed by a software measurement tool that analyzes a computer program during execution to indicate whether program statements have been executed. The software measurement tool can also determine the amount of CPU time consumed by each program segment.

The original intent of the mapping concept was to help computer programmers ensure the quality of their programs. However, auditors can use these same software measurement tools to look for unexecuted code. This analysis can provide the auditor with insight into the efficiency of program operation and can reveal unauthorized program segments included for execution for unauthorized purposes.

Occupations Affected:

Systems programmer   Programming manager
Application programmer

Control Flowcharting

In a complex business environment, it is difficult to thoroughly understand the total system of control of an organization within its total business and operational context. A graphic technique, or flowchart, for simplifying the identification and interrelationships of controls can be a great help in evaluating the adequacy of those controls and in assessing the impact of system changes on the overall control profile. Flowcharts facilitate the explanation of controls to a system analyst or external auditor, or to personnel unfamiliar with specific operational systems; they also aid in ascertaining that controls are operating as originally intended.

The audit area control flowchart technique provides the documentation necessary to explain the system of control. Often an organization's information about controls is fragmented. This makes it difficult to obtain a clear picture of the controls operating within the organization. The availability of an overall picture of controls, using several levels of flowcharts, facilitates understanding.

Occupations Affected:

Communications operator   Operations manager
Systems programmer   Data base manager
Application programmer   Programming manager
Network manager

Job Accounting Data Analysis

Job accounting facilities are available through most computer vendors as an adjunct to their operating systems. The job accounting facility is a feature of the computer operating system software that provides the means for gathering and recording information to be used for billing customers or evaluating systems usage. Examples of information collected by a job accounting facility are job start and completion times, usage of data sets, and usage of hardware facilities. These job accounting systems were designed by the vendors to serve the operating needs of the data processing department. However, much of the information provided by these facilities is of interest to internal auditors.

Two types of job accounting data, the accounting records and the data set activity records, are of interest to the internal auditor. Accounting records consist of records that show which user used which programs, how often, and for how long. They include an identification of the user, the hardware features required by the job, the time it took to perform the job, and how the job was completed. Data set activity records provide information about which data files were used during processing and who requested the use of the data sets. Among the information contained in these records are the data set name, record length, serial number of the volumes, and the user of the data set.

The internal auditor can use data from the accounting records to verify charges for use of the computer resources. They also enable the auditor to verify that only authorized individuals use the computer. Data set activity records provide the auditor with a means to verify that data are being used by authorized individuals.

Occupations Affected:

Transaction operator	Application programmer
Computer operator	Network manager
Peripheral operator	Operations manager
Job setup clerk	Data base manager
Communications operator	Programming manager
Media librarian	Identification control clerk

System Development Life Cycle

In computer application programs, careful development can prevent expensive after-the-fact changes. Data processing professionals are increasingly devoting time to reviewing and checking computer application systems during development to minimize costly modifications after installation. EDP auditors are taking advantage of this approach on the part of data processing to strengthen their own review of the development process. In so doing, the auditor and the data processor are ensured that their computer application system objectives are fully met.

Occupations Affected:

Systems programmer	Operations manager
Application programmer	Programming manager

System Acceptance and Control Group

When the EDP auditor decides to monitor and review the computer application development process, the auditor must determine how to best perform the review. Although the substance of the review is unchanged, the EDP auditor may choose to perform the review personally or to rely on the efforts of another group. To perform the review personally is the choice made by many EDP auditors, even though substantial effort and training may be required to do an effective job. The fact that much of the training required has to do with data processing rather than with EDP auditing has, among other factors, caused the auditors at a large insurance company to choose another approach. The company has established, in the data processing department, a Systems Acceptance and Control (SAC) Group to perform systematic reviews of computer application system developments and to create and maintain effective computer application system standards, particularly in the area of auditability.

Occupations Affected:

Systems programmer	Systems engineer
Application programmer	Communications engineer
Terminal engineer	Programming manager

Code Comparison

Code comparison entails comparison of two copies, made at different times, of the program coding for a particular application. The objective of this technique is to verify that program change and maintenance procedures and program library procedures are being followed correctly. The auditor uses the output of the comparison to identify changes that have occurred between the making of the two copies. The auditor then locates and analyzes the documentation that was prepared to authorize and execute the changes. This technique supports compliance testing rather than substantive testing. Code comparison is especially useful for auditing programs that perform critical business functions and are subject to continuing change.

Occupations Affected:

Computer operator

Job setup clerk

Systems programmer

Application programmer

Terminal engineer

Systems engineer

Communications engineer

Operations manager

Programming manager

Disaster Testing

Most computer service centers develop plans for dealing with disaster. The disaster testing technique tests the validity of these plans by exercising the methods that would be used in such an event. The disasters provided for may include complete destruction of the computer service center.

The objective of a disaster plan is to ensure effective protection against loss of corporate information. The auditor, on an unannounced basis, simulates a disaster in the computer service center to test the adequacy of the center's contingency plans. The test is performed periodically.

Occupations Affected:

Transaction operator

Computer operator

Peripheral operator

Communications operator

Media librarian

Terminal engineer

Systems engineer

Communications engineer

Facilities engineer

Network manager

Operations manager

Data base manager

Identification control clerk

EDP CONTROLS

The following listing refers the user of this guide to descriptions of the eight primary types of EDP controls. Each description also includes a list of specific controls which are examples of that type, a list of occupations which are the object of that type, and a list of occupations which are responsible for that type of control. These descriptions of control types have been abstracted from *Systems Auditability and Control,* published by the Institute of Internal Auditors, Inc. (International Headquarters, 249 Maitland Avenue, Altamonte Springs, Florida 32701), 1977, and prepared by SRI International in consultation with the 11A. The 11A reports give more detailed descriptions of the eight types of controls.

Transaction Origination

Transaction origination controls are used to ensure the accuracy and completeness of data before they enter the computer application system. The scope of the transaction origination control area includes controls up to the point of converting data to a machine-readable format. Management, systems personnel, and auditors are placing increasing emphasis on transaction origination controls to ensure that the information prepared for entry into the system is valid, reliable, cost-effective, and not subject to compromise.

Examples of Controls

Origination procedures	Approvals
Forms design	Identification
Document storage	Error handling
Dual custody handling	Manual review
Source data retention	Batch and balance
Separation of duties	Tagging
Authorization	Transmittal

Occupations Object of Controls

Transaction operator	Communications engineer
Communications operator	Network manager
Terminal engineer	Identification control clerk

Occupations Responsible for Controls

Application programmer	Security officer
Programming manager	EDP auditor

Data Processing Transaction Entry

Transaction entry controls are used to ensure the accuracy and completeness of data during their entry into the computer application system. The scope of the transaction entry control area includes controls up to the point of data entering the communication link or, in a nondata communication environment, entry into computer application programs for further processing.

Transaction entry controls are a combination of manual and automated control routines. They are of particular importance because they control two important application areas: data conversion and edit and validation. Increasingly, the emphasis is on automating as many control routines as possible to take advantage of computer hardware abilities and to promote consistency in the application of controls.

Examples of Controls

Written procedures	Data validation
Protected locations	Batch proof and balancing
Terminal data entry	Error handling
Transcription verification	

Occupations Object of Controls

Transaction operator	Communications operator
Peripheral operator	Communications engineer
Job setup clerk	Network manager
Data entry and update clerk	Data base manager

Occupations Responsible for Controls

Application programmer	Security officer
Terminal engineer	EDP auditor
Programming manager	

Data Communication

Data communication controls are primarily concerned with ensuring the integrity of data as they pass through communication lines from the message input devices to the message reception devices. These controls are important because most data communication equipment is owned and controlled by organizations other than the sending or receiving organizations. These controls are also important because there is a fast-growing trend by many organizations to use data communication services as an integral part of their computer application systems. Consequently, to ensure the accuracy and completeness of data for the entire application system, internal auditors are expected to understand and review this area.

Examples of Controls
Input device identification   Message transmission
Protected locations   Message reception validation
Message identification   and accounting
   and logging   Error handling

Occupations Object of Controls
Communications operator   Operations manager
Terminal engineer

Occupations Responsible for Controls
Systems programmer   Programming manager
Application programmer   Security officer
Communications engineer   EDP auditor
Network manager

Computer Processing

Computer processing controls, which are used to ensure accuracy and completeness of data during computer processing, are the controls that govern computer process integrity and computer process error handling. These controls are applied after the entry of data into the computer application system as application programs process the data. File interface and program interfaces are also included.

The scope of computer processing controls discussed here includes application level controls that are built in and around the central processing unit. These controls are built into each individual application program and control application program data input, processing, and output. Because application controls are unique and specific in one application, they may or may not be transferable between applications. During the continuing development of computer processing controls, it is important to ensure that the principles of internal control (e.g., separation of functions) are being carried forward to the functions performed by the computer application system.

Examples of Controls
Transaction identification   Operation instructions
Computation and logic   Error handling
File balancing

Occupations Object of Controls
Transaction operator   Data entry and update clerk
Computer operator   Communications operator
Peripheral operator   Terminal engineer
Job setup clerk   Communications engineer

Network manager   Data base manager
Operations manager   Identification control clerk

Occupations Responsible for Controls
Systems programmer   Programming manager
Application programmer   Security officer
Systems engineer   EDP auditor

Data Storage and Retrieval

Data storage and retrieval controls are important to ensure the accuracy and completeness of data during the process of data storage and retrieval.

The scope of computer data storage and retrieval controls includes those controls in effect during file handling and file error handling. These controls govern the file-handling processes that are not directly associated with the computer processing of the application system.

Data storage and retrieval controls are of particular importance because they involve a high degree of human intervention and data handling. For this reason it is important to provide the facility and personnel procedures necessary to control the integrity of data files and programs during intermediate storage and retrieval.

Examples of Controls
Library procedures   Backup
File access   Error handling
File maintenance

Occupations Object of Controls
Computer operator   Media librarian
Peripheral operator   Terminal engineer
Job setup clerk   Operations manager
Data entry and update clerk Data base manager
Communications operator Identification control clerk

Occupations Responsible for Controls
Systems programmer   Programming manager
Application programmer   Security officer
Systems engineer   EDP auditor

Output Processing

Output processing controls are used to ensure the integrity of output data from the conclusion of computer processing until their delivery to the functional user.

The functional user is dependent on the prompt delivery of complete and accurate data to conduct the day-to-day business functions. If the organization has proper input and processing controls, computer output is usually correct. However, output controls play an important part in achieving the control objectives associated with the overall computerized record-keeping system. The function of output control is to ensure that processed information includes authorized, complete, and accurate data. The scope of output controls includes the control areas of data processing balancing and reconciliation, output distribution, user balancing and reconciliation, records retention, accountable documents control, and output error handling.

Output controls are important as a control interface between the functional user and data processing. The primary method by which data processing and users ensure that the integrity of data has been maintained during processing is by monitoring application system output.

Output controls are those controls that can be used to control the output and distribution of information from the computer application system.

Examples of Controls

Reconciliation, logging and review	Retention and disposal
Handling and distribution	Accountable document handling
User balancing and reconciliation	Error handling

Occupations Object of Controls

Transaction operator	Terminal engineer
Computer operator	Communications engineer
Peripheral operator	Operations manager
Job setup clerk	Data base manager
Communications operator	Identification control clerk
Media librarian	

Occupations Responsible for Controls

Systems programmer	Programming manager
Application programmer	Security officer
Systems engineer	EDP auditor

Computer Service Center

The accuracy and completeness of records and reports produced by the data processing function depends on the general controls governing computer service center operations and on application controls. Inadequate controls within the computer service center or failure to comply with established controls can result in errors in data preparation and handling, production scheduling, file updating and output report preparation. The controls are functionally independent of application controls but are of equal importance to the accuracy of the results of data processing. The failure of general controls within the computer service center can defeat the objectives of the most elaborate application controls. As such, controls are of great concern to both data processors and internal auditors. The importance of this is demonstrated by survey results, which state the most important goals or objectives of internal auditing when reviewing the data processing department:

- Development of more built-in audit controls
- Enhancement of security (data access, separation of duties, etc.)
- Monitoring methods and procedures to ensure accurate data processing performance.

Computer service center controls can contribute substantially to the fulfillment of all of these objectives.

Examples of Controls

Input/output scheduling	Environment and physical security
Media library	Separation of duties
Malfunction reporting and repair	Billing and charge-out
	Disaster recovery

Occupations Object of Controls

Computer operator	Systems engineer
Peripheral operator	Communications engineer
Job setup clerk	Network manager
Data entry and update clerk	Data base manager
Communications operator	Programming manager
Media librarian	Identification control clerk

Occupations Responsible for Controls

Facilities engineer	Security officer
Operations manager	EDP auditor

Application System Development

The adequacy and effectiveness of controls included in computer application systems are affected by the methods and procedures used during the system development process. Controls over the system development process are important for three reasons:

(1) Good development controls assist in managing costs and schedules.

(2) They help ensure that appropriate application controls are built into application systems being developed.

(3) They ensure that application controls are properly tested before application systems become operational.

By carefully controlling the system development process, one can achieve higher levels of accuracy and reliability in the computer application systems developed and satisfy the goals of developing quality application systems within cost and on schedule.

Elements of the application system development process documented by SRI include project management, programming techniques, development and acceptance testing, program change control, documentation, and data base administration.

Examples of Controls

Life cycle step reviews

Structural program audit trail

Acceptance testing

Program change review

Documentation review

Data base administration

Occupations Object of Controls

Systems programmer

Application programmer

Occupations Responsible for Controls

Programming manager

Security officer

EDP auditor

Appendix I

COMPUTER SECURITY SURVEY QUESTIONNAIRE:
INTERNAL COMMUNICATION

To: All EDP User Department Heads   *From:* Sr. Vice President
Electronic Data Processing

Subject: EDP Security Survey   *Date:* June 30

A consulting firm has been retained to conduct a risk assessment of the EDP environment. The study should yield recommendations to create a more secure data processing climate. One of the major goals of the study is to determine the major effects of loss of data processing services on our business. In terms of your area of responsibility this determination means: What would be the effect on your area if the data processing application systems that support your activities were not available for given periods of time?

The consulting firm has developed a set of questionnaires to help us answer the above question. By reviewing the responses from all users of data processing applications, a relative ordering of systems, by degree of impact on the Bank's business, may be achieved.

The package contains the following items:

- A list of application systems that support your area
- A list of assumptions
- An Estimated Dollar Loss questionnaire
- An Estimated Loss of Control questionnaire
- An Estimated Embarrassment questionnaire
- A Loss Experience questionnaire
- A comment sheet

If the list of application systems for your area is not complete or is incorrect, would you please update the list accordingly. If you have any information to add or a different perspective on the questions raised, would you please include your additions on the comment sheet. If you have any questions concerning the instructions, please call Extension 2882. We will respond quickly to your questions. Please return the completed responses to our office by July 14.

You will be contacted to discuss your responses. In some cases this may entail a brief personal interview. We appreciate your cooperation in this matter.

Assumptions for Questionnaires

For the purposes of the questionnaires please assume the following:

- Loss of data processing services may be due to natural disasters (e.g., storms, floods, etc.) or to the occurrence of man-made events (e.g., programmer error, user error, sabotage, terrorist attack, etc.).

- No manual processing fallback procedures will be available to you in the event of loss of data processing services at the computer centers.

- No electronic data processing alternatives are available in the event of loss of data processing services at the computer centers.

ESTIMATED DOLLAR LOSS QUESTIONNAIRE

Group/Department: _____ Sr. Vice President: _____

Immediate User Area: _____ Officer/Title: _____

Application System: _____

For each time period in the table below, estimate the dollar loss on the business activities for your area, given delay or interruption of the above noted application system. *Then select the SEVERITY CODE from the Dollar Loss Schedule below that most nearly corresponds to the estimated dollar range, and enter the code in each box.* For purposes of this questionnaire "dollar loss" is defined as follows:

Monies expended by your area or revenues lost to your area in terms of retail or commercial customers due to a loss of data processing services. The elements identified as areas for dollar loss include, but are not limited to, the following:

- Expended Funds:
  —Due to fines from government agencies for failure to adhere to regulations or meet deadlines
  —Due to undetected fraud

- Lost Revenue:
  —Due to inability to provide service to customers
  —Due to customers seeking banking services at other institutions
  —Due to lost interest on bank funds

If you identify other elements that can be included, please list them on the comment sheet.

	Less Than One Day	1 Day	2–5 Days	5–10 Days	10–20 Days	20–30 Days	Over 30 Days
Expended Funds							
Lost Revenues							

Dollar Loss Schedule

Severity Code		Dollar Range	Severity Code		Dollar Range
0	=	0 – 3,200	6	=	1,000,001 – 3,200,000
1	=	3,201 – 10,000	7	=	3,200,001 – 10,000,000
2	=	10,001 – 32,000	8	=	10,000,001 – 32,000,000
3	=	32,001 – 100,000	9	=	32,000,001 – 100,000,000
4	=	100,001 – 320,000	10	=	Over 100 Million
5	=	320,001 – 1,000,000			

ESTIMATED LOSS OF CONTROL QUESTIONNAIRE

Group/Department: _____ Sr. Vice President: _____

Immediate User Area: _____ Officer/Title: _____

Application System: _____

For each time period in the table below, estimate the degree of loss of control on the business activities for your area, due to delay or interruption of the above noted application system. *Then select the SEVERITY CODE from the Loss of Control Schedule below that most nearly corresponds to the estimated loss of control and enter the code in each box. For purposes of this questionnaire "loss of control" is defined as follows:*

Losses to your area for which no dollar value can easily be applied but for which a subjective estimate of impact on the business can be made. The elements identified as areas for loss of control include, but are not limited to, the following:

- Loss of Control:—Due to loss of integrity of data (i.e., no confidence that data is valid/accurate)
  —Due to inability to proof accounts
  —Due to out-of-balance conditions
  —Due to lack of necessary information for management decision
  —Due to loss of safeguards against fraud perpetrated by bank employees, bank customers or others

If you identify other elements that can be included, please list them on the comment sheet.

	Less Than One Day	1 Day	2–5 Days	5–10 Days	10–20 Days	20–30 Days	Over 30 Days
Loss of Control							

Loss of Control Schedule

Severity Code		Loss of Control	
0	=	No Loss:	
1	=	Low Loss:	Problem easily handled
2	=	Medium Loss:	Your business activities continue, but with difficulty
3	=	High Loss:	Your business activity stops

ESTIMATED EMBARRASSMENT QUESTIONNAIRE

Group/Department: _____ Sr. Vice President: _____

Immediate User Area: _____ Officer/Title: _____

Application System: _____

For each time period in the table below, estimate the degree of embarrassment that the bank (your area) might suffer due to the loss of the above noted application system for each time period in the table below. *Then select the SEVERITY CODE from the Embarrassment Schedule below that most nearly corresponds to the estimated degree of embarrassment, and enter the code in each box. For purposes of this questionnaire, "embarrassment" is defined as follows:*

Losses to the bank (your area) for which no dollar value can easily be applied but for which a subjective estimate of impact on the business can be made. The elements identified as areas for embarrassment include, but are not limited to, the following:

- Embarrassment:—Due to media exposure of the occurrence of undesirable or compromising events
  —Due to public perception as an unreliable financial institution

If you identify other elements that can be included, please list them on the comment sheet.

	Less Than One Day	1 Day	2–5 Days	5–10 Days	10–20 Days	20–30 Days	Over 30 Days
Embarrassment							

Embarrassment Schedule

Severity Code

0	=	No embarrassment
1	=	Embarrassment but no loss of business
2	=	Minor loss of customer confidence
3	=	Major loss of customer confidence

LOSS EXPERIENCE QUESTIONNAIRE

Please recall the most serious occurrence of delay or interruption of data processing services, since January 19, that caused your area a "significant" loss. *For the purposes of the questionnaire the term "significant" means:*

  a. any loss of $2,000 or more
  b. adverse publicity
  c. loss of customer confidence in
  d. business in your area stopped.

We realize that you may have had other duties not associated with your present assignment and would therefore have no direct knowledge of such events. In this case, may we ask you to consult with staff and/or your predecessor(s) in your position to obtain such information.

Number of significant losses ⎯⎯⎯⎯⎯⎯⎯⎯⎯⎯⎯⎯⎯⎯⎯⎯⎯⎯⎯⎯⎯

Describe below your most serious loss incident.

1. Length of delay ⎯⎯⎯⎯⎯⎯⎯⎯⎯⎯⎯⎯⎯⎯⎯⎯⎯⎯⎯⎯⎯⎯⎯⎯⎯

2. Approximate date of occurrence ⎯⎯⎯⎯⎯⎯⎯⎯⎯⎯⎯⎯⎯⎯⎯⎯

3. Was the delay the result of your organization's actions?

   ⎯⎯⎯⎯⎯⎯ or EDP? ⎯⎯⎯⎯⎯⎯ or other? ⎯⎯⎯⎯⎯⎯

   Explain ⎯⎯⎯⎯⎯⎯⎯⎯⎯⎯⎯⎯⎯⎯⎯⎯⎯⎯⎯⎯⎯⎯⎯⎯⎯⎯⎯⎯⎯

   ⎯⎯⎯⎯⎯⎯⎯⎯⎯⎯⎯⎯⎯⎯⎯⎯⎯⎯⎯⎯⎯⎯⎯⎯⎯⎯⎯⎯⎯⎯⎯⎯⎯

   ⎯⎯⎯⎯⎯⎯⎯⎯⎯⎯⎯⎯⎯⎯⎯⎯⎯⎯⎯⎯⎯⎯⎯⎯⎯⎯⎯⎯⎯⎯⎯⎯⎯

4. Explained reason for delay ⎯⎯⎯⎯⎯⎯⎯⎯⎯⎯⎯⎯⎯⎯⎯⎯⎯⎯

   ⎯⎯⎯⎯⎯⎯⎯⎯⎯⎯⎯⎯⎯⎯⎯⎯⎯⎯⎯⎯⎯⎯⎯⎯⎯⎯⎯⎯⎯⎯⎯⎯⎯

   ⎯⎯⎯⎯⎯⎯⎯⎯⎯⎯⎯⎯⎯⎯⎯⎯⎯⎯⎯⎯⎯⎯⎯⎯⎯⎯⎯⎯⎯⎯⎯⎯⎯

5. Effect of delay ⎯⎯⎯⎯⎯⎯⎯⎯⎯⎯⎯⎯⎯⎯⎯⎯⎯⎯⎯⎯⎯⎯⎯⎯⎯

   ⎯⎯⎯⎯⎯⎯⎯⎯⎯⎯⎯⎯⎯⎯⎯⎯⎯⎯⎯⎯⎯⎯⎯⎯⎯⎯⎯⎯⎯⎯⎯⎯⎯

   ⎯⎯⎯⎯⎯⎯⎯⎯⎯⎯⎯⎯⎯⎯⎯⎯⎯⎯⎯⎯⎯⎯⎯⎯⎯⎯⎯⎯⎯⎯⎯⎯⎯

6. Loss in terms of dollars, embarrassment or other negative impact.

   ⎯⎯⎯⎯⎯⎯⎯⎯⎯⎯⎯⎯⎯⎯⎯⎯⎯⎯⎯⎯⎯⎯⎯⎯⎯⎯⎯⎯⎯⎯⎯⎯⎯

   ⎯⎯⎯⎯⎯⎯⎯⎯⎯⎯⎯⎯⎯⎯⎯⎯⎯⎯⎯⎯⎯⎯⎯⎯⎯⎯⎯⎯⎯⎯⎯⎯⎯

Appendix J

EXAMPLES OF SCENARIOS

1. Program Taking: Programmer/Employer

A programmer gave two weeks' termination notice to his employer. During his last week of employment, he was found using the computer to copy the production programs of his employer onto his own personal tape owned by him. He indicated that he was making a copy of the programs to take with him to his new employer. It was explained to him that the programs were proprietary, and his personal tape was erased and returned to him. On the last day of his employment, he was found copying the account number and password file. The copied material was taken from him and he was escorted out of the building to terminate his employment.

2. Insurance Fraud: Life Insurance Customer/Automated Premium Accounting System

A life insurance customer received a check for $100 from an insurance company with a notice explaining that this was a refund of a surplus collected in his premium account. The customer believed it was an error and returned the uncashed check to the insurance company, explaining the error. The next month the customer received another check for $100. The customer cashed the check and wrote a personal check for $100. He sent this check to the insurance company without explanation. The check was deposited in his premium account, and the following month he received a premium surplus check for $200. He cashed the check and returned the $200 to the company with a personal check. The following month he received a check for $400. After several months of similar actions, the amount had grown geometrically, and he deposited the check in a numbered bank account in Switzerland and enjoyed a trip to Brazil.

3. Lapping Fraud: Supervisory Teller/Branch Bank

A supervisory teller engaged in a lapping fraud. He accepted money from savings account customers and entered the correct amount in the on-line teller machine and customers' passbooks. When the customer left, he put a blank passbook in the teller machine, entered a correction showing a smaller amount deposited and pocketed the difference. This practice was carried on for several years until the teller was juggling more than 50 accounts with shortages. He was using the stolen money to gamble, hoping that he would win a large amount of money and restore the money to the savings accounts. At the end of each interest period he moved the shortages

294

from the accounts for which interest was to be calculated to accounts where the interest would be calculated on the first day of the new period. This resulted in the correct amount of interest applied to the accounts. On the first day of each new period he moved the shortages to the former type of accounts so that the latter accounts would also have correct interest applied to them. Occasionally the auditors would discover one of the short accounts when doing confirmations with savings customers. The supervisory teller would explain that an error had been made in that account, and he would correct it by creating a shortage in another account. The auditors expected occasional errors of this type since the teller was responsible for training new tellers for the bank. The fraud was eventually detected by accident when the teller's betting habits became significant and were reported to bank management.

4. Salami Fraud: Programmer/Credit Card Company

A programmer responsible for maintenance of a credit card accounting system placed a Trojan Horse (hidden instructions in a computer program) into a portion of the credit card accounting production program, and also in the master backup copy of the program. The program increased the interest charges by a few pennies on several thousand accounts and credited the accumulated funds to his personal credit card account he had established under a fictitious name. This was done in such a way that the controls were not violated and the control totals of interest and credits balanced. He occasionally used his account to legitimately use the accumulated credits. The fraud continued for several years and was never discovered.

5. Data Extortion: Computer Operations Supervisor/Employer

A computer operations supervisor gave notice of his termination. On the weekend before his termination he drove a truck to the loading dock of the computer center and removed all master file tapes and disks of the financial system of the company. He then drove the truck to the remote backup storage facility where he used a memo signed by himself to gain access to the facility and removed all of the backup files, and loaded them on his truck. He hid over 300 magnetic tapes and 48 disk packs in a remote location. On Monday he placed a telephone call to corporate headquarters and demanded $500,000 for the return of the tapes and disks. Management concluded that it would require several million dollars to reconstruct the entire financial data base of the company. They paid the ransom and recovered the tapes and disks.

6. Terrorist Attack: Terrorists/Multi-National Company

Terrorists attacked the computer center of a multi-national company. The computer center was housed in a building in an industrial area separated from other offices of the company. Access was controlled by a uniformed guard and electronically operated doors into the facility. The well-dressed individuals explained to the guard that they had a surprise birthday party planned for one of the computer operators and were carrying a number of large boxes wrapped as gifts. The guard admitted them to the lobby and asked to inspect the contents of the boxes. At that point, the individuals opened the boxes, removed automatic weapons, incapacitated the guard temporarily, and entered the computer center. They forced all of the employees in the computer center at gunpoint into the lobby, where they were temporarily held. The entire computer center, including the tape library and programming offices, were drenched with gasoline. A fuse was set at the main entrance. The attackers fled, giving instructions to employees to leave the building. The attackers fled in cars, the employees left the building, and the building exploded and burned, completely destroying its contents.

7. Taking Trade Secrets: Terminal Operator/Financial Institution

A financial institution uses a computer system to record and process investment decisions and transactions made by traders and investment analysts. Printouts of results are produced at a remote lineprinter terminal in an office where manual handling completes the processing. A terminal operator discovered the great short-term value of the output information and found a buyer for it who could make great profits from its use. The operator obtained the information contained in 200 one-page reports each day in a combination of the following ways: handwritten copying, removal of carbon paper from the multipart forms, use of multipart forms with an extra copy, and causing computer reruns and second printings. The operator delivered the information to the buyer outside of the computer building twice each day.

8. Timekeeping-Payroll Fraud: Timekeeper/Employer

A clerk prepared hours-worked records for 300 employees. He filled in forms for each employee, entering name, employee number, and numbers of hours worked. The forms were checked manually, based on employee names. The data were keyed into the computer timekeeping and payroll system where all controls and processing were based on employee number. The clerk filled in forms showing fictitious overtime hours using names of employees who often work overtime; however, he entered his own employee number. Manual checking revealed no discrepancies, and the overtime was credited to the clerk in the system. This proceeded for several years without detection.

Index